W9-BMV-263

NATURAL
HEALING

CHRISTOPHER HOBBS, L.AC.

Acknowledgements

*I could not have completed this book without the valuable help of my partner,
Beth Baugh, who worked hard to pull together diverse information
about the historical and other uses of the herbs, and lent her keen editorial and
stylistic eye to the entire project. Michael Amster, medical student, combed medical
libraries from Palo Alto to Davis and contributed the best science has to offer.
Dan Blumberg, MD, our friend and holistic psychiatrist, reviewed and contributed
to the section on psychoactive medications. Lesley Tierra contributed an elegant
section on the uses of Chinese patents and insomnia. Finally, thanks to
Doree Pitkin for stylistic editing.*

In this book, the author is not prescribing herbs for any medical condition, but rather is reviewing their historical and modern record of use. The writer and editors of this book emphasize that a total program for health, which can often effectively include an herbal program, is the only lasting and sure way to assist the body in its healing process.

Stress and Natural Healing
Christopher Hobbs

Cover design: Bren Frisch
Illustrations: Susan Strawn Bailey and Gayle Ford
Book design: Dean Howes

Text copyright 1997, Christopher Hobbs

Botanica Press is an imprint of Interweave Press

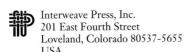 Interweave Press, Inc.
201 East Fourth Street
Loveland, Colorado 80537-5655
USA

Printed in the United States of America

Library of Congress Cataloging-in-Publication Data

Hobbs, Christopher, 1944–
    Stress and natural healing : herbal medicines and natural
therapies / by Christopher Hobbs.
        p.   cm.
    Includes bibliographical references and index.
    ISBN 1-883010-38-1
    1. Stress management.   2. Herbs—Therapeutic use.   3. Alternative
medicine.   4. Naturopathy.   I. Title.
RA785.H625
615.5—dc21   199797-14001
                                                                        CIP

First Printing: 7.5M:697:PP

FOREWORD

By Svevo Brooks

SEVERAL YEARS AGO, I came across a medical pamphlet written midway through the present century. The author, a distinguished physician with four decades of clinical practice, concluded that there were but three principal causes of illness: telephone, calendar, and clocks. These, he said, had become controlling forces in society, denying citizens precious rest. People were no longer dying of old age or physical ailments, but dying from hurrying. Their nervous systems had worn out.

Fifty years have passed since these observations were made, but they seem relevant today. What household is not regularly invaded by a ringing telephone? Who amongst us is not at least partially enslaved by the demands of the clock? How often do we wake up fully rested?

As the pace of life quickens, we more deeply need calm, uninterrupted moments for the renewal they imparts to our spirits. Yet the time allotted to rest is ever diminished. Leisurely walks, afternoon naps, the opportunity to stop and inhale the fragrance of a flower—these small interludes, once commonplace, are increasingly rare.

The book you're about to read is an attempt to lure you, however briefly, from the bustle of everyday life. Like a walled garden or an inviting path, these simple ideas, gleaned from the wisdom of Mother Nature, will lead you to quiet places and experiences. You'll experience the calming effects of plant aromas, the balm of a good night's sleep. In Mother Nature's sequestered garden, you'll sip rest-inducing herb teas, discover the relaxing benefits of bodywork, and rediscover a remarkable tonic, a short nap.

It is from the basic rhythms found in Nature and human nature that Christopher Hobbs has drawn inspiration for this important and useful book. The insights and prescriptions that follow will draw the reader closer to Nature and in so doing bring welcome measures of comfort and repose.

INTRODUCTION

THIS BOOK is about relaxation, an important key to health. Stress and tension prevail throughout our society today; in fact, the very structure of modern society is stressful. Overpopulation, overcrowding, noise, environmental pollution, crime—none promote relaxation. Reactions to stress take many forms. The resulting pain and misery, loss of work-place productivity, and costly burden on our health-care system affects everyone directly. We need some stress, or challenge, to stimulate creativity and foster individual growth and maturity. But when challenges become overwhelming, body systems begin to fail, leading to anxiety, insomnia, fatigue, ulcers, high blood pressure, and other symptoms. First, we look to coffee to overcome exhaustion, and alcohol to calm us. Then we resort to over-the-counter medications such as aspirin and Maalox for a little relief. The physician often finds no specific, observable pathology.

More than ever we need to learn to relax, and to do so in healthy, life-affirming ways that do more than temporarily mask the symptoms of stress. Many people today are turning to alternative medicine in quests for self-empowerment and abundant well-being. They are finding that holistic, natural methods of promoting relaxation strike at the very roots of stress and support the fullness of health despite the stresses and strains of contemporary life.

This book cuts across the mainstream into new and exciting areas of research and practical self-help methods. It will help you to understand the meaning of stress and act to protect yourself against the damage it can do. First we address the workings of the nervous system, the ways that stress affects it, and the potential health problems that can result. Then, mainstream medical treatments are compared with holistic approaches to these disorders. Natural ways to promote relaxation by using proven dietary and herbal programs, as well as visualization, conscious breathing, meditation, and exercise, are explored. As many are now discovering, these natural, holistic alternatives are powerful tools in building a life of good health.

Contents

Chapter 1

THE NATURE OF STRESS

STRESS IS one of the most studied and discussed phenomena in human experience. The word itself, according to the *Oxford English Dictionary (OED)*, probably derives from the middle-English words *destresse* or *stresse*, which appear interchangeably in fourteenth-century texts. Other English words from this lineage include strict and constrict. The current definition of stress in the OED is given as "hardship, straits, adversity, affliction."

Today, *stress* refers to the undue pressures of living in a fast-paced society. The idea that these pressures create an impact on people is not new. Hans Seyle, who began his research into stress in the 1930s, was the first to describe biological stress and explain its effects on health. In his classic book *The Stress of Life*, originally published in 1955 and revised and reprinted in 1978, he defines stress as "the nonspecific response of the body to any demand." Nonspecific, in this case, refers to any event or stimulus, whether it be external (such as a touch or a noise) or internal (such as an emotion). Fundamentally, stress is the wear and tear of living. Some people are prepared, through genetic favor or diligent attention to health, to cope well with the stresses of living; others are ill-prepared indeed.

Today, stress has taken on very specific meanings. The word stress is used to describe both an experience (usually a hard, difficult, or very intense one) and the *result* of that experience on the body. The modern expression "stressed out," although overused and vague, refers to a state of anxiety, worry, or exhaustion that has resulted from difficult or challenging experiences. The term implies the existence or potential rise of unpleasant symptoms.

STRESS AND VITAL ENERGY

Stress, by itself, saps energy. When we are able to deal with life's challenges calmly and efficiently, we expend energy at a lower rate than if we are dealing with the challenges and experiencing stress. Under stress, we become exhausted much more quickly than we do otherwise, and recover energy more slowly. Certainly stress creates symptoms such as digestive upset, insomnia of various types, fatigue, and muscle tension. These symptoms reflect the disruption of energy and consequent disruptions of body systems.

What is the source of our energy? Ancient writers and modern healers agree that we receive most of our vital energy as a gift from our ancestors, a gift that originates in higher realms of awareness—what we call God, the Goddess, or the Universal Spirit. This hereditary vital energy is thought to be finite. We receive only so much for a lifetime, and there are no refills, although we can supplement our ancestral supply from several sources. When we invest the time, energy, and effort to learn how to take each breath deeply, fully, and consciously, we receive vital energy from the air. This energy is called *prana* by practitioners of the ancient East Indian system of healing known as Ayurveda. They emphasize that small, shallow, unconscious breaths bring little energy into the body, while deep, conscious breathing enhances energy and calms the body's systems.

During meditation, we can reach and be nurtured by the original source of all energy and vitality. Deep meditation opens a pathway to a wisdom higher than the conscious mind can fathom, quiets the restless mind, and allows the body to rest and heal itself.

Ancestral vital energy is supplemented by food, water, air, and perhaps other natural sources, such as trees and Mother Earth herself. Think of the rejuvenating qualities of a wilderness trip—the silence broken only by the sounds of Nature, conscious appreciation of the cycle of sunrise and sunset, and the glimmering brilliance of the stars on dark, cloudless nights. Such contact with Nature imparts vital energy.

Vital foods impart this energy as well. Some wild foods or superfoods, such as nettles, dandelion, yellow dock greens, and green foods like spirulina and wheatgrass juice are especially rich in energy. Maintaining strong digestion ensures that we receive vital energy from food.

Table 1-1. Social Readjustment Rating Scale

Death of spouse	100
Divorce	73
Marital separation	65
Jail term	63
Death of close family member	63
Personal injury or illness	53
Marriage	50
Fired at work	47
Marital reconciliation	45
Retirement	45
Change in health of family member	44
Pregnancy	40
Sex difficulties	39
Gain of new family member	39
Business readjustment	39
Change of financial state	39
Death of close friend	37
Change to different line of work	36
Change in number of arguments with spouse	35
Mortgage over $60,000	31
Foreclosure of mortgage or loan	30
Change in responsibilities at work	29
Son or daughter leaving home	29
Trouble with in-laws	29
Outstanding personal achievement	28
Begin or end school	26
Change in living conditions	25
Revision of personal habits	24
Trouble with boss	23
Change in working hours or conditions	20
Change in residence	20
Change in schools	20
Change in recreation	19
Change in church activities	19
Change in social activities	18
Change in sleeping habits	16
Change in number of family get-togethers	15
Change in eating habits	15
Vacations	13
Christmas	12
Minor violations of the law	11

THE STRESSORS OF EVERYDAY LIFE

The most commonly quoted listing of potential stressors in daily human life was created by Holmes and Rahe in 1967. In this classic chart (see Table 1-1), potential stressors are rated according to input from interviews and other research studies with test populations and human volunteers (Elliott & Eisdorfer, 1982).

Doubtless this chart could be updated to reflect contemporary life; for instance, in 1967 a mortgage of $60,000 was considered huge, but by today's standards it is small. Nonetheless, the chart gives an indication of the typical factors in life that cause varying levels of stress.

Adding the numbers after each factor present in an individual's life over the period of one year yields a general indication of

Table 1-2. Typical Stressors Used in Research

Threatening, unpleasant films
Understimulation/Demand underload
Overstimulation/Demand overload
Noise, unexpected or uncontrollable
Prestige or loss of status
Electric shock
Uncontrollable situations
Natural Events
Physical illness (including surgery, hospitalization)
Threats to self-esteem
Traumatic experiences
Stress-event sequences
Bereavement
Losses of any type (physical, psychological, or social)
Migration
Retirement
Status change (job change, salary change, marriage)
Chronic and chronic intermittent stressors
Daily "hassles"
Role strains
Social isolation
Sleep deprivation

stress level and prediction of future major illness or accident. For instance, a score of 150 to 300 indicates a moderately high stress level and a 50/50 chance of major illness or accident during the next two years. A score of 300 or more brings the odds to 80 percent probability of severe physical consequences of stress.

Another study by the Institute of Medicine, National Academy of Sciences, identifies factors used in studying stress among humans (see Table 1-2) (Elliott & Eisdorfer, 1982). Compiled from numerous clinical and research studies, the list includes subtle social factors that researchers have linked to common diseases.

The Physical Consequences of All Stress

By consistently maintaining a high level of wellness and understanding how stress can work for instead of against health, we can sustain energy and youthfulness throughout life. Stress affects the body in very real, physical, ways and the reactions that take place in tissues, organs, and body systems are rooted in our very humanity. The general wear and tear of life can be highly individual. We will develop diseases such as asthma, hepatitis, cancer, and heart disease in response to physical or emotional stresses, de-

pending on inherent individual weaknesses and environments.

Each person, regardless of constitutional type, habits, and ideas, is subject to a very fundamental response to living which Seyle calls the "stress syndrome" or the GAS (general adaptation syndrome). The GAS is particularly associated with the nervous and hormonal systems and represents a predictable way in which people respond to life on a biochemical level. The GAS occurs in three phases:

1. The alarm stage (AG) is the initial acute reaction to stress. The body's defense systems are on full alert. The symptoms of this phase include sensations of anxiety—increased heart and breathing rate, heightened mental awareness, and sweating—and digestive upset. Your body activates the nervous and hormone systems to secrete protective hormones such as epinephrine and norepinephrine and to keep the body on guard. You promptly feel more alert to everything around you, but should you be injured—turn an ankle, for instance—you would be much less sensitive to pain than usual, for pain messages are minimized. If this experience is a rare event, the tension and soreness will disappear after a few days, and the normal, healthy person will not be much the worse for the it.

2. The stage of resistance (SR) follows the AG, occurring when the body begins to adapt to the stress and deal with the stressor.

Because the intense symptoms of the alarm stage are gone, a person who is in the stage of resistance may deny that the stress continues. Nonetheless, the body responds to the continuing stress at a deeper level. The stress hormones are still being released in small amounts, affecting the body in various ways. These ways include depressing the immune system, decreasing bone strength, compromising brain functions such as memory, and decreasing energy levels. Headaches, insomnia, irritability, and stiff muscles are all signs that the body is responding in this way. Many who live in developed countries constantly exist in various states of resistance.

3. When the stage of resistance is exhausted, the final stage of exhaustion (SE), or burnout, sets in.

The symptoms of the stage of exhaustion are similar to those of the alarm reaction, but the repercussions are much more severe because the body's strength is depleted from weeks, months, or perhaps years of excessive wear and tear. Some try to relieve the stress with alcohol, entertainment, and fatty foods, hoping to calm their feelings of anxiety. Others seek sedatives to resolve insomnia, or seek prescription medications.

Some people, stimulated by the intensity of the stress itself and depending on reserves of hereditary strength, can sustain the stage of resistance for a very long time, but most, without relief from the stress, eventually break down, even to the point of "nervous breakdown;" a complete rest may be the last resort. Individuals who reach exhaustion may age prematurely and risk developing life-threatening diseases such as cancer, heart disease, and diabetes. Selye characterizes this final stage as the "breakdown of the organism, with a complete loss of resistance" (1978).

Mice that are chronically stressed in laboratory experiments develop ulcers and eventually submit passively to a stressor, like electric shock, that is entirely avoidable, as if they are "giving up" (Zhukov & Vinogradova, 1994). Humans can give up, too; we see this in alarming suicide rates that are rising in many parts of the country.

What is the link between emotional and physical stress and disease processes? Scientific investigation has sought to clarify the answers to this question for many years, and we now know that the physical, emotional, and mental results of stress are unrelenting. If we allow ourselves, consciously or unconsciously, to live with high levels of stress, we may well end up with serious and long-term health consequences.

The Physiology of Stress

The body's biochemical and neurological responses are important factors in the stress we feel, but many stressors do not alone cause symptoms and disease. Rather, the body's *response* to a stressor may be the major factor in the disease process. For instance, suppose you've been lifting a number of heavy boxes and feel a little muscle stiffness the next day. You evince a certain smugness at having been able to lift so much with so little negative impact on the body. Later, however, you reach for a pencil and a sudden, sharp pain radiates down your back.

The lifting and the muscle spasm are quite likely related. When you placed stress on the muscles of your back by lifting the boxes, your body responded to your wishes but damage was still being done. The physical stress placed on your back as you lifted the boxes perhaps over-stretched muscles or tore the muscle tissue. Overnight, inflammation and swelling occurred. When you tried to stretch out those muscles again by reaching for the pencil, the muscles rebelled with painful spasms. The reaching triggered the pain, but the damage to the muscles and ligaments occurred previously.

Some types of stress create direct damage to the body and simultaneously cause emotional and physical stress. Loud noise, for instance, can damage the eardrums, especially if sustained, while it causes emotional distress, too. Even negative emotions can cause direct injury to the body. Depression, for instance, decreases one's immunity to physical illness.

In other words, symptoms and manifestations of disease are caused not only by the stressor—the virus or the noise—but also by the body's attempt to stave off the stressor. Thus, disease can be considered in two parts—the direct result of action on the tissues by pathogens, and the body's reaction to the pathogens.

The most dramatic examples of this syndrome are autoimmune diseases, in which the body's immune system sends antibodies to attack pathogens, only to destroy all the tissues around the original target area. This process can be very circumscribed, as in the case of autoimmune-based kidney or liver disease, or symptoms can occur throughout the body.

We do not fully understand autoimmune illnesses, and many debate which illnesses belong in the category. Some researchers (i.e., Duesberg, 1996) claim that the human immunodeficiency virus (HIV) is not capable of causing all the symptoms of the AIDS disease; instead, desperate attempts of the immune system to rid itself of the virus create the manifestations and symptoms of AIDS.

Within the workings of the numerous neurological and hormonal feedback loops throughout the body, a stressor may play a minor role in producing symptoms. The mind often plays a role by amplifying symptoms. This habit may be learned early in life. For instance, if a person feels an ache at the temples, reminiscent of an earlier pain that preceded a major migraine headache, then the tension created by the expectation of a headache might lead to a reaction by the blood vessels. This makes the ache feel like pain and provokes stress, leading to more worry. The feedback loop continues until a migraine is produced. It is now impossible to measure the role of the mind in the process of disease and the intensity of symptoms, but it is likely to be significant.

The best way to break this familiar loop process may be the practice of meditation, wherein one creates a separation and detachment from one's own thoughts. Other stress-releasing techniques, such as yoga, conscious breathing, massage, or acupuncture may also be valuable. It is much easier to stimulate subtle changes in the level of internal and external tension and ameliorate emotional and psychological states than to try to directly affect biochemical processes in the body by taking various medications.

THE STRUCTURE AND FUNCTION OF THE NERVOUS SYSTEM

The nervous system and the hormonal system act in harmony as a major control mechanism of the body. Through countless chemicals and nerve fibers, these systems transmit information from sensors in our skin, eyes, ears, and taste buds to the central nervous system. The central nervous system processes this information and sends action signals back out to the body, including the hormonal system. The nervous system may also store information for future use in the form of memories.

The nervous system creates and maintains both tension and relaxation in the body. It is broadly divided into the central nervous system (CNS) and the peripheral nervous system (PNS). Each system carries out different functions and is located in different areas of the body. These divisions are made for the sake of discussion and study; in reality, both the CNS and PNS are integrated into a complex but unified system that also can affect the hormonal and immune systems.

The CNS consists of the brain and spinal cord, both so essential to life as to be encased in the bone of the skull and vertebrae, respectively. As the "center" of the nervous system—much like a computer's central processing unit (CPU)—the CNS functions as a "control panel" for the body, receiving all sensory input from the PNS via the nerves, then returning responses, and storing input.

The PNS consists of the peripheral nerves that radiate from the spinal cord into every area of the body. Ganglia, the nerve plexes or junctures where many nerves meet, are centers of intense neurological activity. It has been suggested that the ganglia are the chakras discussed in yoga, although the chakras are said to reside in the subtle, not the physical, body. Nonetheless, the ganglia may well be loci through which the chakras are "connected" or associated with the physical body.

The PNS is divided into the autonomic division and the somatic division. The somatic division receives sensory input from the periphery of the skin, muscles, and joints, and transmits that information to the CNS. In turn, the CNS sends output in the form of reflex or motor impulses to the skeletal muscles, resulting in movement. Thus the somatic division is under voluntary control. The autonomic division transmits sensory information from the internal organs to the CNS. In turn, impulses are sent back to smooth muscle cells of these organs. The autonomic division functions automatically, at a subconscious level. For instance, it is the autonomic division that is responsible for keeping out heart beating, our lungs breathing, and our intestines digesting, all without our conscious input. Although some control can be exerted over the autonomic system by those who meditate or practice biofeedback, most people are generally unaware that the heart continues to beat.

Every organ in the human body is connected to the sympathetic and parasympathetic nerve branches. Balance—called homeostatic equilibrium in physiology—is achieved by maintaining just the right degree of activation of each branch. If either branch is overactive or underactive, a disease state arises.

Hormones and neurotransmitters are chemical messengers important in every phase of human biological function. Some of these compounds, such as vasopressin, epinephrine (adrenaline), norepinephrine, and oxytocin, act as both neurotransmitters and hormones. The nervous system, through the action of the neurotransmitters, influences the secretion of hormones, which then act on a specific target tissue to bring about a response. These hormone levels are tightly controlled by what is called "negative feedback," keeping the body within homeostasis or healthy equilibrium.

The effect of any hormone is to regulate a target cell or tissue by regulating its metabolism or affecting levels of certain proteins, and its effects can be specific or widespread. Each hormone binds to specific sites, called receptors, on specific cells. The cells which have no receptors for that particular hormone remain unaffected by it. When the hormone binds, it forms a complex that activates a specific response. For instance, during puberty, testosterone directs muscle cells to grow more rapidly, increasing the size and strength of the muscles. Although the hormone circulates throughout the body, its effect is limited to specific tissues and cells.

Hormones are created from raw materials supplied by foods in the diet. For instance, steroid hormones come from cholesterol, a component of fat; amine hormones and protein hormones from amino acids. Diet can directly influence the production of these compounds, and thus every aspect of biological function, although the effects are often subtle.

A neuron is composed of three parts: axon, dendrite, and nerve body. Nerve impulses travel only one way; from the dendrite end to the axon end of the nerve. These two ends are separated by the nerve body. Where an axon meets the nerve body of another neuron, a synapse or synaptic cleft occurs. Thus, the dendrite receives the impulse conducting it toward the cell body, and an axon conducts the nerve impulse away from the nerve body to the next neuron.

Neurotransmitters are made in the neuron and stored in axonal vesicles located near the synaptic cleft. When an electrical impulse reaches the end of the axon, these neurotransmitters are released into the synaptic cleft. Here, they travel across the tiny space to the next neuron where they bind with a specific receptor. Depending on the neurotransmitter and the type of receptor, this next neuron is either excited or inhibited. So that these neurotransmitters are not continuously stimulating the connecting neuron, they are rapidly broken down by enzymes in the synaptic cleft. Thus, each new impulse traveling along a neuron becomes a distinct event, rather than a continuous blur of stimulation.

A final aspect of neurotransmission relating to stress and health is the phenomenon of *synaptic fatigue*. When a neuron is continuously and rapidly stimulated, it eventually loses the ability to respond as it runs out of its store of neurotransmitters. A single neuron contains enough neurotransmitter to last only minutes if continually secreted. One's individual biological potential, or capacity to produce neurotransmitters, may be an important part of what the Chinese ancients called "ancestral Qi."

The human nervous system excels in sensitivity, finesse, and complexity, but, like a modern computer-regulated automobile, these qualities offer many more ways to break down. As research continues into the chemistry and function of the nervous system, it may become clear that the foods we eat, our environment and our physical and emotional activities have a far greater impact on the nervous system than we now believe.

Nerve Function

When a stimulus is perceived, the CNS sends impulses, or "messages," along nerves in the form of electrical waves. These waves or action potential, as they are called, occur by the opening of ion channels or gates on the surface of neurons.

The cell membrane (surface) of a neuron contains tiny pumps that actively remove sodium ions from the cell and put potassium ions into the cell. During an action potential, these gates open up, allowing positively charged sodium ions to rush into the cell. This stimulates additional sodium gates along the length of the neuron to open also. This causes a sudden change in the electrical current of the cell; it can actually be measured on an oscilloscope. This initial part of the action potential is called depolarization.

As rapidly as the cell membrane was depolarized, it becomes repolarized. This occurs by the rapid movement of positively charged potassium ions out of the cell, returning the electrical potential to its previous state. An action potential moves along the length of a neuron at an extremely rapid pace until it reaches the next neurotransmitter, or the effector—in this case, a skeletal muscle fiber. Here the neurotransmitters are released, move across the synapse, and cause an action potential in the muscle fiber; the response causes the muscle to contract.

Although scientists know of more than fifty different neurotransmitters, each with a different molecular structure and function, the ones we are interested in are acetycholine and norepinephrine. Acetylcholine is a neurotransmitter primarily involved in the transmission of impulses in the parasympathetic (rest and digest) nervous system. It is also used in motor neurons connected to sweat glands and blood vessels found in the skeletal muscles. Nerves using acetylcholine are called cholinergic fibers.

Norepinephrine, on the other hand, is found in nerves of the sympathetic (fight or flight) nervous system. Nerves using norepinephrine are called adrenergic fibers.

Smooth muscle cells of the blood vessels, heart, and intestines are generally connected by both cholinergic and adrenergic fibers. In different tissues, the same neurotransmitter can either stimulate or inhibit a nerve impulse, depending primarily on the receptors to which it binds. An inhibitory response can occur by stabilizing the membrane potential, preventing an action potential from occurring. One way this occurs is by affecting the permeability of the neuron to other ions such as calcium, potassium, and chloride, thus preventing the movement of sodium ions. This, in turn, stabilizes the voltage across the neuron membrane; stimulation is blocked. Thus, hyperpolarization occurs instead of depolarization.

A BIOCHEMICAL VIEW OF THE NERVOUS SYSTEM

Chronic stress is likely to affect every cell of the body, but when considering the biochemical effects of stress on health, researchers often focus on the two major control centers, the nervous and hormone systems. These systems interact with one another and with every other system of the body. They also directly affect the immune system. Scientists have recently discovered that immune cells possess binding sites for stress hormones, suggesting one avenue by which immune suppression can result from chronic stress. Because much of the organ control and regulation come from these two systems, they are a good starting place when considering the biochemical effects of stress.

The understanding that stressful situations activate the sympathetic branch of the autonomic nervous system and the adrenal medulla to release the neurotransmitters epinephrine and norepinephrine was first developed by Cannon and de la Paz in 1911 (Puglisi-Allegra & Oliverio, 1990). The discovery of other consequences of stress soon followed.

Seyle (1978) developed the idea that stress also activates the hypothalamic-pituitary-adrenal cortex (HPA) system. Neurological input from the higher centers of the brain (for instance, when perceiving danger) or from external sensory input activates the hypothalamus, which sends minute amounts of control hormones to the pituitary gland. This gland then sends out adrenocorticotropic hormone (ACTH), inducing the adrenal cortex to produce glucocorticoids (like the hormone cortisol).

Each of these two sets of hormones plays a role in the flight-or-fight mechanism, alerting us to the possibility of danger and preparing us for action. Epinephrine and norepinephrine act together with glucocorticoids to provide more energy to the muscles. They do this by metabolizing stores of protein, carbohydrates, and fatty acids into

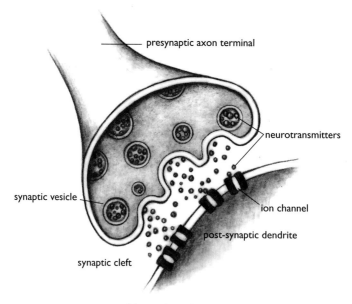

presynaptic axon terminal

neurotransmitters

synaptic vesicle

ion channel

post-synaptic dendrite

synaptic cleft

Nerve Impulses

Table 1-3. Major Hormones

Hormones	Source	Effects
Cortisol	Adrenal gland	Stimulates gluconeogenesis activity in the liver and metabolism of lipids, carbohydrates. Net effect, raises blood sugar levels. Maintains integrity of blood vessels, kidney function. Promotes healing by halting the immune response.
Adrenocorticotropic hormone (ACTH)	Pituitary gland	Affects the adrenal cortex, promoting the synthesis and secretion of sex steroids, glucocorticoids, and mineralocorticoids.
Testosterone	Testes, adrenal gland	Major male sex hormone
Estrogens	Ovaries, adrenal glands	Major female sex hormone
Luteinizing hormone	Pituitary gland	Stimulates secretion of both estrogen and testosterone.
Prolactin	Pituitary gland	Affects functioning of fertility and sexual potency.
Growth hormone	Pituitary gland	Stimulates growth of muscle and bone. Stimulates cell division. Increases protein synthesis. Decreases sugar uptake by muscles while increasing the metabolism of fat reserves for energy.
Melatonin	Pineal gland	Affects the circadian rhythms and quality of sleep. May affect immune system and gonadal function.
Epinephrine	Adrenal glands	Increases metabolism, blood glucose, heart rate, blood pressure, shunts blood away from the interior organs to the skeletal muscles.

Note: Except where indicated, volunteers' blood levels of these substances normalized when the volunteers became accustomed to the stressor. Coping mechanisms seem to have a direct effect on how rapidly these chemicals and effects are normalized (Ursin et al, 1978).

glucose. The end result is increased blood glucose. The brain also responds to stress by secreting additional peptide hormones such as endorphins, substance P, and vasopressin. These hormones regulate pain and blood pressure.

Neurotransmitters refer to a group of molecules involved in sending nerve impulses from one nerve to another, or from one nerve to a muscle. In addition to epinephrine and norepinephrine, neurotransmitters include serotonin, dopamine, and acetycholine. These molecules are made and stored in nerve endings and secreted when a nerve impulse is generated. This is a short-lived response, because the neurotransmitters are rapidly degraded by enzymes (see Table 1-5). Some neurotransmitters can control mood and emotions. By understanding the mechanisms involved, scientists have created popular mood-altering drugs such as Prozac and Zoloft, which interfere with the function of these neurotransmitters.

Panksepp (1990) has suggested an even greater complexity of the "stress response." Centered in the brain's limbic system, composed of the amygdala and hippocampus, are distinct areas that apparently control the release of some hormones and respond to

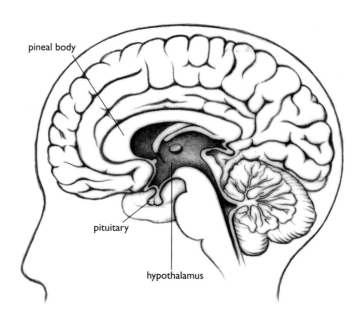

Important glands within the brain

pineal body

pituitary

hypothalamus

the release of others, particularly stress hormones. Although these centers are poorly understood, in animal studies they have influenced a number of stress reactions, perhaps because they contain numerous receptor sites for glucocorticoids such as cortisol. In addition, these brain centers are known to be involved in instinctual behavior and emotions. They are likely to be associated with responses to both stressful and pleasant situations.

The body's complexity continues to unfold as research goes on, and questions develop rapidly. How does the brain create emotions? Can emotions be reduced to chemical compounds? It appears that varying stressors—danger, grief and loss, excessive anger, and submission to authority, to name a few—may stimulate different combinations of chemicals within the body, yet the various combinations work seamlessly together in a healthy individual. Scientists study healthy systems to learn how to alter and restore those that have broken down.

The Nervous System in Action: Fight or Flight

For humans to survive and evolve into today's thinking and feeling beings, nature created and refined internal systems of alarm

Table 1-4. An Overview of a Nerve Impulse

1. In response to a stimuli, the sensory receptor of the peripheral nervous system initiates a nerve impulse.

2. This nerve impulse is transmitted along the sensory neuron to the central nervous system via an electrical current.

3. In the CNS, the sensory neuron transfers the impulse to an interneuron through the release of a neurotransmitter. The neurotransmitter travels across the synaptic cleft, binding to receptors on the interneuron and initiating an electrical current.

4. The nerve impulse is then transferred from the interneuron of the CNS to the motor neuron of the peripheral nervous system. Again, this is accomplished by the secretion of neurotransmitters from the interneuron, which are taken up by the motor neuron.

5. The motor neuron (or effector) reacts appropriately. This may involve muscle contraction or relaxation or glandular secretion.

and protection. Unlike animals such as tigers and sharks, who have the advantage of claws or razor-sharp teeth, humans have had to rely on cunning and ingenuity to survive over the millennia. Our nervous systems detect potential danger through noises, smells, and even extra-sensory information. It is no wonder that mankind is so sensitive to stressful situations today.

Over the eons, our primitive brain centers, such as the diencephalon, have not changed dramatically; but the cortex, the higher reasoning part of the brain, has developed and become a powerful influence on behavior. For instance, if a person is driving at seventy miles per hour on the freeway, the primitive part of the brain can interpret this experience as dangerous—and of course it is. However, the cortex—the reasoning part of the brain—knows that by driving in the correct lane and using caution, an accident is unlikely. The cortex cannot, however, correctly assess the powerful reaction of the diencephalon to this experience. Thus the sympathetic nervous system is continuously aroused, while the rational mind is determined to keep driving to the destination.

According to the neuropsychologist A. T. W. Simeons (1960), this incongruity among the parts of the brain is a major factor in the damaging effect of some kinds of stress on health. The more primitive brain centers overestimate the threat of potentially dangerous situations, leading to increased muscle tension, heart rate, brain function, and other physical activity; simultaneously, the higher reasoning center, the cortex, interprets these physical reactions as abnormal and disregards them, thereby increasing the strength of the alarm reaction and leading to even more damaging reactions in the body. When these reactions continue daily and are added to the mental and emotional feedback loops previously mentioned, a strong relationship between exposure to chronic stress and severe disease is suggested.

The fight-or-flight mechanism, the body's primary internal coping mechanism for dealing with threats, involves the activation of the nervous system and the increased production of neurotransmitters. Under stress or threat of danger, the brain sends a signal to the adrenal glands to secrete more epinephrine into the blood. This kicks the sympathetic nervous system into "high gear." The adrenal glands, located atop the kidneys, link the actions of the hormonal, nervous, and immune systems. As the systems work together, the body prepares either to run from danger or to stand and fight.

Activation of the sympathetic nervous system is a good thing if you're being attacked by a mugger or about to be hit by a car, but chronic activation of the system can be lethal in the long run. It depletes the body's energy reserves and reduces circulation to the internal organs. Digestion slows down and perhaps stops, depriving the body of needed nutrition and disrupting elimination. Sleeplessness and anxiety may follow. Stress may also lead to high blood pressure, other cardiovascular problems, and im-

mune-system disruptions. Some drink too much alcohol under stress, take up smoking, or smoke more. Eventually, vitality drops and fatigue and illness can set in. Table 1-5 lists some of the effects of stress on the production of the body's pharmacy—the hormones and neurotransmitters.

INDIVIDUAL RESPONSES TO STRESS

What allows an intense experience to become destructive rather than instructive? Seyle asserts that most experiences, in themselves, are not stressful in a harmful sense; instead, one's re-

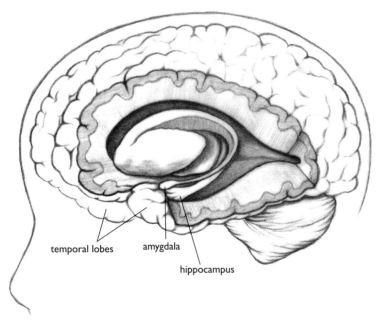

temporal lobes   amygdala

hippocampus

Interior brain structures

action to an experience determines whether the stress is positive or negative. Sometimes stress brings positive, healing effects and promotes increased maturity and strength. The excitement of receiving a promotion, falling in love, or enjoying a meaningful experience can create stress, but in a positive way that we interpret as opportunity. Stress also allows us to react quickly and with great strength in a threatening situation, such as pulling a child from the path of an oncoming car. Stress can motivate our growth and development and increase our feelings of satisfaction in our accomplishments.

Reactions to negative stress need not be damaging; responses are often highly individual. Some people maintain health despite having experienced stressful or even life-threatening events. These individuals often feel a strong sense of meaning in their lives, a belief in themselves, and a commitment to living life well. Along with a strong, vigorous attitude and a close connection with their inner world, these survivors have a highly developed sense of self-control.

Some people seek for fun what others would call severe stress. Thrill-seekers engage in sports such as rock-climbing, hang-gliding, and sky-diving. Many people find that their most profoundly creative energy emerges when they are faced with challenges. Or are these folks simply addicted to adrenaline and other stress hormones? Like all aspects of human nature, the varied responses to stress are complex and individual.

Personality One factor in whether stress becomes positive or negative is certainly personality. Those who are characteristically impatient, competitive, and hot-tempered are more susceptible to the negative impact of stress than those who respond calmly. The impatient person, popularly known as Type A, responds quickly, intensely and actively, while the Type B is likely to hold off action, think the situation through, and formulate a plan to solve the problem. Type A, confronted with a stressful situation, moves quickly to the fight-or-flight bodily response and eventually is more likely to develop certain kinds of ulcers, digestive problems, and cardiovascular illnesses than the Type B.

Genetic Factors A person's genetic makeup or constitution is also likely to play a role in how stress affects health. When the individual has abundant vital energy, based on a bountiful genetic gift, many physical and emotional stressors simply seem small. The energy can be directed toward the stress without depleting the individual's body or spirit.

Without an adequate supply of vital energy, it is difficult to deal with the smallest of life's hassles without feeling exhausted or overwhelmed. Elliott and Eisdorfer (1982) mention that in animal studies, production of stress hormones markedly varies in different strains of mice, indicating that genetics may determine how stress affects the individual.

Coping Skills. Some people learn how to cope with stress in positive ways and thus are less affected than others. These individuals are likely to have habits of optimistic, hopeful thought. They seek the support and help of others when facing stress and think of different ways to overcome the situation before acting. They tackle problems one by one and give themselves time to adjust to changing situations.

Overall, those who manage stress well face the situation patiently and calmly, direct energy toward it, and give time to the resolution of the stressful situation. This holds true even with illness. If you have a cold, for instance, you can moan and groan about it and gulp down painkillers, antihistamines, and antibiotics hoping to hasten your recovery, keep up all your activities, and get over the cold. But

this behavior will further weaken or imbalance your body's delicate internal ecosystem, which is struggling to fight off the virus.

On the other hand, you can embrace the powerful potential for healing and increased wellness that are present within your body. For instance, when cold viruses take hold, the sufferer often feels fatigued and unmotivated toward productive activity. A runny nose, slight fever, and frequent perspiration also occur.

Working with Nature and following her direction can turn the experience of having a cold from a dreary one into a positive experience of rest and healing. Perhaps the fatigue indicates the need to rest, to stop the outward flow of vital energy and redirect it inside for stocktaking of the internal world. The mucus discharge from the nose is the body's attempt to wash out the irritating virus; fever and sweating are the body's way to burn the virus out and flush it away. Taking antihistamines and other medications to reduce fever, then heading off to work, confounds the body's efforts and delays healing.

Instead, at the first sign of a cold, support healing by resting and letting your body do its work to reorganize and redirect its internal resources. Visualize beneficial healing, retreat from activities, and rest. Eat lightly, and take herbs. With this help, internal cells will be repaired, restored, and reinvigorated throughout the tissues and organs. The immune system, activated by the viral pathogens (disease-causing agents), will activate to keep the body's other systems in good working order. The discomfort of the cold will be shorter, milder, and less troublesome if you cooperate with Nature.

THE NERVOUS SYSTEM ACCORDING TO TRADITIONAL CHINESE MEDICINE

An examination of Eastern and Western medical belief shows how modern science can confirm and even clarify ancient wisdom. Traditional Chinese Medicine (TCM) is a complete system of diagnosis and therapies (therapeutics) developed by observation and clinical experimentation over thousands of years.

In Chinese medicine, health is defined as the correct balance between the yin (passive, nutritive) and yang (active) energies of the body. All the organs and body systems known to modern Western medicine are recognized by TCM, but the Chinese understanding of human anatomy is less than Western medicine's because

TCM was developed with very little dissection and no microscopes. Also, the TCM concepts of genetics and biochemistry are limited; ancient Chinese doctors simply did not have the tools to study such things.

Yet TCM is in some ways more advanced than Western medicine. TCM includes correlations among mental, emotional, and physical states of being. Because ancient Chinese physicians had only observable, external cues as diagnostic tools, they paid great attention to patterns of disharmony manifested in a patient's pulse, tongue, and facial features as well as physical and psychological symptoms.

A core concept of TCM is Qi (pronounced "chee"), which translates roughly as "vital" or "life" energy. Western medicine has no equivalent for Qi because, scientifically speaking, we don't know exactly what it is. Many TCM practitioners view Qi as a subtle energy that is neither electricity nor any of the other known energies. Others think it may involve bioelectric and geomagnetic interactions.

TCM asserts that Qi circulates among and nourishes the internal organs; this corresponds to the complex of circulation and metabolism which supplies every cell in the body with oxygen and nutrients and carries away waste

Table 1-5: Important Neurotransmitters

Neurotransmitter	Source	Function	Effect on Secretion
Acetylcholine	Nerve endings	Conducting nerve impulses across the junctions between nerves and muscles.	Increase
Catecholamines			
Norepinephrine (noradrenaline)	Nerve endings, adrenal glands	Binds to alpha adrenergic receptors, causing constriction of blood vessels, inhibition of gastrointestinal muscles, contraction of gastrointestinal and bladder sphincters, and increased heart activity.	Increase
Epinephrine (adrenaline), norephinephrine	Adrenal glands	Binds to beta adrenergic receptors, stimulating the heart muscle and dilation of bronchial system.	Increase
Dopamine	Central nervous system, adrenal gland.	Affects mental health. May be involved in psychosis and movement.	Increase
Other amino acids derived from neurotransmitters			
Serotonin	Central nervous system	Constricts the blood vessels involved in sleep and sensory perception	Increase
Glycine	Central nervous system, especially the spinal cord	Inhibits neural excitation in the central nervous system.	Unknown
Gamma-aminobutyric acid (GABA)	Central nervous system	Inhibits neural excitation in the central nervous system.	Increase
Neuropeptides			
Substance P	Sensory neurons, brain, intestines	Mediates pain, touch, temperature, and inflammation. Binds to opiate receptor, produces insensitivity to pain when under stress.	Probable increase
Endorphins and enkephalins	Brain	Produce sense of euphoria and pain relief in certain situations. Responsible for "runner's high".	Decrease

Note: Except where indicated, the blood levels of these substances normalized after volunteers became accustomed to the stressor. Coping mechanisms seem to have a direct effect on how rapidly these chemicals and effects are normalized (Ursin et al, 1978).

OVERCOMING STRESS

I had a very intense bout with influenza at an early age. My fever hovered around 103 for nearly three days. I got out of bed in the middle of a very dark night and walked down the hall. Huge, fuzzy, colored balls swirled all around me. These were sent by alien beings, I thought, and I felt I had to hide from them. I managed to open a closet door and burrow into a pile of clothing to avoid discovery by the aliens.

The experience was intense and scary, but as I huddled in the clothing, a new sense of strength and awareness came over me. Perhaps the adversity and adventure of my inner battle with the real aliens (viruses) helped produce a strengthening of my immune function, heightening my sense of self-protection.

Looking back, I feel that by meeting the challenge of the illness, usually considered destructively stressful, I instead took the opportunity to grow and develop. I believe that we can use stress to grow beyond our self-imposed limits to a point where what was once unimaginable becomes possible.

products. The TCM concept of the balancing forces of yin, the cooling, nurturing force, and yang, the warming, active force, also corresponds to Western understanding of nervous-system function. In modern terms, yang corresponds to sympathetic activation, while yin corresponds to parasympathetic activation.

The parasympathetic branch (yin) instructs the organs to slow down, rest, take up nourishment, and recuperate as needed. On the other hand, the sympathetic branch (yang) diverts blood and energy to the heart, lungs, and major skeletal muscles. TCM recognizes that an overabundance of yin or yang results in poor health, just as Western medicine sees eventual detriment in a sustained state of sympathetic alertness.

In TCM theory, "vital essence," or nutritive substance (yin), is said to be created out of "vital activity" (yang), or the workings of the glands and muscles and the circulation of blood and lymph throughout the body. Conversely, vital activity is created out of vital essence through the digestion and metabolism of essential nutrients.

Parasympathetic tone, correlated with yin, promotes the digestion, circulation, and absorption of nutrients throughout the body. And sympathetic activation is needed, in turn, to make the body move, ingest, digest, secrete, and circulate blood.

TCM addresses the imbalances that occur when either yin or yang are excessive. Yin excess is characterized by mental and physical sluggishness, excessive mucus, and depressed metabolism. Yin deficiency, on the other hand, results from excessive, sustained stress. Some individuals are "yin deficient" types who are constitutionally predisposed to this imbalance. They are often very thin, energetic, and prone to mood swings. They may tire suddenly.

TCM's understanding of nervous disorders differs from that of Western medicine. In Western medicine, the heart is the muscular, physical organ that pumps blood. TCM concurs with that definition but also expands it to refer to an energy system; thus the TCM concept of Heart is capitalized to distinguish it from the organ. In TCM, the Heart is the residence of the Mind and Spirit (Shen). Most sleep and nervous disorders stem from an imbalance within the Heart system.

TCM also teaches that the "five emotions" can act as disease-causing agents (see Table 1-6). Accordingly, any emotion, in excess, can lead to disease in an organ. Similarly, if the emotion is blocked, disease can result. For instance, if we never feel joy or love, our Heart "hardens." If we feel too much joy, a state known as mania, our Heart and nervous system can run amok.

Table 1-6: Emotions as Pathogens

Emotion	Organ Affected	Potential Result of Excessive Emotion
Anger	Liver	Headaches, irritability, red itchy eyes
Fear	Kidney	Weak knees, low back pain, ringing in the ears
Joy, mania	Heart, nervous system	Insomnia, depression, anxiety
Sadness, grief	Lungs	Asthma, chronic bronchitis, emphysema, constipation
Thinking, worry	Digestion	Digestive problems, fatigue, depression

CHAPTER 2

EVERYDAY STRESS AND HOW WE DEAL WITH IT

FEW OF US escape the stress pervading our society today, although each individual interprets stress and its effects somewhat differently. Overall, however, the most typical sources of stress can be grouped into very broad classifications.

Childhood Stress As children grow to adulthood, they often carry with them the deeply felt stress of negative childhood experiences, especially those that occurred in the context of the family. Children respond quite differently to typical experiences such as being teased; one may find the experience amusing and a sign of being included. Another child may find being teased unbearable and carry this aversion into adulthood, experiencing instant, intense stress upon hearing well-intended, humorous comments.

Unfortunately, this kind of stress often spills over into adult relationships. Early in life we learn ways of approaching others, interpreting events, and solving problems. Sometimes we continue these habits long after experience proves them ineffective.

This type of ingrained stress is difficult to resolve because it has been practiced over and over, to perfection. Overcoming it first involves identifying and unlearning subconscious habits and defense mechanisms. Then new, more relaxed responses and habits must be learned.

Those seeking to overcome and manage stress often need professional help and support to do so. Many systems of psychotherapy strive to free one's innate health and ability to love. Such psychotherapy is most effective when combined with a spiritual practice such as Zen, Yoga, Sufism, Buddhism, or Gnostic Christianity that clearly defines levels of awareness that exist beyond the realm of Western psychology.

Job Stress Everyone knows what this is! For most of us, the core of job stress is the fact that we need employment to support ourselves and our families. Overt or covert threats to our source of income are very stressful indeed, and the daily work can be high-pressure, too.

Some jobs, such as police work and the endless deadlines of the newspaper business, are inherently stressful. Others are stressful because they are boring and repetitive. Swing-shift workers who frequently change schedules experience both physical and emotional stress. Those who are given a good deal of responsibility in their work, but no authority with which to carry it out, are often stressed as well.

Some workplaces subject employees to damaging physical stress. Repetitive motion injuries have disabled many. Some workers are routinely exposed to radiation, toxic chemicals, high levels of noise, and damaging vibrations. Although workers have more protection from workplace hazards than they did twenty years ago, by no means are all workplaces benign and safe.

Many dream of alleviating job stress by finding work that is personally satisfying and that generates an adequate income. Finding work that brings out talents and abilities is worth the effort. Another positive way of dealing with job stress is giving up the fruits of our labors, the triumphs and defeats, for the higher good.

Environmental Stress Environmental stress arises from interactions between the individual and the environment. It includes seeing and breathing air pollution; tasting and consuming impure tap water, food, and beverages; hearing the noise of traffic and heavy equipment; and many other intrusions on one's peace and quiet. Much of this is beyond the control of the individual, but each person has the power to live in harmony with the Earth by recycling, limiting driving, planting trees, consuming less, eating organic food, and joining with others to benefit the Earth. We must work together to overcome the powerful forces that create pollution, set priorities, and take into consideration the long-term effects of polluting the environment.

The techniques of natural healing support the health of the Earth as well as the health of individuals. The manufacture of pharmaceutical drugs creates toxic by-products that can ultimately find their way into the air, water, and food supply. In contrast, the organic cultivation of medicinal herbs and the use of other natural healing methods pollute neither the environment nor the body.

Our environment also includes other people, and particularly in urban areas the constant friction of the overcrowded concrete jungle leads to explosive conflict. Community and neighborhood organizations, churches, and local support networks help channel frustration and anger into constructive action. To create healing for this planet of its everyday wars and disharmony, we must endeavor to heal ourselves, our families, and our communities. Simply being aware of sociopsychic stress and the resources available for dealing with it are important first steps toward counteracting its harmful effects.

Physical Stress Physical stress often results from overuse of one area of the body or from exposure to a substance that overtaxes the body's ability to remain healthy. It can also result from the workplace, from chores at home, from playing strenuous games, or engaging in quiet, pleasant activities such as needlework.

Protecting ourselves from stress requires first that we directly face the stress and examine it deeply. Only then can we begin to eliminate the stress from daily life. The quick-fix solutions to stress offered by our society are often destructive and contrary to good health. Instead, we must build health in order to survive our stressful environment and to clear the way for good decision-making about our lives.

SUBSTANCE USE AND ABUSE

Daily, a majority of the population uses legally sanctioned drugs to get through the day and to slow down at night. When our stomachs hurt and digestion is upset, we swig antacids. Can't sleep? There are plenty of sleep aids available at the drugstore, or the doctor will write a prescription. Pep up in the morning with a couple of cups of coffee. Later, how about a stiff drink to calm you down?

Faced with stress, most people will grapple with the situation right up to the point of overwhelming frustration. If the situation does not resolve in an acceptable way, individuals seek relief from the emotions they feel: frustration, annoyance, a sense of failure. Some experience stomach pain and poor digestion, headaches, insomnia, overwhelming fatigue, and even worrisome chest pains.

Our society offers plenty of options to relieve the symptoms of stress: antacids, sleeping pills, alcohol, tobacco, sugar, marijuana, cocaine, and more. By using these substances, we can pep ourselves up, become numb, or otherwise avoid the direct impact of stress. The problem is that these substances actually compound the effects of stress, even as they seem to relieve them. Nonetheless, contemporary society is fascinated with uppers and downers.

The use and abuse of stimulants and sedatives has become a complex problem involving intense political, social, and medical controversies. As a society, we don't even agree on which substances qualify as "drugs" and which do not, much less on how to regulate them. Some who speak out against "drugs," such as marijuana, see no harm in drinking alcohol, arguably the most socially destructive of the legally sanctioned drugs. Others rail against legally sanctioned drugs but praise the purported health benefits of illegal drugs such as marijuana. Legislators, health professionals, and neighbors profoundly disagree.

The debate about drugs takes other twists and turns. Consider, for instance, the debate raging among the tobacco industry, health advocates, and the government. Health advocates produce study after study showing that smoking kills. Lawsuit after lawsuit wends through the courts, seeking to establish the harmfulness of tobacco. The govern-ment—bureaucrats and legislators alike—holds hearings, forms committees, collects evidence, and makes speeches. The tobacco industry, however, funds a powerful political lobby and influences legislation and regulations; thus it continues to advertise and sell an addictive, carcinogenic drug.

However, we may be on the verge of change. At this writing—early in 1997—the United States Food and Drug Administration has proposed that tobacco be regulated as an addictive drug. If the proposal succeeds, we may see stricter regulation on the sale and advertising of tobacco, reduced government subsidies, and increased fines and penalties for the sale of tobacco to minors (Barnett, 1997; Glantz, 1997). In addition, a number of states are suing tobacco companies to recover millions of dollars lost when smokers become ill and must be supported by public health care services (Van Voris, 1997).

The deadlock of our national debate about drugs makes progress very difficult. It's a trying and emotional topic. While nearly everyone believes that adults should have the right to choose which products they consume, at what point does the use of stimulants and downers by others affect our right and our choice not to be exposed to them? Drunk drivers kill twenty thousand people each year—should we accept these deaths as necessary to protect "rights?" As in other issues of right and wrong, facts conflict or are nonexistent. How much of a given substance leads to addictive or abusive behavior? When is occasional use considered safe?

The following chapter reviews substance use and abuse in an objective manner so that every reader, regardless of personal viewpoint, can examine the facts about the stimulants and downers that, for many, comprise primary and ongoing ways of coping with stress.

PICK ME UP: THE STIMULANTS

The most popular stimulant is caffeine, which is readily available in coffee, tea, carbonated beverages, and over-the-counter medications. About one-third of Americans each consume approximately 300 milligrams of caffeine daily, the equivalent of three cups of coffee. Other stimulants include tobacco, sugar, ephedra (ma huang), appetite suppressants, and illicit drugs such as cocaine.

Western explorers first entered the steamy South American rain forests, home to the coca plant, in the mid 1800s. A Dr. von Tschudi, an ethnobotanist, described a 62-year-old native man whom he employed to do hard physical tasks. To his astonishment, the man worked day and night for five days without taking nourishment and with only a few hours of sleep. Then the man accompanied Dr. von Tschudi, on foot, for 150 kilometers through the mountains. The unusual fellow was perfectly willing to continue without food, provided he received a continuous supply of coca leaves (Anrep, 1879).

Judging by their use of stimulants, many Americans now aim to achieve the productivity of Dr. von Tschudi's employee. Imagine, in today's busy society, having four to five hours more of productive work time each day! Statistically, the use of stimulants is rising; current per capita consumption of coffee is now more than ten pounds annually. At the same time, Americans are getting less sleep than ever before. In a study comparing the lifestyle habits of men in the 1930s to those of men in the 1980s, contemporary men are less concerned about rest and sleep. Unsurprisingly, the majority suffered from daytime fatigue and tiredness (Bliwise, 1996). The pervasive social attitude that sleep is expendable encourages increasing rates of stimulant consumption.

Stimulants increase mental activity, body metabolism, and awareness by increasing central nervous system activity. They are easily abused because of their addictive qualities. A new user of cocaine, for instance, experiences an explosion of energy for the first few weeks of drug use. However, as the body's internal chemistry adjusts to the stimulant, it demands more cocaine to maintain the same high. Drug dependency has occurred; the user will now find it difficult, and perhaps impossible, to stop taking the drug. Cocaine is a potent example, but less powerful stimulants such as caffeine cause a similar effect.

While dependency is a serious danger to those who take stimulants, the substances create other, more subtle effects. For example, stimulants provoke anxiety symptoms and undue tension (Smith, 1988). Long-term users of stimulants often suffer from chronic irritability, insomnia, and fatigue, because stimulants drain the energy reserves of the body faster than they can be replenished. Some stimulants, such as nicotine, are known to cause cancer.

Fighting fatigue with stimulants short-circuits the body's efforts to sustain health. Fatigue indicates the body's need to rest and often signals impending illness. Following an infectious disease, such as the flu or a cold, you should allow sufficient time for full recovery. Resuming a busy life too soon after an illness may cause repeated infection and result in longer bed rest. Honor and respect illness and fatigue as an opportunity to recover and heal.

Nicotine

Nicotine is a highly addictive stimulant that occurs naturally in the tobacco plant. It enhances alertness and relaxes muscles. Over sixty species of tobacco belong to the genus *Nicotiana*, but only two can be used for human consumption. *Nicotiana tabacum* is the tobacco typically consumed in the United States. Once harvested, tobacco leaves undergo curing and fermentation for processing into cigarettes, cigars, snuff, chewing tobacco, and pipe tobacco. Although the percentage of Americans who smoke tobacco has decreased to about twenty-five percent of the population, the use of snuff or chewing tobacco has increased. In other countries, tobacco smoking is increasing rapidly or remaining stable.

History The introduction of tobacco to the Western world corresponds with the establishment of the British colonies in

North America. In the late fifteenth century, European explorers of the new continents discovered the plant, a traditional part of Native American life. Nicotine's pleasant effects quickly captivated Europeans; London alone had over 7,000 tobacco shops in the early part of the seventeenth century. Tobacco plantations along the southeastern coast of North America soon became the world's major suppliers. Tobacco also went to the Far East via Japanese trade routes.

During these early times, tobacco was used medicinally and considered by some a panacea for certain ailments. Some believed that it was possible to breathe life into another with breath carrying tobacco smoke. In the nineteenth century, however, it was proven that the lethal dose of nicotine is as little as 40 milligrams. Tobacco was attacked by clergymen, educators, and some physicians. Early clinical research claimed that delirium tremens, perverted sexuality, impotence, and insanity were linked to chronic use of tobacco. Medical use of tobacco ended with the conclusion of the Civil War (Maisto, 1991), but recreational tobacco use continues today.

Today's attitude towards tobacco varies greatly. In the United States and Canada, many know that tobacco causes a variety of cancers, emphysema, and heart disease. Education provided by physicians, schools, and media campaigns on the risks of using tobacco has encouraged many people to quit smoking, or perhaps not to start, probably resulting in fewer smokers as compared to the pre-education high of fifty-five percent in 1955 (Shopland & Brown, 1985).

Beyond North America, tobacco use remains popular. In Japan, smoking is such an established part of society that a person is offered a smoke with a ceremonial cup of tea (Maisto, 1991). In most parts of the world, tobacco is highly revered despite thousands of clinical studies and millions of deaths that prove its faults. One tobacco researcher comments that, "[N]o country that has ever learned to use tobacco has given up the practice" (Maisto, 1991).

Dangers of Tobacco A cigarette may contain about 20 milligrams of nicotine, most of which escapes in the smoke. This can be a toxic amount, however, if the tobacco is accidentally swallowed by an infant. Tobacco has stimulatory effects on the central nervous system, which may progress to convulsions and coma. Continual stimulation at the level of the muscles may lead to respiratory paralysis, preventing breathing. Hypertension and irregular heart beats are also associated with acute tobacco toxicity. Continual smoking leads to chronic nicotine toxicity.

Cigarette smoking is the single most preventable cause of disease, especially disease of the heart and lungs. Its use has an enormous socioeconomic cost to the public. Smoking is associated with peptic ulcer, lung cancer, cardiovascular disease, and sudden death due to heart failure. Insurance companies have compiled data on the differences in survival rates for males aged 35 to 75. At the age of 55, 10 percent of smokers are dead, compared to 4 percent of nonsmokers. At age 65, the differences widen to 28 percent and 10 percent. And by age 75, the difference is twofold, 50 percent and 25 percent (Maisto, 1991).

Statistics provided by the Office of Smoking and Health (USDHHS, 1987) disclose that over 170,000 heart-related deaths, 130,000 cancers, and 50,000 cases of chronic obstructive lung disease are caused by cigarette smoking (USDHHS, 1987). These statistics do not take into account the number of deaths caused by the use of other tobacco products.

Another danger of smoking is secondhand smoke. It was once thought that smokers were only harming themselves, but today it is known that exhaled smoke contains all the deadly elements inhaled by the smoker. According to the USDHHS, heavy exposure to passive tobacco smoke may be the equivalent of smoking one to two cigarettes a day (USDHHS, 1987). Passive smoke is especially harmful for those with asthma, bronchitis, or allergies. Of special concern are children whose parents smoke. One study shows that children living in an environment of passive smoke are more likely to have bronchitis, pneumonia, and some impairment of pulmonary function (Bonham & Wilson, 1981).

Almost every American has been affected by the smoking-related death of a loved one. So why are people still smoking? Why? Because nicotine is one of the most addictive drugs known.

Caffeine

The most widely consumed psychoactive substance in the world, caffeine, is used to induce wakefulness and relieve fatigue for short periods. Caffeine is a pervasive part of our culture. Its popularity exceeds that of nicotine and alcohol combined, with an annual global consumption estimated in excess of 120,000 tons of the alkaloid from all sources

(Gilbert, 1984). In the United States, the per capita consumption of coffee is 1.7 cups per day, or 3.3 cups per coffee drinker (Narod et al. 1991). A *Consumer Reports* survey found that caffeine is compounded into more than 1,000 over-the-counter products (1987). The latest addition to the caffeine market is bottled water boosted by a substantial amount of caffeine. Table 2-1 reports the amount of caffeine in common products.

History Plants that contain caffeine, including coffee *(Coffea arabica)*, chocolate *(Theobroma cacao)*, tea *(Camellia sinensis)*, and yerba maté *(Ilex paraguariensis)*, have been prized for many centuries. Yerba maté is popular among the indigenous peoples of South America and remains the national drink of Brazil, Argentina, and Paraguay. Europeans in the eighteenth century referred to yerba maté as the "green gold of the Indios" and recognized its use as a "slimming remedy which facilitated losing weight in a natural way and stilled the distressing feelings of hunger and thirst" (James, 1991). Caffeine entered the pharmaceutical domain when the compound was isolated from yerba maté in 1820 (Bisset, 1994).

Prior to the sixteenth century, European caffeine sources were

TABLE 2-1. Amount Of Caffeine Per Serving

Beverage or product	Amount
Dripped Coffee	110 mg/cup
Percolated Coffee	75 mg/cup
Instant Coffee	65 mg/cup
Decaffeinated Coffee	2 mg/cup
Tea	30 mg/cup
Cocoa	20 mg/cup (plus theobromine)
Chocolate bars	20 mg/bar
Jolt	71 mg/12 ounces
Mountain Dew	52 mg/12 ounces
Sunkist Orange	42 mg/12 ounces
Dr Pepper	38 mg/12 ounces
Pepsi Cola	37 mg/12 ounces
Coca Cola, Diet Pepsi	34 mg/12 ounce

Note: 7-up, Sprite, Fresca, Diet Sunkist Orange, and Hires Root Beer contain no caffeine (Gilbert, 1976).

limited to tea and yerba maté. When traders from the Arabian peninsula introduced coffee in the 1500s, its popularity grew so quickly that within 25 years over 3,000 coffee shops had been established in Europe (Smith, 1985). Colonists began cultivating coffee in the mid-seventeenth century at plantations in the Dutch East Indies. Coffee is now cultivated in Latin America, South America, Africa, India and Hawaii.

Biological Effects Caffeine is a xanthine, related to theophylline found in tea and theobromine found in cocoa. These xanthines stimulate the central nervous system (CNS), causing wakefulness, increased mental activity, stimulation of the cardiac and respiratory systems, and diuresis (urination). The drug also interferes with the ability of the CNS to regulate behavior, pain sensation, muscle control, and sleep (Brody, 1994). Caffeine is addictive, and withdrawal symptoms include lethargy, headache, irritability, and depression. Some researchers implicate caffeine in premature births.

Caffeine is thought to stimulate the body by increasing the release of norepinephrine and epinephrine. These neurotransmitters are involved in the sympathetic nervous system, the division responsible for the "fight or flight" response. Summarized below are the numerous physiological effects of caffeine:

Xanthines such as caffeine can affect the central nervous system, the heart, the gastrointestinal tract, the kidney, smooth muscle, and skeletal muscle. These compounds have both negative and positive effects, however, and have been used therapeutically for asthma, congestive heart failure, and pulmonary edema (fluid in the lungs). In the central nervous system, low doses of xanthines stimulate the cerebral cortex, causing increased alertness. Xanthines can increase the force of the heart, thus increasing blood flow to the body as well as raising blood pressure. Some people have experienced irregular heart beats due to caffeine. Xanthines stimulate digestion through the secretion of gastric juices and digestive enzymes; this may be why people enjoy coffee as an after-dinner drink. There is a slight effect on the kidneys, promoting diuresis, or the formation of urine. Smooth muscle cells relax in response to xanthines. This leads to dilation of the blood vessels and the bronchi, improving blood flow and breathing. Because of this, xanthine-based drugs are used therapeutically to treat asthma. In skeletal muscle, xanthines increase the strength of contraction. Withdrawal of caffeine can cause headache, lethargy, and irritability among those who drink six cups of coffee or more per day.

Caffeine is quickly absorbed by the body and has a half-life of about five hours. This means that after five hours, half of the original amount of caffeine remains in the body. Therefore, its stimulating effects are present for only four to six hours after consumption. Because caffeine is metabolized in the liver, the health of that organ influences the half life. A weak or diseased liver will increase the amount of time it takes to remove or metabolize caffeine. On the other hand, cigarette smoking increases the liver metabolism and the rate that caffeine is removed.

Rapid liver metabolism does not indicate liver health; instead, it may signal impending disease and degeneration from excessive use of toxic substances. For example, smokers metabolize caffeine over fifty percent faster than nonsmokers because their inhalation of toxic smoke and nicotine elevates the levels of liver enzymes. Increased liver metabolism is also a sign that the chronic caffeine user has developed a tolerance to the effects of the drug (James, 1991).

Adverse Effects and Toxicity

There is much controversy surrounding the safety of caffeine, particularly in reference to long-term use. Caffeine is currently approved as a direct food additive for cola-type beverages on the FDA's Generally Recognized As Safe (GRAS) list. In 1986, an FDA advisory review panel on nonprescription products reported that caffeine is safe and effective as a stimulant when administered in doses of 100 to 200 milligrams every three to four hours, with a daily maximum of 600 milligrams (Feldmann & Davidson, 1986).

The short- and long-term side effects of caffeine are well documented. Occasional users who consume between 100 and 400 milligrams of caffeine per day may experience symptoms of enhanced alertness, increased mental activity, irritability, tremors, quickened pulse, urge to urinate, anxiety, restlessness, insomnia, nausea, and digestive disturbances. Other less visible signs include high blood pressure, cardiac abnormalities, increased cholesterol levels, and gastric acid secretion (Feldmann & Davidson, 1986).

The side effects experienced by long-term users of caffeine are similar to those of a short-term user, but usually less noticeable because of the body's tolerance.

Long-term users experience decreased mental alertness and less control of their moods and behavior, because the nervous system depends on caffeine for stimulus. Other common symptoms include increased sensations of pain, poor muscle control, and disturbed sleep. Some of caffeine's side effects may increase with age. For more information on the side effects of caffeine, see Table 2-2. (next page).

Sugar

The only simple sugars our ancestors had were fruits, fruit juices, and as a rare treat, honey. Refined sugar did not become part of the Western diet until the twelfth century, although its cultivation is documented in India during the third century B.C. Today sugar is manufactured from three primary sources: sugar cane, sugar beets, and corn. The sugar industry's most popular and cheapest sweetener is high-fructose corn syrup.

Food manufacturers have turned the natural craving for sweet foods into an immensely profitable industry. By including refined sugar in most processed food products, including spaghetti sauce, ice cream, cookies, most drinks, and bread, food manufacturers increase their sales. Despite improved labeling requirements, ingredient lists seldom contain the word *sugar*, and instead include *glucose*, *fructose*, or *sucrose*, all euphemisms for simple sugar.

The average American consumes more than 120 pounds of simple sugars and sweeteners a year, or the equivalent of 35 teaspoons a day (Vickery, 1991). It is the largest single component of the American diet, representing 16.4 percent of total calorie intake (Schwantes, 1975). The most popular form of sugar is white granulated sugar (sucrose), which contains 48 calories per tablespoon and no protein, vitamins, or minerals.

Sugars such as molasses, honey, maple syrup are also simple sugars and should be used with discretion, but they are enriched by small amounts of minerals and vitamins. Brown rice syrup and barley malt syrup offer the same benefits. Fruits also contain simple sugars, along with dietary fiber, vitamins, and minerals. Once the taste buds become accustomed to refined sugar, however, natural sugars seem bland by comparison; when switching from refined to natural sugars, a period of adjustment may be necessary.

Because refined sugar is an integral part of the average diet, sugar is the most accessible and abused of all stimulants. Yet sugar

—continued on p. 44

Table 2-2. Caffeine and Medical Studies

There are over 2,500 medical studies of caffeine. A majority of these focus on three main topics: birth defects, cardiovascular effects, and withdrawal and dependency. The following table summarizes the most recent clinical studies and the current debate in each area of research.

Birth Defects

Human clinical studies have shown that caffeine may cause miscarriage, slow the growth of the developing fetus, or cause heart irregularities. Animal studies have shown that large doses, equivalent to 600 mg/day in humans, cause low birth weight and premature delivery (Morris & Weinstein, 1983).

In 1981 the Food and Drug Administration advised women to limit caffeine intake because research shows a relationship between caffeine consumption and low birth weight (Caan et al, 1989). Many studies have been performed following the 1981 ruling, which both support and oppose the FDA recommendation. Research is still inconclusive as to the carcinogenic effects of caffeine. The current guidelines recommend that women do not consume more than 300 mg/day (Resch & Papp, 1983). Regardless, it seems prudent to discontinue drinking coffee during pregnancy. Caffeine does cross the placenta and enter fetal circulation.

Study Focus	Research Conditions	Results	References
Low birth weight	Case-control study of 9,564 pregnancies	Modest effect of caffeine consumption on fetal growth	Caan et al (1989)
Low birth weight and complications	More than 12,000 women who consumed 4+ cups of coffee/day.	No increased risk of adverse outcomes of pregnancy	Linn et al, (1982)

Cardiovascular Effects

An effect of caffeine's stimulus is an increase of cardiovascular activity. Common effects on the cardiovascular system include increased heart rate and blood pressure, heightened force of cardiovascular contraction, and increased blood flow output.

The health concern surrounding caffeine and the cardiovascular system focuses on whether caffeine has a long-term negative effect on cardiovascular function. The results of almost 100 clinical studies on this topic are inconclusive. Many studies provide evidence that caffeine does increase blood pressure, although not enough to cause a heart attack. A large study sponsored by Kaiser Permanente with over 66,000 participants supported this conclusion. On the other hand, a clinical study from the Netherlands found that caffeine increases blood pressure and promotes arteriosclerosis and blood clotting (Bak & Grobbee, 1990). With so many contrasting studies, it is difficult to make a recommendation concerning the long-term effects of caffeine on the cardiovascular system.

Study Focus	Research Conditions	Results	References
Cardiovascular disease	4,000 individuals over a 12-year period	No relation between coffee intake and heart attacks	Dawber et al (1974)
Coronary heart disease, such as myocardial infarction and angina.	1,040 male medical students followed for 28 to 44 years.	Quantitative association between coffee intake and coronary heart disease.	Klag et al, (1994)

Correlation of behavior and health	700 heart-attack patients compared to 13,000 healthy patients	Patients who drink 5+ cups/day had 50% greater risk of heart attack than those who abstained.	Feldmann & Davidson, 1986
Caffeine and incidence of cholesterol	Tests on thousands of men and women conducted by Kaiser Permanente in 1985	A substance in coffee other than caffeine is responsible for increase in cholesterol	Is Coffee Safe? *Consumer Reports* Sept. 1987

Tolerance, Dependency, and Withdrawal

During long-term use of caffeine, the body undergoes adjustments, gradually becoming tolerant to and dependent on its effects. For instance, the numbers of adenosine receptors, a receptor targeted by caffeine, increases in chronic users of caffeine, while becoming less sensitive to it (James, 1991). Another example of tolerance and dependency is demonstrated by the results of a study measuring the effects of caffeine on the adrenal glands of rodents. This experiment showed that chronic users of caffeine had adrenal glands double the size and weight of nonusers, because the caffeine forced the glands to secrete extra adrenaline (Friedman, 1979). In summary, the body makes subtle adjustments, such as increasing adrenal gland size and the availability of adenosine receptors, to help the body tolerate and accommodate the heightened influx of the caffeine.

Caffeine dependency develops at surprisingly low dosages in humans. A recent clinical study demonstrated how chronic users consuming as little as 100 mg/day can experience dependency and withdrawal symptoms (Griffith, 1990). Another study concluded that people who consume low-to-moderate amounts of caffeine (2.5 cups daily) experience withdrawal symptoms such as depression, anxiety, low vigor and fatigue, and moderate or severe headaches (Silverman et al, 1992). Previous to these studies, withdrawal symptoms were only recognized with chronic users in excess of 600 mg/day.

Study Focus	Research Conditions	Results	References
Withdrawal symptoms and syndrome	62 adults, habitual consumers of 2.5 cups of coffee/day. Double-blind study conditions.	Effects of withdrawal included depression, low vigor, fatigue, and moderate to severe headaches	(Silverman et al, 1992).
General health benefits of substantial reductions in caffeine.	Studied the effects of coffee and tea reduction in the relief of tension and anxiety symptoms.	Great improvements in anxiety, irritability, sleep disturbance, headaches, and abdominal symptoms	(Smith, 1988).

Note: Other areas of controversy regarding caffeine use include caffeine use in children, resulting in severe irritability and poor sleep patterns; correlation between caffeine use and fibrocystic breast disease in women between 30–50 years of age; correlation of coffee drinking and bladder cancer (D'Avanzo, 1992). Population studies correlating consumption of coffee with reduced exercise and increased consumption of alcohol, cigarettes, saturated fats, and cholesterol (Puccio, 1990); patients with panic disorders display particular sensitivity to the negative side effects of caffeine (Boulenger et al, 1984).

is an essential component of life. Carbohydrates are biochemicals composed of carbon, hydrogen, and oxygen. They are essential to life because they are the only molecules that directly provide energy. Fats and proteins must first be transformed into carbohydrates to provide energy. The source of these carbohydrates is green plants, which, by using carbon dioxide and light, can synthesize glucose and carbohydrates. The simplest of the carbohydrates are the monosaccharides, also called simple sugars. Glucose is a monosaccharide. When two monosaccharides are joined together, they form a disaccharide; for instance, two glucose molecules joined together form the disaccharide maltose. Longer chains of monosaccharides are referred to as polysaccharides. Starch is an example of a polysaccharide.

Eating simple sugars promotes the release of insulin by the body. The role of insulin is to help transport sugar into the cells to be used as fuel. Excess sugars that cannot be used as energy immediately are converted into glycogen or fats. Because simple sugars are rapidly metabolized, the result is a swing in the amount of glucose in the blood from an extreme high to an extreme low. This can lead to a sudden burst of energy, followed by a lack of energy shortly thereafter.

Biological Effects In moderation, simple sugars are safe to consume, but in large amounts they can lead to obesity, heart disease, infection, tooth decay, and diabetes. For example, Dr. John Yudkin, a cardiovascular specialist and Professor of Nutrition at the University of London, theorizes that sugar is an important factor in the etiology of heart disease. He supports this hypothesis through clinical studies reporting that

- Men afflicted with coronary heart disease typically consume an unusually high amount of sugar
- Sucrose, although it is a complex carbohydrate, induces elevated levels of blood fats including cholesterol, which may influence the development of heart disease
- Analysis shows that global trends of sugar consumption correlate with the development of heart disease (Yudkin, 1971)

Simple carbohydrates may decrease the efficacy of the immune system. One study performed under *in vitro* conditions found that simple sugars inhibit some types of cellular immunity (Baba, 1979). Another researcher noted that a single slice of chocolate cake can cut the body's germ-fighting action by more than fifty percent for the first few hours

Table 2-3. Sugar Content of Various Products

Product	Size	Sugar in teaspoons
Soft Drink	8 ounces	4
Candy Bar	1 bar	6–8
Chocolate Cake	1 slice	15
Brownies	1 square	3
Ice Cream	1/2 cup	5–6
Apple Pie	1 slice	12
Peanut Butter	3 Tablespoon, Jiffy	3
Jelly	1 Tablespoon	3
Dried Apricots	4–6 halves	4
Raisins	1/4 cup	4
Prunes	3–4	4
Regular Doughnut	1	4
Jello	1/2 cup	4
Orange Juice	1/2 cup	2
Fruit cocktail	1/2 cup	5

while the body is metabolizing the sugars (Schwantes, 1975).

People who have rapid metabolisms are especially sensitive to sugar. For them, eating refined sugar is like eating a slow poison. It can lead to chronic problems such as low-grade urinary tract or yeast infections, insomnia, nervousness, and other health deficiencies. People of other constitutional types are also sensitive to refined sugar, but not to the same degree.

Ephedra (Ma Huang)

The herb ephedra has been used in Traditional Chinese Medicine for thousands of years to treat colds, allergies, and asthma. It is an effective bronchodilator and a stimulant as well.

The two active alkaloid constituents of ephedra, ephedrine and pseudoephedrine, are now synthesized for use in many cold, allergy, and asthma medications. Ephedra or its synthetic compounds may also be found in weight-control products, herbal stimulant preparations, and numerous fake psychedelic products such as Herbal Ecstasy.

Supplements containing ephedra have been scrutinized in the past few years because of the way the herb has been promoted. "Natural" stimulant formulas, weight-loss concoctions, and herbal psychedelics come in many forms: pills, powders, teas, sodas, and herbal extracts. Over 100 companies have promoted such products as safe, natural food supplements and as safe alternatives to caffeine. However, ephedra may be more harmful than caffeine because it not only stimulates the central nervous system but also increases the metabolic rate and has a longer-lasting effect. This may be a good combination for a weight-loss product, but it can produce a number of undesirable side effects, including malnutrition and fatigue. Some manufacturers of ephedra products have not been forthright in providing consumers with complete and honest information.

Young people sometimes use ephedra products for a legal psychedelic experience. Ephedra does not alter consciousness as hallucinogens do. It mimics the action of epinephrine and also affects the central nervous system like amphetamines do. In recent years, approximately fifteen deaths nationwide have been associated with herbal psychedelic products. In response, many local and state governments have begun to regulate ephedra-containing supplements and stimulants. New York State, for example, has outlawed ephedra-based products, including carbonated beverages containing ephedra. Other states such as Illinois have required products containing the stimulant to be available only by prescription. In April, 1996, the FDA officially warned consumers of the danger of ephedra taken in excess, especially to people with high blood pressure, heart disease, and diabetes. An FDA advisory committee is currently debating new nationwide regulations for the sale and use of ephedra based products.

One of the key ephedra issues is safe dosage. Qualified herbal practitioners and acupuncturists use ephedra wisely, combining it with other herbs to minimize its side effects. In 1996, the American Herbal Products Association, a voluntary national trade association for manufacturers of herbal products, took the step of requiring members to place a warning label on their ephedra-based products. Most herbalists support the traditional, appropriate use of ephedra in products designed to help relieve the symptoms of colds and flu.

Amphetamines

Amphetamines belong to a class of stimulants that also has a history of abuse. As street drugs, they can be found as ice, methylphenidate, ecstacy, and phenmetrazine. Amphetamines are long-lasting stimulants and enhance physical performance and concentration while causing restlessness. Side effects of amphetamines include anxiety, increased heart rate, and hypertension. Withdrawal may produce depression, lethargy, anxiety, and psychosis. Alcohol and other depressants are often used by those who abuse amphetamines to counteract their effects.

Appetite Suppressants

Over-the-counter appetite suppressants can contain amphetamine-like stimulants such as phenylpropanolamine hydrochloride and caffeine. Many people who try appetite suppressants and weight-control drugs have a low tolerance to stimulants and rapidly find that they need to take more and more to prevent overeating. Some are bothered with irritability, restlessness, sleeplessness, and other symptoms of overstimulation. Withdrawal symptoms from the drugs may include depression, anxiety, and other complications. Because long-term weight control requires caloric reduction and physical exercise (Feldman & Davidson, 1986), treating obesity with these or other drugs may be of limited value.

Cocaine

Cocaine is a highly addictive stimulant derived from the coca plant of South America, an integral part of indigenous culture. Traditionally, the native people have chewed the leaves mixed with powdered chalk or ash to help carry the plant's drug into the bloodstream.

Today, the leaves are chewed regularly in Peru and Bolivia for their fatigue-relieving and therapeutic value. Chewing coca leaves provides a long-lasting, low-grade euphoria that reduces appetite, increases physical stamina, and counteracts symptoms associated with "mountain sickness" and oxygen deprivation, a benefit in the high mountain habitats of South America.

Ethnobotanists have discovered abuse of coca that parallels the abuse of morphine in our culture. Passionate coca chewers such as the Coqueros tribe use coca to produce an intoxication marked by visions; the abuse also produces premature aging, apathy, and insanity. Typically, individuals chew several small bundles of leaves per day, taking in about sixty grams of leaf or 400 milligrams of cocaine (Murray, 1986). Although cocaine has many negative qualities, the coca plant itself—in low doses—has some therapeutic value, including mood improvement, increased energy, decreased appetite, and increased sexual stimulation.

Cocaine was isolated from the coca leaf in 1860. At that time, it was noted to have anesthetic properties. Its use, however, was as a treatment for morphine addiction and as a euphoriant. Currently, it is used as an anesthetic for surgery of the nose and eyes. Because it also acts as a vasoconstrictor, it can limit bleeding during surgery.

By 1914, cocaine's addictive qualities and association with increased crime had prompted forty-six states to enact legislation regulating its use and distribution. That same year, Congress passed the Harrison Narcotics Act banning nonmedical use of the drug and requiring strict accounting of medical dispensing to patients (Musto, 1973), and cocaine was forgotten as a law-enforcement problem. In the 1970s, however, it became one of the most frequently abused street drugs.

Today, powdered cocaine is favored by users, who inject it into their veins after mixing it with water, or snort it up their noses. Free-base or crack cocaine is rendered alkaline, or basic, making it more potent and absorbed more quickly into the bloodstream when smoked. Crack dosages range between 10 to 500 mil-ligrams, depending upon drug quality and the user's tolerance.

Cocaine is considered the most potent central nervous system stimulant of natural origin (U.S. Department of Justice, 1992). The drug acts on the CNS by inhibiting the re-uptake of the neurotransmitters norepinephrine and dopamine at the synaptic cleft. As discussed in the previous chapter, norepinephrine can cause both excitatory and inhibitory effects on neurons. Among these effects are increased motor activity and increased heart rate and blood pressure. Dopamine, a precursor of norepinephrine, can cause increased motor activity, vasodilation or constriction at higher doses, and psychosis. It is often associated with enhanced pleasure.

Cocaine has been associated with violent crimes. It is a short-lived drug, thus requiring the user to repeat and perhaps expand the dose throughout the day for euphoria to persist. Its ability to cause addiction is higher than that of amphetamines, and overdoses that can lead to death are more possible. Its use was once limited because of its high cost, but now cocaine and crack have become the drug of choice for drug users of all income levels. Cocaine users are of two sorts: Those who use it sporadically, at a party, for in-

TABLE 2-4. Additional Sources of Caffeine

Common Name	Species	Caffeine Content
Tea	Camellia sinensis	1–5%
Guarana	Paullinia cupana	3%
Chocolate	Theobroma cacao	2%
Kola nut	Cola acuminata	1.5%
Coffee	Coffea arabica	1.5–2.5%
Yerba maté	Ilex paraguariensis	.5–1.5%

(Bruneton, 1995)

stance; and those who use it chronically as part of a lifestyle involving other drugs.

Cocaine's long-term effects are similar to those of amphetamines, only worse: delusions, insomnia, fatigue, and anxiety. It often creates profound physical changes, including lowered pulse rate, decreased body temperature, and depressed breathing. Because the body responds to cocaine withdrawal with an effect that is opposite to the drug's action, these symptoms can be life-threatening. The withdrawal phenomenon holds true psychological features, as well; when facing withdrawal, chronic users become severely depressed and anxious.

Withdrawal symptoms also include nausea, convulsions, seizures, and hallucinations or paranoia. Because cocaine abusers often seek out and become addicted to other drugs such as opiates (heroin), barbiturates, anxiolytics, nicotine, caffeine, and alcohol, symptoms of both addiction and withdrawal are often intermixed, complex, and difficult to treat (www.ussc.gov/crack/chap2.htm). Eventually the chronic cocaine user must stop using the drug or die.

Other Natural Stimulants

Other natural stimulants include kola nut, chocolate, guarana, yerba maté, and black tea; all contain caffeine as the major stimulant and are used as coffee is used in the United States (see Table 2-4). Many herbs also contain the alkaloidal stimulants theophylline and theobromine. These compounds are similar in structure and function to caffeine.

LET ME DOWN:
THE SEDATIVES

As much as Americans love the fast lane and all the stimulants that go along with it, we can't continue indefinitely without rest.

To help unwind and relax, we can find downers or sedatives any time, day or night. Sedatives are a broad class of drugs that depress and slow down the functions of the nervous system. The most popular sedative, by far, is alcohol, but prescription drugs such as Xanax and Valium are gaining popularity. Various over-the-counter sleeping aids sell well, too. The following section reviews the most widely used and abused sedatives.

Alcohol

Alcohol is the world's most popular sedative and second only to tobacco as the cause of preventable diseases. About eighty percent of adults in the United States consume alcoholic beverages, and five to ten percent of adult males have alcohol-related problems. In moderation, alcohol can reduce the symptoms and hormonal changes that accompany stress. Its use has also been associated with a reduced risk of heart attacks and heart disease.

Alcohol is addictive and produces a tolerance that requires more of it to produce the same effects. Alcohol's main target is the central nervous system, where it creates the effects of sedation, relief of anxiety, slurred speech, uninhibited behavior, and impaired judgment. Moderate use of alcohol produces significant changes in the blood that reduce clotting. Because it dilates blood vessels, alcohol can cause hypothermia in cold weather.

Chronic, long-term consumption of alcohol leads to reduced ability of both the liver and the intestines to function properly. This may make a person more susceptible to other toxins and can lead to malnutrition. Alcohol harms the entire body, with effects to the nervous system, blood, heart, hormones, and immune system. Chronic use of alcohol also increases the risk of cancer, especially of the mouth, throat, and liver. Fetal alcohol syndrome can occur in infants of mothers who abused alcohol during the pregnancy.

The destructive results of alcohol abuse strike not only the user but society as well. Yet the federal government can do little to regulate alcohol because of its popularity and political clout. Alcohol claims over 150,000 lives each year, some directly, through cirrhosis of the liver and other damage to the body; and others indirectly, through accidents, abuse, violent crimes, and suicide (Vickery, 1990). Consider the following statistics:

- Drunk drivers are involved in over 2,600,000 automobile crashes each year, victimizing

4,000,000 innocent people and killing about 20,000 (Orozco, 1996).

- One-third of Americans are nondrinkers; one third are occasional drinkers who consume less than three drinks a week; and the remaining third, the heavy drinkers, consume ninety-five percent of all alcohol sold in the United States. Approximately fifty percent of this third tier consume more than fourteen drinks per week (Maisto, 1991). (Note: A drink is considered to be a half ounce of pure alcohol, which equates to one twelve-ounce can of beer, a five-ounce glass of wine, or a cocktail containing one and one-half ounces of spirits.)

- Approximately three in every 1,000 infants are born with fetal alcohol syndrome, a deformity caused by drinking during pregnancy. These children are both physically and mentally permanently handicapped (USDHHS, 1987).

- Alcohol abuse is a factor in fifty percent of all divorces and in many cases of spousal and child abuse (Vickery, 1990).

- A 1987 Gallup poll found that one in every four American homes has been touched by alcohol-centered problems (Vickery, 1990).

- The cost of alcohol abuse to the nation is estimated at more than $200 billion a year, sixty-five percent of which is due to lost employment and productivity (Maisto, 1991).

- The effects of alcohol abuse spread across generations. Children of alcoholics are four times more likely to become alcoholics themselves than are the children of nonalcoholics (Maisto, 1991).

History Alcohol has been an integral part of human culture for thousands of years. Written accounts and archeological evidence suggest that humans were making alcoholic beverages by at least 6,000 B.C. The first alcoholic beverages were probably made from fermented fruit juices. The Egyptian civilization developed the first barley-grain beers, and the Chinese mastered the production of distilled spirits around 1000 B.C. Apparently, Western Europe did not begin consuming alcoholic beverages until the eighth century A.D. (Maisto, 1991).

Since earliest times, alcohol has worn a double-faced mask. Alcohol's merry face helps us celebrate life events and smooth many social, political, and business activities. Alcohol's tragic face shows when individuals who drink too much damage themselves, their families, and their communities.

These serious problems have brought repeated condemnations of alcohol by the church, lawmakers, physicians, and philosophers (Keller, 1979). The nineteenth-century American Temperance Movement sought to counteract alcohol's negative influence on society, and its hard-fought successes eventually led to the passage of the Eighteenth Amendment to the Constitution in 1919, prohibiting alcohol. The amendment was short-lived, however, due to the excessive crime and bootlegging that surrounded the illegal manufacture and sales of alcohol. The Twenty-first Amendment, restoring alcohol to legal status, was passed in 1933.

Cultural acceptance of alcohol steadily increased until the mid-1980s. Recently, however, the general trend is toward limiting alcohol use because many take the negative consequences of excess alcohol seriously. Organizations such as Alcoholics Anonymous (AA) and Mothers Against Drunk Drivers (MADD) have brought attention to the impact of alcohol abuse on the individual, family, and society. Even with growing consciousness of the dangers of excessive alcohol, ample work remains to be done to understand how alcohol problems develop, how they are maintained, and how they can be prevented and treated.

Biological Effects Once swallowed, alcohol is rapidly absorbed through the gastrointestinal lining into the blood stream. Alcohol is carried throughout the body via the circulatory system, freely crossing membranes. In fact, it permeates the body so fast that within minutes of taking a few sips it can be detected in most tissues. The effects of alcohol are diverse and can result in both stimulation and sedation.

Alcohol is a toxic substance that would kill unless broken down by the body. Fortunately, the liver secretes a variety of enzymes specifically designed for this task, transforming alcohol into an inert compound that can be released via the lungs (creating a telltale breath odor) and urine. The fastest the liver can break down alcohol is approximately one drink per hour. Individuals who drink more store the excess alcohol in their blood and tissues.

Law enforcement officers rely on the slow-paced breakdown of alcohol when analyzing blood, urine, and breath to gauge sobriety. In most states, drivers are considered guilty of "driving under the influence" (DUI) if their blood-alcohol concentrations (BAC) exceed 0.10 percent (Maisto, 1991).

The amount of alcohol required for a person to behave drunkenly depends on body size and fat and amount of tolerance that has built up. Table 2-5 describes the typical acute effects of alcohol associated with rising blood-alcohol concentrations (Maisto, 1991).

Alcohol-related illnesses may take months or years to develop, especially since each person has a unique lifestyle and inherited constitution. Yet it is safe to say that the body is immediately affected by both occasional and long-term excess alcohol. Trying to define a "safe" level of alcohol consumption, a Canadian group from the Addiction Research Foundation suggests that more than two drinks a day is risky; other physician groups contend that more than one drink a day is unhealthy (Maisto, 1991).

Much credit should be given to chronic abusers of alcohol and

Table 2-5. Acute Effects of Alcohol Associated with Different Blood Alcohol Concentrations

% Blood-Alcohol Content	Effects
.01–.02	Slight change in feeling; sense of warmth and well-being.
.03–.04	Feelings of relaxation, slight exhilaration, happiness. Skin may flush warm and red.
.05–.06	Effects become more noticeable. More exaggerated changes in emotion, impaired judgment, and lowered inhibitions. Coordination may be altered.
.07–.09	Reaction time increases, muscle coordination impaired. Sensory feelings of numbness in cheeks, lips, and extremities. Further impairment in judgment.
.10	Definite deterioration in motor coordination and reaction time. Person may stagger and speak slowly.
.15	Major impairment in balance and movement. Large increase in reaction time. Detriment in judgment and perception.
.20	Difficulty staying awake; substantial reduction of motor capabilities; slurred speech, double vision, difficulty standing without assistance.
.30	Possible loss of consciousness.
.40	Unconsciousness, loss of sensation throughout body.
.45–.50	Total depression of circulatory and respiratory functions. Death.

other drugs who are dedicated to kicking their habits. The feeling of self-empowerment created by getting free of an addiction and the resulting increased sense of self-worth makes the effort especially life-affirming.

Benefits Alcohol has some therapeutic benefits. Moderate amounts of alcohol were once believed to be good for general health, tonifying the body and mind. For some it was thought to be the panacea for many of life's ills. Times have changed, and today we know a lot about the dangers of alcohol, as well as its medical value.

In cough syrups, alcohol enhances absorption of the active ingredients of the medicine. Invaluable as a solvent and preservative, alcohol is widely used in the production of both Western and herbal medicines (Jacobs & Fehr, 1987). Without alcohol, many valuable medical preparations could not be manufactured and effective.

Some recent findings indicate that moderate alcohol consumption may yield specific health benefits. Studies show that a drink a day can help decrease the risk of cardiovascular disease. One hypothesis holds that light alcohol consumption increases the production of high-density lipoproteins (HDLs), which help remove damaging cholesterol from artery walls. Another group of French studies shows that moderate drinkers of red wine have a lower incidence of heart disease. This body of work hypothesizes that red wine contains anthocyanidins, coloring pigments or tannins, which confer a protective effect by helping prevent the build-up of LDL cholesterol, reducing the blood's tendency to clot and preventing free-radical damage to vessels and heart tissue (Kahn, 1995). Researchers clearly state, however, that while red-wine consumption shows a protective effect against some types of heart disease, it does not benefit longevity or overall quality of life (Criqui et al. 1994).

It seems safe to conclude that fermented drinks containing a small amount (ideally, less than five percent) of alcohol can be a minor part of an overall health program that also includes aerobic exercise, diet improvement, and meditation.

Pharmaceutical Drugs

Pharmaceutical drugs are often prescribed by doctors for patients who are experiencing insomnia, anxiety, or nervousness because of stress. The first type, barbiturates, are addictive and extremely dangerous when taken with alcohol. Barbiturate addiction, like alcoholism, is characterized by narrowing obsession with obtaining the drug, insomnia, anxiety, paranoia, and suicidal thoughts. The benzodiazepines, which include Valium and Librium, create physical and psychological dependency. At first users experience feelings of well-being and peaceful sleep, but these benefits demand higher and higher doses of the drug. Withdrawal can be life-threatening and should be attempted only with medical supervision. Clearly, these medications are powerful if misused or if the individual has an adverse reaction.

Drug manufacturers warn against the use of these products for long periods of time, yet doctors prescribe them for months or years. One report states that more than a third of people over 65 are given at least a six-month supply of benzodiazepines (Keltner & Folks, 1993). Medical doctors may misuse these drugs because they provide an easy way to tranquilize the patient.

Sensitivity to pharmaceutical medications can develop over months or even years; then, suddenly, some unexplained symptom arises. When the symptom disappears when the drug is discontinued, physicians are often reluctant to acknowledge that the drug was the probable cause of the problem. The fact that two or three drugs, or even five or six, are sometimes prescribed together greatly compounds the risk of unwanted side effects. Many multiple-drug interactions have never been studied, so the patient becomes the guinea pig for pharmaceutical companies. More than 100,000 patients die annually from drug reactions or post-surgical infections (Faltermayer, 1994). Many pharmaceuticals are highly toxic to the liver (hepatotoxic) and lead to liver disease if used for a prolonged period. Even minute amounts of some drugs can subtly affect the mind and body (see Table 2-6 next page).

In fact, the term sleeping aid is a misnomer. Over-the-counter sleep aids and prescription drugs such as antidepressants and benzodiazepines such as Valium, Halcion, and Restoril do not actually produce healthy sleep. Instead, the drugs depress the central nervous system so that the patient loses consciousness in a parody of sleep. The most restorative stage of sleep, REM, is decreased in this state. The quality of sleep is thus severely diminished.

Ironically, long-term use of sleeping aids worsens insomnia. When the medication is discontinued, a condition called rebound insomnia often results. For many, it is worse than the sleeplessness

Table 2-6. Side Effects of Common Over-The-Counter and Prescription Drugs for Stress-Related Disorders

Drugs by Class	Side Effects	Alternatives
Analgesics		
Aspirin	Stomach irritation; large dose, ringing in ears, clotting defect, liver and kidney toxicity	Massage, yoga, willow-bark extract, corydalis extract
NSAIDS: Ibuprofen, acetominophen	Indigestion, nausea; liver damage with extended use or use with alcohol	As above
Ulcer Treatments		
H2 Blockers *reduce stomach-acid production*		
Cimetidine (Tagamet)	Diarrhea, dizziness, confusion	Marshmallow tea, licorice tea
Nizatidine (Axid)	Minor digestive upset	Cabbage juice, DGL licorice extract
Ranitidine (Zantac)	Headache, rash, nausea	Marshmallow tea, licorice tea
Mucosal Protective Agents *Protect the mucosal lining*		
Sucralfate (Carafate)	Constipation, dizziness, dry mouth, nausea, allergic skin reactions	Cabbage juice, DGL licorice extract
Bismuth subsalicylate (Pepto Bismol)	With long-term, frequent use: dermatitis, joint pain, weakness, diarrhea	Cabbage juice, DGL licorice extract
Antibiotics *used against* H. pylori *infection*		
Erythromycin	Superinfection (yeast), allergic reaction, diarrhea, cramps	Recommended antibiotics for ulcers are most effective when two antibiotics and Pepto-Bismol are used simultaneously. Side effects depend upon the antibiotic chosen.
Metronidazole	Metallic taste, superinfection (yeast), allergic skin reaction, headache, loss of appetite, diarrhea	
Amoxycillin	Allergic skin reaction, superinfection (yeast), colitis	
Tetracycline	Allergic reactions, mild to severe; colitis; tooth discoloration in children under age 8; irritation of mouth and/or tongue; loss of appetite, digestive upset, diarrhea	
Antidepressants		
Tricyclics		
Desipramine	Confusion, disorientation, aggravation of bipolar and schizophrenic disorders, heart arrhythmia, low white-blood-cell and platelet counts	St. John's wort
Amitriptyline (Elavil)	Drowsiness, blurred vision, dry mouth, constipation, impaired urination, confusion, weight gain	St. John's wort
Nortriptyline (Aventyl)	Light-headedness, drowsiness, blurred vision, dry mouth, constipation, impaired urination, skin rash, weight gain, dental cavities	St. John's wort

Drugs by Class	Side Effects	Alternatives
Monoamine Oxidase Inhibitors (MAOI)		
Phenelzine (Nardil)	Dangerous interactions with many drugs and foods, insomnia, light-headedness, fluid retention, possible high blood pressure, headaches, drowsiness	St. John's wort
Selective Serotonin Reuptake Inhibitors		
Paroxetine (Paxil)	Lowered blood pressure and fainting, skin rash, headache, heart palpitations, appetite loss, sweating	St. John's wort
Sertaline hydrochloride (Zoloft)	Decreased appetite, male sexual dysfunction, skin rash, headache, nausea	St. John's wort
Fluoxetine (Prozac)	Decreased appetite, minor weight loss, headache, allergy, drowsiness, fatigue, disrupted sexual function	St. John's wort
Anti-hypertensives		
Beta-blockers		
Propranadol (Inderol)	Lethargy, cold hands and feet, slow heart rate, light-headedness	Note: Do not make any changes in your blood pressure medication before consulting with your professional healthcare practitioner.
Centrally Acting Sympathoplegics		
Methyldopa (Aldomet)	Drowsiness, dry mouth, stuffy nose, light-headedness	Garlic, hawthorn
Vasodilators		
Hydralazine (Apresoline)	Headache, loss of appetite, tachycardia, digestive upset	Passion flower
Antispasmodics		
Carisprodol (Soma Compound)	Drowsiness	Kava-kava
Cyclobenzaprine hydrochloride (Flexeril)	Drowsiness, dry mouth, dizziness	Kava-kava
Sedative/Hypnotics		
Benzodiazepines		
Diazepam (Valium)	Dependence, drowsiness, lethargy, next-day "hangover"	Valerian, California poppy
Alprazolam (Xanax)	Drowsiness, headache, dry mouth, fatigue, blurred vision	Valerian, California poppy
Triazolam (Halcion)	Amnesia, tachycardia, depression, confusion	Valerian, California poppy
Zolpidem tartarate (Ambien)	Dependency with long-term use, rebound insomnia upon abrupt withdrawal, drowsiness, blurred vision	California poppy
Miscellaneous		
Buspirone (Buspar)	Mild drowsiness, lethargy, fatigue	California poppy, hops
Lorazepam (Ativan)	Sedation, dizziness, unsteadiness, next-day "hangover"	California poppy

that motivated the patient to seek medication. The benzodiazepines are particularly difficult in terms of rebound insomnia as well as anxiety and agitation upon discontinuation because these drugs quickly change the internal chemistry of the body and create dependency. Consequently, benzodiazepines and other sleeping aids should be discontinued gradually.

Although pharmaceutical drugs are beneficial in some cases, the need for most of them can be eliminated by following a total program for health. These drugs should be reserved for life-threatening situations and intractable cases that do not respond to natural remedies.

Over-the-Counter Sleeping Medications

Medications to disguise the effects of stress are all around us. Even the simplest convenience store today stocks at least one stomach medication, headache remedies, and a product that promises to help you sleep; you can find an astonishing array of these items at any grocery or discount store. It's profitable because most of us, when stressed, will reach for such products to get rid of the symptoms we feel. Yet we're not cured by these products; in fact, some of them create other, and sometimes worse problems for us. The side effects of over-the-counter (OTC) remedies can be very troublesome (see Table 2-6, previous page).

The top selling over-the-counter medications are sleeping aids. Over fifty types are available without prescription and many others with prescription. Nonprescription sleeping aids are the most commonly abused of all OTC drugs. Long-term users quickly develop dependency (Feldmann & Davidson, 1986).

When one understands how sleep medications work and how they affect the mind and body, it is hard to believe that so many take them. First, there is controversy surrounding nearly every sleeping aid on the market, because many are ineffective.

A majority of OTC sleeping aids are antihistamines, which are designed to treat cold symptoms. In this process, they also depress the central nervous system and cause drowsiness, depending on the dose. OTC sleeping aids do not actually bring about sleep as it is biologically defined, which is why many report, after using them, that they slept but do not feel rested. Side effects of antihistamines include allergy to the drug, excitability, and lowered blood pressure.

For example, Sominex and Nytol were first designed to prevent allergic irritation and inflammation caused by the histamine response. Their major side effect, drowsiness and sedation, led to marketing these drugs for treatment of insomnia.

Many sleeping aids are addictive and have numerous, unpredictable side effects. Occasionally people report euphoria, excitement, and uneasiness upon taking the drugs. Not everyone responds alike, and some will be stimulated by small amounts of the drug.

The digestive-system aids are equally dangerous, particularly because medications that regulate or stop the flow of stomach acid have recently been made available without prescription. Many people are taking these medications at prescription levels and above without medical evaluation of their need for the drugs. Thus, whatever pain they feel in the stomach goes undiagnosed, and the medications they gulp down may be harmful, not helpful to their condition.

The side effects of Tagamet, Axid, and Zantac can include digestive upset such as diarrhea and nausea. Headaches occur, as do dizziness and confusion. Some have reported rashes. Even Pepto-Bismol, a product that our grandparents probably used, can cause diarrhea, weakness, joint pain, and skin irritation if taken frequently

for a sustained period. Clearly, these medications should not be taken without the advice of a health-care professional.

Many simple, effective, and nontoxic natural remedies can induce sleep and calm the symptoms of stress. Some people become so accustomed to the effects of the drugs that they are astonished at how clear-headed they feel once the drug is completely eliminated. Many experience improved memory, too. Natural healing offers many excellent alternatives that should be explored before one turns to drugs.

CONCLUSION

Reducing stress and its effects on health is a challenge for nearly everyone. The uppers and downers that most of us use for this purpose not only fail to truly reduce stress, they can make our stress symptoms worse! We can become trapped in a miserable cycle of experiencing stress, trying to treat the stress, and finding the stress escalating, not subsiding.

To break the cycle, we must step out of it and pursue alternatives, rebuild our vital energy, and practice the methods and habits that bring about stress reduction. Much as we have developed habits of stress, we can now build habits of calm, quiet health.

CHAPTER 3:

RELIEVING STRESS NATURALLY

ALTHOUGH STRESS may be an integral part of contemporary life, we can turn to ancient and proven natural ways of relieving stress and preventing or treating its symptoms. All the systems of the body require periods of rest and periods of activity in order to function well. It is the periods of rest that most find difficult to achieve, primarily because the frenetic activities of modern life have become so habitual that they seem essential. Without periods of revitalizing rest, we become ever more vulnerable to bouts of serious illness. Without health, all that we now work so frantically toward will be lost, and the effort meaningless.

We can counteract stress and bring abundant health into our lives in a number of ways. One of the most important is doing our inner work—connecting with a higher wisdom, resolving old hurts, reaching for understanding, asking forgiveness for wrongs and forgiving others. Inner work that is ignored creates turmoil in our lives, and for many this is the first and foremost source of stress.

Dealing with stress also requires practical, daily attention to supporting our bodies' efforts to heal and maintain health. We can do this first by using natural herbs and foods properly, by assuring ourselves adequate and healthful rest, and by using techniques that are specific to creating peace and calm in our lives. Before we can achieve an abundance of health, we must focus on controlling the stress we feel.

HERBAL MEDICINE

Medicinal herbs have long been used by the majority of people in the world for disease prevention and restoration of health. Eighty percent of people in the Third World, as well as 900 million Chinese, rely on herbal medicine for their primary healthcare (Farnsworth, 1985). Until recently, in the United States the use of medicinal herbs has been largely supplanted by pharmaceutical drugs. Due in part to concern about the potential harm of prescription drugs and in part to new awareness of health alternatives, interest in healthful herbs is increasing rapidly.

Please note that this book reviews the historical and modern record of the use of herbs to support good health; the author is not prescribing herbs for any medical condition. A total program for health, which can often effectively include an herbal program, is the only lasting and sure way to achieve and maintain good health.

Constitutional Herbalism

Constitutional herbalism is a person-centered approach to using herbs that considers differences in individuals—and differences in the nature of particular herbs. Benjamin Franklin's famous saying, "I would rather know what sort of person has a disease than what sort of disease a person has," reflects an approach to healing that has ancient roots. Numerous cultures have long recognized that the individual's basic constitutional properties, based on genetic predisposition, early training, acculturation, and present condition influence not only the kind of disorder that is likely to develop, but

the most effective way of healing as well. That is, the person's individual constitution must be considered by the health practitioner when evaluating, diagnosing, and prescribing.

One of the most important principles of natural healing concerns the state of vital energy flow throughout the body. Vital energy, known as Qi in Traditional Chinese Medicine, is thought to permeate every fiber and aspect of our being, even to the cellular and molecular level. As a guiding principle in herbalism and natural healing, it is useful to consider three main energy states or conditions that can occur in the body and to a large extent determine the development and outcome of symptoms and determine how healthy we are or to which diseases we may be susceptible: stagnation of vital energy, deficiency of vital energy, and excess of pathogenic substances affecting the body.

To maintain abundant health, vital energy must flow smoothly, regularly, and abundantly, but not excessively. When vital energy becomes stuck and does not flow regularly and smoothly, the resulting condition is called *stagnation*. Stagnation of vital energy often leads to pain, stiffness, and discomfort in various parts of the body. To remove stagnation, we use herbs, foods, and activities that *regulate* or smooth vital energy. Examples of herbs useful for this condition include ginger, wormwood, and fringe-tree bark.

When a person has insufficient vital energy to support all the internal functions of the body, or if there is a lack of vital energy in any organ or organ system, the condition is known as *deficiency*. During aging, we use up vital substances as well as vital ancestral energy, so we are more likely to be deficient than younger people. Symptoms that commonly occur with deficiency syndromes include fatigue, depression, lack of interest in life, insomnia, and anxiety.

To remove deficiency, we use an important class of herbs called *tonics*. These include astragalus, reishi, shiitake, or small amounts of gentian. Tonics help make up the deficiency by supplying minerals and polysaccharides that support and nourish body processes. Many foods can act as tonics, including fish, green vegetables, or beans.

Considering the third condition of *excess*, we must first introduce the "six pathogens" (disease-causing agents). The pathogens may originate in our environment, or they may be generated from within the body. An environmental stimulus may be too much sun in the summertime, or exposure to a toxic agent in the air. An internally generated pathogen could be a burst of anger or the overstimulation of the metabolism caused by excess sugar or accumulation of metabolic by-products such as ammonia, brought about by the metabolism of protein.

Hot: Pathogenic heat that accumulates though our metabolic processes. Heat is accentuated by stimulants such as sugar, caffeine, and stress, which all increase metabolic rate through sympathetic activation. Pathogenic heat is associated with and can be accentuated during the summer season. Symptoms associated with pathogenic heat include infections, headaches, skin rashes, mouth sores, heart disease, arthritis, and other inflammatory diseases.

Cold: Pathogenic cold can penetrate our body's defenses and harm our digestion, respiratory tract, kidneys, or other internal processes, slowing them down and inhibiting the necessary circulation of blood and vital energy, leading to impairment of function or even disease if sustained.

Coldness is associated with winter. Symptoms include digestive pain, diarrhea with watery stools, kidney pain, and pain in other parts of the body.

Dry: Pathogenic dryness can occur after exposure to air conditioning. It is most likely to occur in the fall. Dryness can lead to such symptoms as dry mouth, nose, and throat, with bleeding, dry cough, and dry skin.

Damp: Pathogenic dampness results from exposure to damp climates, or when the dampness of the environment penetrates the body. We are more likely to be exposed to excessive dampness in the spring. Symptoms include excessive mucus, runny nose, night urination, a feeling of heaviness in the limbs, loose stools, and edema.

Toxins: Pathogenic toxins can be generated internally from incomplete digestion or overeating. They may also originate from elements in the environment, such as pesticides, herbicides, or heavy metals.

The Five Emotions: The emotions correspond with the five solid internal organs. Excessive or deficient emotions can lead to imbalance and disease if they are intense or prolonged. For instance, the Heart may become hardened by a lack of joy, or diseased from too much joy, which is known as mania. The five emotions and their corresponding organs include: Joy, Heart; Anger, Liver; Sorrow or Grief, Lungs; Fear, Kidneys; Pensiveness (includes worry and too much thinking), Digestion.

We can suffer from an excess of any of these pathogens, which can lead to unpleasant symptoms as diverse as headaches and high blood pressure. It is also possible for a generally deficient person to experience an excess in a specific pathogen or combination of pathogens. For instance, when a 60-year-old person has created a deficiency of the immune system or hormones through the overuse of vital resources, he or she often comes down with the flu.

There are several ways to eliminate a pathogenic excess and correct the imbalance, including draining the excess pathogen through the bowels with the use of *purgatives* (cascara, rhubarb), through the urine with gentle herbal diuretics called *aquaretics* (dandelion leaves, cleavers, parsley root), or through sweating them out with *diaphoretics* (yarrow, ginger). Ridding the body of the excess pathogens can restore balance and relieve symptoms. Table 3-1 summarizes (next page) the energy states of the body.

Using Herbs Instead of asking, "What is echinacea good for?", the question becomes, "For whom is echinacea suitable, and under what circumstances?" Instead of automatically giving echinacea to anyone who has the

Table 3-1. Energy States of the Body

Condition	Substance or Function	Typical symptoms	Healing Herbs or Foods
Stagnation	Vital energy (Qi), vital substances such as blood	Pain	Stimulating, regulating, or cleansing
Excess	Hot, cold, dry, damp, toxins, the five emotions	Infections, poor digestion, excessive mucus, emotional and mental imbalances	Draining
Deficiency	Vital energy, vital substances	Fatigue, depression, anxiety, insomnia	Tonifying, building

symptoms of an upper respiratory tract infection like cold or flu, one considers the person first, *then* the symptoms. If the person is normally healthy, without long-term chronic immune weakness, and simply has an acute viral infection, then echinacea can aptly be used to stimulate the immune system and help remove the infection. This herb directs the force of the immune system toward the surface of the body, where the viral attack is occurring.

If, however, the person has a history of recurrent colds or upper respiratory tract infections, it is necessary to consider the possibility of chronic immune weakness. In this case, an immune stimulant like echinacea would not be appropriate and could actually lead to immune-system *suppression*. Instead, one would look for herbs that work at a deeper level to bring the patient's partic-ular constitutional type and present condition into balance.

It takes many years of study to fully understand the intricate concepts involved in Traditional Chinese Medicine or Ayurveda, but several basic concepts can help make herbal remedies more effective. A central concept states that some people need building up with tonic herbs and formulas; and some need heat or energy removed or redirected by the use of specific or stimulant herbs or formulas.

Determining accurately an individual's constitutional type is a complex process which includes many questions, observations, and specialized knowledge. The Resource Directory includes several books that are helpful in learning about constitutional types, but individual diagnosis requires the services of an herbalist or Ayurvedic practitioner. In general, however, constitutional types are classified as excess or deficient.

Excess is characterized by energy, or nutritive force, that interferes with an individual's normal function. Such individuals rarely report feeling chronically fatigued or run down, and the body weight is typically normal. Physical examination reveals that the tongue is a deep red, possibly with a yellow coating toward the back, and the pulse is strong. This individual generally avoids spicy foods, hot drinks, and so on.

People who tend to have excess nutritive force usually benefit from using cooling herbs that move and direct energy, such as goldenseal and Oregon grape root. Examples of nervines, herbs that have a calming effect on the central system, for an excess constitution are passion flower and skullcap. California poppy, another excellent nervine, will work with either excess or deficient types.

A person with a deficiency constitution suffers from lack of nourishment, nutrient assimilation, functional energy, and vitality. He or she typically feels run down and chronically tired. The tongue may be livid red with no coating (a thin, white coating is normal) or pale, a very light pink. The pulse is thin, small, and deep; the health practitioner must press

hard to feel it. This individual often has internal coldness and generally avoids cold weather. People exhibiting these symptoms are often helped by tonic herbs such as astragalus, reishi, and ligustrum. Examples of nervines for a deficiency condition are California poppy, reishi, and linden flowers.

What's Your Type?

Over the centuries, a number of systems defining constitutional types have developed in the world's healing traditions. Today, Western herbalists use three basic systems to determine a person's constitutional attributes. First is the Ayurvedic system of kapha, vatta, and pitta; second, the Western system of mesomorph (physical type), ectomorph (mental type), or endomorph (digestive type); and third, the Chinese five-element system of water, metal, wood, fire, and earth types. The Resource Directory points out more information sources on constitutional types. A basic knowledge of your constitutional type helps when choosing appropriate diet, herbs, and lifestyle.

Table 3-2 summarizes a system of constitutional types based on that of Traditional Chinese Medicine. This system effectively determines the appropriate temperature and nature of foods and

Table 3-2. Basic Constitutional Types

Constitutional Type	Best Foods	Foods to Avoid	Best Herbs
Yang-excess (Physical type)	Raw vegetables, salads, fresh fruit in season, balanced diet with fish, chicken, vegetables, fruit, grains	Red meat, stimulants	Calming herbs (California poppy, passion flower); cooling herbs (burdock, dandelion, Oregon grape root, yellow dock)
Yang-deficient (Spiritual type)	Small amounts of cold, raw foods, eat mostly cooked foods and some red meat; if desired fish, chicken, spicy foods, grains, stir-fried vegetables, tofu	Raw fruits and vegetables, especially straight from the refrigerator.	Earthy herbs (roots such as burdock, warming, yang-promoting herbs such as red ginseng, aconite, cinnamon, ginger, teasel root
Yin-Excess (Digestive type)	Stir-fried vegetables, raw vegetables	Foods high in simple sugars (fruits, juices)	Ginger, cinnamon, cardamon
Yin-Deficient (Nervous Type)	Yams, baked squash, fish, sea vegetables, protein foods such as beans, sugar-free yogurt	Refined carbohydrates in any form (sugar, pasta, breads, baked goods), any stimulants such as coffee, ephedra, cocaine	Rehmannia, eleuthero, American ginseng, Chinese wild yam, kudzu root

herbs for an individual. Here, the term "yin" (vital substances) is taken to signify the feminine attributes of nourishment, fluids, coolness, and important nourishing and regulating substances such as hormones, neurotransmitters, and enzymes. The concept of yin signifies both the substances themselves, their functions, and how they are created and stored. "Yang" (vital energy) designates the complementary male attrib-utes of activity, energy, and heat. Yang also refers to the process of using up the yin substances.

As a practical example, imagine a large, robust, outgoing person with a red complexion, loud voice, and quick temper, all yang attributes. This type of person, who has a yang-excess constitution, is considered to have too much heat and yang energy. That is, the metabolism is rapid and raises the body's temperature in a subtle but harmful way. When balanced and healthful, this person's yang manifests as heat, passion, intellect, forcefulness, and heightened body awareness.

Now imagine a slightly-built person who is pale, timid, low-voiced, and indecisive; one whose manner and movements are tentative, and whose sex drive is marginal. This is a yang-deficient type who resides more in the spirit than the physical world.

People can also embody an excess or deficiency of yin energy. Imagine a large and fleshy person who carries excessive water and fat. This type is slow, sluggish, fleshy, and purposeful in movement and is known as a yin-excess type. Under normal circumstances, people with this constitutional type tend to have a well-developed digestive system; food and nourishment are very important to them.

Finally, imagine a person who is thin and wiry, perhaps strong, purposeful, often passionate, and quick of movement. This yin-deficient type, with a high metabolic rate and a well-developed nervous system, often has problems with anxiety, nervousness, and sleeplessness.

The individual's constitutional type has practical implications for healing. The ways of healing one type are not necessarily the best for another type. For instance, suppose that an individual who is yang-excess develops a chronic urinary-tract infection. To support healing the infection, the yang-excess individual should avoid hot foods, such as very spicy curries, that contribute to generating heat in the body. Sugary foods also can stimulate metabolism and promote heat production. When excessive heat in the body is a problem, eating sugary foods like cookies and ice cream is like throwing gasoline on a fire. Cooling vegetables such as cucumbers, salads, neutral grains, legumes, and some fresh fruit in season contribute to balancing the body's temperature and allowing healing to occur.

THE ACTIVE CATEGORIES OF HERBS

There are five categories of herbs and herb formulas.

Cleansers remove wastes and pollutants from tissues and organs with minimal effects on bodily processes. Examples are ionic substances, such as pectin, soluble fiber such as psyllium seed, and insoluble fiber such as psyllium husk to remove excess toxins from the body.

Heroics blast through energy blocks or stagnation and dramatically move or inhibit energy.

Strong and potentially irritating, heroic herbs should be prescribed only by practitioners who understand their actions and dangers, and then used only for a limited time.

Specifics perform one function for a limited time, moving energy or blood to stimulate a body process in a particular way. For example, echinacea stimulates the immune system. Specific herbs are used to treat acute conditions for short periods of time, generally in cycles of ten days on and three days off for up to three cycles. Additional examples include feverfew, goldenseal, Oregon grape root, St. John's wort, valerian, and wild oats. These herbs can remove excess, harmonize or regulate vital energy, and interact with the body's vital fluids to remove stagnation.

Nutritive tonics nourish specific cells, tissues, organs, and the whole individual, creating a state of balance in the body. They provide nutrients for function and repair. Nourishing tonics are sweet herbs and include astragalus, burdock, Siberian ginseng, hawthorn, nettles, and reishi. These herbs can help remove deficiency.

Stimulating tonics affect specific cells, tissues, organs, and the whole individual. They are slow, gentle invigorators that strengthen a person, increasing the efficiency of body organs, tissues, or systems. Examples are black cohosh, ginger, ginkgo, and turmeric. These herbs help remove deficiency and stagnation.

HOW TO USE HERBS

Commercial Preparations Herbs are commercially available in several forms. Bulk herbs are simmered or steeped in water to make tea. Herb powders are placed into capsules or pressed into tablets. Herb tinctures are extracted in alcohol and water; place about thirty drops into one cup of water and drink as a tea. Essential oils are generally distilled by professionals. They're very strong and must be used according to directions.

Homemade Herbal Preparations It is best to prepare herbs in vessels made of nonreactive materials, such as stainless steel, glass, or ceramic. Particularly avoid aluminum, as it may interact with the herbs and spoil them.

Herbal infusions or teas are made by pouring boiling water over leaves and flowers. Use one teaspoon of herb or herbal blend to one cup water. To determine how much herb to add to a measured amount of water, use the general formula of 1:10, where

CALMING HERBS FOR CHILDREN

Many children suffer from hyperactivity, for which many are given strong, synthetic sedatives such as Valium or Ritalin. Parents who prefer an alternative to these drugs can turn to herbal medicine, which is safe and mild, yet effective, so it is especially appropriate for children. Many herbalists recommend the following herbs for hyperactivity. All are available in natural food stores as single herbs or in formulas. I have found that liquid extracts are especially useful for children, because they can be disguised in tea or juice. The dose can easily be regulated from one drop to fifty, depending on the child's age and weight.

These herbs are safe when used properly. Remember to start with the lowest therapeutic dose for a few days, and check for individual reactions to the herb.

Red Clover Blossom:	A gentle nerve relaxant, this herb purifies the blood of toxins. It is suitable for long-term use. Prepare as a tea: one teaspoon per cup of water, steeped twenty minutes. Give the child half a cup each morning and evening.
Chamomile:	Makes a gentle and relaxing tea that tastes good and is very safe. Chamomile is a classic herb for children.
Linden blossom:	Makes a pleasant-tasting, calming tea. Linden blossom is also efficacious when added to baths; pour in a strong tea, or tie an ounce of herb in cheesecloth and place in the bath.
California Poppy:	A sedative recommended for hyperactivity and difficulty with sleeping.
Lemon Balm:	A lemon-tasting herb with a mild relaxing effect.
Wild Oats:	Hyperactive children should be given this nervine tonic. It makes a mild, pleasant-tasting tea and can be drunk freely. As an alternative, place five drops to three droppersful of liquid extract into water, juice, or one of the relaxing teas.
Hsiao Yao Wan:	This famous Chinese patent remedy is used to cool "liver fire," which can make kids angry, irritable, and perhaps even downright obnoxious. It is widely available in herb stores. Give the child 6-8 pills three times a day for a few weeks.

the 1 is one part of the herb by weight, and the 10 is the water by volume in ounces. Alternately, you may use the herb measured in grams and the water in milliliters.

Cover the pot and let the herbs steep for ten to thirty minutes. Then strain and drink the liquid or refrigerate for later use.

Decoctions are made by simmering roots, stems, and barks in water for twenty to forty-five minutes, then allowing the mix to steep for another fifteen minutes off the flame. The typical proportion is one ounce of herb to one pint of water.

Tinctures are generally made by steeping fresh or dried herbs in a mixture of alcohol and water; for most herbs, 100-proof vodka makes a satisfactory menstruum, or mixture. Use one part of herb or herb blend to five parts liquid, all measured in ounces. Keep the mixture in a warm place out of direct sunlight, and shake daily for at least two weeks. Then squeeze the liquid through a linen cloth or press it out with a hydraulic press. Tinctures will keep for two or three years.

Herbal oils are made by infusing herbs in a vegetable oil, such as olive, almond, or apricot-kernel oil. The herbs are chopped or pureed, covered with oil, and placed in a glass container, then left in the sun or another warm place for two weeks and shaken daily. The liquid is then filtered and placed in a glass container for storage.

Dosages and Schedule of Use

Deciding on the proper dosage of herbs and herbal preparations is extremely important. The dose determines whether an herb or preparation will have no effect, a substantial therapeutic effect, or a toxic effect, although there is typically a wide range of safety. When starting a program with an herb or preparation, use common sense. Check for individual sensitivity by starting with a low dose and working up to a full therapeutic dose. When discontinuing a remedy, taper off the dose to allow the body to become readjusted. For children, the younger and smaller the child, the smaller the dose.

Infants need only a few drops of a tincture or a teaspoon or two of tea as a dose. Calibrate the dose for children and adults based on overall strength and vitality. A person with lots of vitality can tolerate a higher dose because the body has sufficient energy to handle it. In other words, for such a person the herbs can release and move energy, not deplete it. Generally weak and deficient persons should take a lower, gentle dose. People who are sensitive to herbs and medicines in general also are best treated with small doses.

Finally, it is vital to know the nature of the herb or herb formula before deciding on dose. Herbs such as poke root, which can cause vomiting and stupor if misused, are very harsh and have a narrow range of safety. Others such as peppermint have a wide range of safety. However, even "safe" herbs can produce unwanted side effects if used to excess. For instance, psyllium husk is a safe and effective source of dietary fiber when taken in appropriate quantities. Too much psyllium, however, can bring on diarrhea. Tables 3-3 and 3-4 (next page) summarize average doses for adults and children.

Safety and Contraindications

Some have the perception that herbs are always mild and wholesome and may be taken without concern for side effects or reactions. This is simply not so; herbs can be very powerful. Several cautions are in order:

- First and foremost, herbs contain potent chemicals that can have serious, even lethal effects; after all, caffeine, alcohol, ephedrine, and tobacco are all natural products. Do not

Table 3-3. Adult Dosages of Herbs

The exact safe and effective dose of commercial tinctures, herb powders, capsules , tablets, and other kinds of herb extracts is often difficult to pinpoint. This is because the potency and quality of the herbs and herb extracts can vary from company to company, and individual response to herbs can vary, too.

Choose the product based on reputation of the firm that produces it. When in doubt, consult the nutritional specialist working in a natural food store or shop, or ask your herbalist. Again, it is always best to start with a minimum dose for several days, then work up to a therapeutic dose over another few days.

Form of Herb	Dosage
Fresh herbs from the garden	One or 2 medium-sized leaves
Dry herbs (nibbling)	Up to 1 gram
Teas	One cup to 1 quart per day
Powdered herbs	Two to 4 caplets, 2 to 3 times per day
Liquid extracts	One to three droppersful, 2 to 3 times per day
Powdered extracts	One to 2 tablets, 2 to 3 times per day (00-size capsules)
Highly purified standardized extracts	One tablet, 2 or 3 times per day

Table 3-4. Children's Dosages, Tinctures

Age of Child	Dose
1 month	2 to 5 drops tincture
1 to 3 months	5 to 10 drops
3 to 6 months	10 to 15 drops
6 months	15 to 25 drops
1 to 3 years	25 to 35 drops
3 to 5 years	35 drops to 1 dropperful
5 to 10 years	1 to 1.5 droppersful
10 to 15 years	1.5 to 2 droppersful
16 and above	Adult dose

Note: These doses are average doses and are usually given two to three times daily, as needed. When beginning a herbal treatment, start with the minimum therapeutic dose and continue at that dose for several days, watching carefully for individual reactions. If reactions occur, discontinue use.

use herbs without educating yourself thoroughly; better yet, work with a qualified health practitioner to develop an herbal regimen specific to your needs.

• Drug-herb interactions can be dangerous and little is known about them. Herb-herb interactions are also possible, and can have serious consequences.

• Abruptly substituting herbal therapy for drug therapy may prompt a withdrawal reaction. Tapering off over a period of two or three weeks is much better, and breathing techniques, meditation, and exercise can facilitate the readjustment. When one has used drugs over a period of years, it may take several months to feel truly free from after-effects.

Most commercial products containing herbs use ingredients that are not toxic, but there are a few exceptions. The American Herbal Products Association (AHPA), a trade organization for herbal manufacturers, is very concerned about herbal safety. Member companies follow a code of ethics and agree to carefully monitor the quality and identification of the ingredients in their products. Unfortunately, not all herbal products sold in North America are manufactured by AHPA members. If you want to know whether the manufacturer of the herbal products you buy is an AHPA member, call the organization's national office at (301) 951-3204.

Many herbs, even some available in herb stores, should be used cautiously (see Table 3-5). Other more potentially toxic herbs may be sold by herbalists, licensed acupuncturists, and naturopathic physicians. Make sure to carefully follow your herbalist's or the manufacturer's instructions regarding dosage and the period of use of any product you use. If you have doubts or questions, be sure to investigate the herb.

Although rare, it is possible for some people to have an adverse, idiosyncratic reaction to an herb that is considered safe. If you experience symptoms such as rash, headache, upset stomach, nausea, or diarrhea while taking thera-peutic quantities of an herbal remedy, cut the dose in half (if symptoms are mild) and continue to take it. If symptoms are severe, discontinue and call your health-care practitioner.

Some herbs can interact or interfere with pharmaceutical medications. If you are taking medications, be sure to tell your herbalist or natural health practitioner about the medication and dosage. Physicians are rarely trained in herbal medicine, so most are not a good source of information on herbal toxicity, side effects, or contraindications. You may find a professional herbalist in your area by contacting the American Herbalist Guild (AHG) (see Resource Directory).

Table 3-5. Herbs to Use Cautiously

Herb	Potential Difficulty
Lobelia	Emetic, use with caution
Chapparal	Liver stimulant, use with caution, do not use during pregnancy
Comfrey	Contains liver toxins, use with caution, do not use during pregnancy
Coltsfoot	Contains liver toxins, do not use during pregnancy
Ephedra	Stimulant, contains ephedrine
Kola nut	Stimulant, contains caffeine
Guarana	Stimulant, contains caffeine
Tobacco	Contains toxic, addictive nicotine; extremely dangerous

STRESS AND FOODS

Because diet is likely to be closely linked with stressful events, what we eat has a huge impact on body chemistry and ultimately on health. Under stress, we tend to choose foods that aren't the best for us; with care and consideration, however, we can learn to use food in support of healing and good health.

We now know that a number of important neurotransmitters, which affect mood and mechanisms for coping with stress, are built from amino acid molecules found in protein foods. An example is serotonin, made by the body from the amino acid L-tryptophan, found in soy, dairy products, and meat. This neurotransmitter is essential in coping with anxiety, depression, and insomnia.

All cells, organs, and systems of the body are governed by the principle that continual overuse or use in one direction to the exclusion of others will break down the body's normal, self-regulated state of health.

Experimenting with foods as sources of amino acids as part of a normal, healthy diet is an excellent way to work toward overcoming the effects of stress. In natural food stores, many amino acids are available in pure form as a supplement. The guidance of a qualified natural health practitioner is valuable in determining whether pure amino-acid supplements are helpful for you; such products are not without risk. Table 3-6 summarizes information

Table 3-6. Amino Acids

Amino Acid	Foods	Action	Uses
GABA	Absent in foods	Calming to the brain	Anxiety, depression, hypertension
Glycine	Turkey, wheat germ, carrot, cottage cheese, celery, almonds	Sedative to brain	Depression disorders
Leucine	Wheat germ, milk, avocado, yogurt, chicken, almonds, walnuts, cheese	Promotes protein synthesis and slows effects of stress	Low energy resulting from severe stress
L-Tryptophan	Soy, pinto, and mung beans; tempeh, tofu, lentils	Influences serotonin concentration in the brain	Pain, insomnia, depression

Information in this chart taken from The Healing Nutrients Within by E. R. Braverman.

about important amino acids that help with such stress symptoms.

THE HEALING QUALITIES OF HERBS AND FOODS

Throughout history, healers have considered the use of herbs and foods as part of their arsenal against discomfort and illness. Today, our concern for the healing secrets of plants and foods is great; expeditions to remote and threatened areas search for previously unknown plants that may have uses in healing.

Adaptogens

The word *adaptogen* was coined by the Soviet scientist N. V. Lazarev in 1947. He said that a substance must fulfill three criteria to be classified as an adaptogen, which is a substance that allows the body to adapt efficiently to stressful situations:

- Cause only minimal side effects
- Increase the body's overall immune function by a wide range of actions rather than by a specific action
- Restore balance to all bodily systems while placing additional burden on none.

Since then, researchers have conducted thousands of scientific tests on Siberian ginseng and other herbal adaptogens. These herbs have proved to be remarkably effective in preventing a variety of stress-related ailments; they also increase stamina and athletic performance.

In general, by supporting adrenal function, adaptogens help

Adaptogen Tea

Siberian ginseng root	4 parts dried herb, by weight
Schizandra fruit	4 parts dried herb, by weight
Echinacea root	1 part dried herb, by weight
Wild Oats	1 part dried herb, by weight
Ginkgo	1 part dried herb, by weight
Licorice	1 part dried herb, by weight

If your herbs are whole, prepare them by chopping them fine. Mix the herbs well and store. Simmer 1 ounce of the herb mixture in 2 cups water for 20 minutes, then strain. Drink 1 cup of the tea, 2 or 3 times daily.

counteract the debilitating effects of stress. They help the body's cells produce energy more efficiently, then turn around and help the cells eliminate wastes. Adaptogens work anabolically to help the body build muscle and tissue and use oxygen more efficiently. Finally, adaptogens enhance the regulation of biorhythms.

The general tonifying effects of adaptogens are familiar to Western medicine. Until about fifty years ago, doctors commonly prescribed medicines known as roborants (which strengthen the body), tonics (which restore normal tone to tissue), and alteratives (which improve the processes of nutrition and repair). What we now call adaptogens combine at least some of the major functions of roborants, tonics, and alteratives.

Russian researchers have identified several herbs as powerful adaptogens. They include Siberian ginseng *(Eleutherococcus senticosus)*, ashwaganda *(Withania somnifera)*, schisandra *(Schizandra chinensis)*, reishi *(Ganoderma lucidum)*, gotu kola *(Centella asiatica)*, and rehmannia *(Rehmannia glutinosa)*.

These adaptogenic herbs can be incorporated into a daily nutritional regimen with other nutritional and herbal supplements. Displaying few contraindications or cross reactions with other supplements, adaptogens can be taken as tinctures, capsules, or teas. Adaptogen Tea is a recipe for an adaptogenic formula that can be made at home to help protect the body against stress.

Nervines and Calmatives: Relaxing and Antistress Herbs

In the classical herbalism of the early twentieth century, any herb that affected the nervous system

MILK THISTLE, THE GREAT PROTECTOR

The liver is often stressed during the use of pharmaceutical drugs. One herb that can help protect and support the liver during this time is milk thistle *(Silybum marianum)*. It is available in liquid extract or standardized extract form, usually in capsules or tablets.

Milk thistle is well-suited to help the body deal with the accumulation of internally metabolized toxins and by-products and the creation of free radicals caused by stress. Studies of milk thistle extract show that it helps regenerate and strengthen the liver, enabling the organ to more easily eliminate fats, alcohol, prescription drugs, chemical pollutants, X-rays, and other stresses.

in any way was called a nervine. For further clarification, the nervines can be divided into six subcategories.

Sedative nervines, the calmatives, reduce anxiety and have a calming effect on the central nervous system. These herbs are frequently used in formulas for nervousness, sleeplessness, and mild anxiety. Examples are California poppy, valerian, hops, kavakava, and lavender.

Analgesic nervines help reduce nerve or muscle pain, although they can be used for any kind of pain. Typically, these herbs will not work so well or so quickly as aspirin, but a well-designed formula containing some of these herbs can be helpful in reducing pain and promoting healing with few side effects. Examples include Roman chamomile, valerian, St. John's wort (used externally and internally), corydalis, and Jamaican dogwood.

Stimulating nervines stimulate and raise the tone of the sympathetic nervous system and also raise the sympathetic tone. Small amounts of these herbs combined in a formula can enhance mental and physical performance and reduce fatigue. Examples are guarana, rosemary, kola nut, ephedra, coffee, and tea. They should be used in conjunction with adrenal tonics and adaptogens like gotu kola, eleuthero, or ginkgo that can help counteract any detrimental effects on the adrenal system.

Tonic nervines nourish the nervous system and should be taken for extended periods of time—at least three months—in order to help nourish and support the function of the nervous system. Examples include wild oats, passion flower, celery, and sea vegetables such as nori and wakame.

Psychotropic nervines enhance intuition and dreams. They are sometimes used for people who are trying to remember their dreams, perhaps to gain understanding about the meaning of unconscious images. Examples include kava-kava and mugwort.

Soporific nervines can help one fall asleep faster, wake up less often, go into a deeper sleep, enhance REM sleep, and yield more refreshing sleep. They may not work for everyone but are very useful when combined with stretching, breathing, meditation, and other methods of relaxing. Examples of soporific nervines include valerian, catnip, hops, St. John's wort, and California poppy.

THE ENERGETICS OF FOODS

In Traditional Chinese Medicine, herbs and foods are considered to have particular qualities according to hot or cold nature, flavor, and special healing constituents. Some herbs and foods are cooling in the presence of excess heat; others are warming and useful when the body is too cool. Sweet and pungent flavors, for example, are warming, while salty or sour flavors are cooling. Herbs are also known to have directions; that is, the action of the herb may be toward the surface of the body or toward the interior. It may push energy and bodily fluids up in the body (i.e., expectorants), or push down (i.e., laxatives). Herbs and foods may also influence the function of specific organs or have an overall helpful effect. The proper use of these herbs and foods creates balance within

Table 3-7. Foods to Relieve the Symptoms of Stress

Food	Temperature	Uses
Calms Digestion		
Lettuce	Cool	Calms energy, removes heat
White basmati rice	Neutral	Calms, soothes stomach, intestines
Soy products	Neutral	Cancer protectant, balances hormones
Cultured, sugar-free yogurt	Cool	Ensures healthy intestinal flora
Adrenal Tonics		
Aduki beans	Warm	Nourish adrenals
Yams	Warm	Nourish, strengthen digestive organs
Regulates Digestion		
Ginger	Hot	Activates, warms digestion
Fennel	Warm	Relieves indigestion and gas
Orange peel	Warm	Alleviates nausea, prevents stagnation
Protects Digestion, Liver		
Milk thistle	Neutral	Protects, restores liver
Turmeric	Warm	Relieves inflammation, protects liver
Garlic	Hot	Kills parasites, promotes circulation of energy, lowers cholesterol
Sea vegetables	Neutral	Soften cysts, lumps, and tumors
Supports Nervous System		
Sea vegetables	Neutral	Provides mineral ions to promote nerve function
Oats	Warm	Strengthen nervous system
Celery	Cool	Tonifying to the nerves
Regulates and Supports Hormones		
Soy products	Neutral	Reduce cancer risk
Prevent Infections		
Garlic	Hot	Acts as antibiotic and antiseptic

the body, leading to improved health.

These active qualities of herbs and food are called "energetics." Traditional herbalists consider the energetic properties of herbs and foods at least as important as their active constituents and uses, because energetics help determine which foods are best suited for different types of individuals. Choosing just the right foods for the individual constitution and present condition will allow the basic natural healing principles of herbs and foods to improve health. If the body systems are underactive and not producing enough heat for the body to function correctly, warming, cooked foods will dispel the cold.

The temperature of the metabolism is important because the body's systems, including the nervous system, may become seriously impaired when their environment is not normal. Many enzyme systems cease functioning at a less-than-optimal temperature; other body systems lose efficiency and thus demand more energy to function.

Specific beneficial compounds of herbs can be extracted and standardized. In this form, they are known as "phytopharmaceuticals," literally "plant medicines." One of the best examples is genistein, a phytoestrogen that has hormone-balancing effects and is found in soy products. Table 3-7 (previous page) is a summary of foods and some of their constituents that can be useful for supporting and balancing the body when under stress.

Stress and Digestion

Symptoms of stress seem to target the digestive system. Protecting the digestive tract from the effects of stress requires preventive measures. When body systems function under stress and heavy performance demands year after year, they become depleted and exhausted. The best prevention for system overuse is to vary activities so that every system receives a time of rest as well as a time of work. For optimum health, the digestive system needs periods of activity interspersed with periods of rest and recuperation.

Herbs to Support Digestion

Because ongoing stress can disrupt the digestive tract, supplying energy and nutrients to restore and maintain its normal functions is essential to health. In Traditional Chinese Medicine, herb and herb formulas of two major classes are commonly recommended: *regulating* and *strengthening* herbs and formulas.

Qi (vital energy) herbs and formulas regulate the action of the digestive processes, making its work more efficient. Table 3-8 gives examples of herbs and formulas from both Western traditions and Traditional Chinese Medicine that can be used regularly.

Another class of herbs and formulas is digestive vitality tonics. These help overcome the effects of stress by increasing the power of the digestive tract to break down foods, assimilate important nutrients, release energy from food to the cells and organs, and eliminate wastes. Some of these popular herbs and formulas are summarized in Tables 3-9 and 3-9A.

Healing herbs can also have specific effects against the symptoms of stress. Stomach aches often occur when the body is under stress because the digestive tract produces more acid and enzymes than necessary to digest food. This surplus irritates the tissues of the stomach and sometimes the entire digestive tract, leading to symptoms of burning and discomfort. Table 3-10 indicates herbs and formulas for overcoming this problem by soothing the digestive tract.

Stress can also cause cramping and knotting of the stomach, small intestine, and large intestine, leading to constipation, discomfort, and pain. Table 3-11 lists some herbs, known as antispasmodics, that act to relax the digestive organs. Table 3-12 (next page) summarizes the herbs useful for protecting the digestive tract against the ravages of stress.

Tonic Foods

Deficiency occurs when a bodily function is overworked to the point that it breaks down, having lost the ability to function. A "tonic" is then required to restore natural function and efficiency.

Table 3-8. Herbs and Herb Formulas to Regulate Digestion

Name of Herb or Formula	Uses
Escape Restraint Pill (yue ju wan)	Abdominal distention, feeling of fullness in chest and abdomen, pain, belching, reduced appetite, indigestion
Atractylodis	Poor appetite, nausea, fatigue
Orange peel	Food stagnation
Cyperus	Epigastric distention
Four-seed tea	Flatulence, indigestion
Peppermint	Nausea, indigestion

Table 3-9. Herbs and Herb Formulas to Strengthen Digestion

Name of Herb or Formulas	Uses
Four Gentlemen	Fatigue, poor appetite, pale complexion
Bitters Tea Formula	Weak digestion, poor appetite, low energy
Digestive Power Formula	Weak digestion, poor appetite, low energy
Bu Zhong	Weak digestion
Liver-Digestion Formula	Poor and/or painful digestion, gas, bloating
Gentian root	Weak and/or painful digestion

Table 3-9A. Herbs for Increasing Digestive Strength (TCM)

Herb	Action	Uses
Artichoke leaf	Cooling	Increases bile activity and digestive efficiency
Astragalus	Warming	Tonifies spleen and stomach
Bitters	Cooling	Activates bile to improve digestion
Centaury	Cooling	Improves digestive function
Ginger	Warming	Supports digestion, relieves nausea
Ginseng, red	Warming	Improves cold, deficient digestion

Table 3-10. Herbs to Soothe Digestion

Name of Herb or Formula	Uses
Herbal Soothing Tea	Irritable bowel syndrome, indigestion
Flax-seed tea	Constipation, gastritis, irritable bowel syndrome
Mallow-leaf tea	Gastritis
Marshmallow root	Ulcers, gastritis
Licorice	Weak digestion, ulcers, gastritis
Plantain leaf	Gastrointestinal irritation

Table 3-11. Antispasmodic Herbs

Herb	Uses
California poppy	Intestinal cramps
Chamomile	Colic, nervous stomach
Skullcap	Poor digestion (acts as a mild bitter tonic)
Valerian	Nervous stomach
Wild yam	Flatulence

Table 3-12. Protecting Digestion Against Stress: A Natural Healing Summary

Symptom or Ailment	Prevention Methods
Constipation	Increase soluble and insoluble fiber in the diet. Use abdominal massage. Yoga, stretching. Eat dinner early (before 7 P.M.). Eat breakfast at least 1 hour after rising. Exercise before breakfast. Avoid overeating.
Painful Digestion (dyspepsia)	Practice abdominal massage for 5 to 10 minutes daily. Focus on consciously relaxing the abdominal area. Drink peppermint and/or chamomile teas daily. Observe good food combining. Keep meals simple, avoid coating foods with oil, avoid eating sugary foods along with protein foods. Avoid spicy foods. Avoid cold beverages around mealtimes. Take "bitters" before each meal.
Gas	Observe good food combining. Drink peppermint and/or fennel tea after dinner. Soak beans overnight, rinse daily for 2 to 3 days until they begin to sprout, then cook. Use digestion-strengthening herbs (bitters, ginger tea) before meals.
Heartburn	Avoid spicy foods and fried foods. Avoid coffee and other stimulants. Practice conscious breathing and take a relaxing break before meals. Use antispasmodic teas (chamomile, wild yam, California poppy) when needed.
Ulcers	Avoid stimulants (coffee, tea). Take relaxing breaks frequently. Practice meditation. Use anti-inflammatory herbs to soothe irritation in the upper gastrointestinal track (2 to 3 cups per day of licorice tea, marshmallow-root tea, or plantain tea); aloe vera gel. Use antibacterial or immune-stimulating herbs if the ulcer is associated with the bacteria *H. pylori* (echinacea, garlic, golden seal). Drink freshly-juiced organic cabbage juice, 8 ounces twice a day for 10 days.
Swallowing Difficulties (dysphagia)	Use anti-inflammatory and antispasmodic teas such as California poppy or chamomile in small amounts, about a half cup, 6 to 10 times daily. Focus on consciously relaxing the esophagus. Drink peppermint and/or chamomile teas daily. Work on resolving emotional issues that may be troubling you.
Irritable Bowel Syndrome	To reduce spasms, take peppermint oil in enteric-coated capsules as directed on bottle. Massage abdomen daily for 5 to 10 minutes. Visualize the relaxation of the bowels whenever needed. Check for food allergies by eliminating suspected foods one at a time. Drink peppermint and/or chamomile teas daily. Drink antispasmodic teas such as California poppy or chamomile several times a day, or use the herbs in tincture form.

Tonics act with a strengthening and invigorating effect, and many substances and activities can produce more energy: certain herbs and foods, a quick cold shower, physical exercise, rest, and expressions of love and caring with others.

Foods can have a very positive tonifying effect on the digestive tract. An overstimulated metabolism or a yang-excess or yin-deficient constitution will benefit from foods that are cooling and calming in nature. Tables 3-13 and 3-14 give the temperature and

TABLE 3-13. The Energetics of Beverages

Beverage	Temperature	Taste	Notes
Coffee	Hot	Bitter, acrid	Contains the stimulant alkaloid caffeine
Tea	Hot	Astringent	Contains caffeine
Cola drinks	Hot	Sweet	Contain caffeine and refined sugar
Milk	Cool-cold	Sweet	Allergic reactions are common
Mineral water	Cool	Salty	None
Distilled water	Neutral	Bland	Will not leach out minerals
Vegetable juice	Warm-cool	Sweet, salty	Root vegetables have more sugar so are warm and sweet
Fruit juice	Cool	Sweet (sour)	High amounts of simple sugar
Rice milk	Cool	Sweet	High amount of simple sugar
Soy milk	Neutral	Sweet	Some people have allergic reactions

Calming Herbal Extract

3 parts California poppy tincture
1 ½ parts kava-kava tincture
2 parts valerian tincture

2 ½ parts hawthorn tincture
1 part reishi tincture

Combine the tinctures and bottle. Take up to forty drops in a soothing herbal tea three or four times a day.

Table 3-14. Energetics of Common Foods

Food	Temperature	Taste
Animal Products		
Red meat	Hot	Salty, sweet
Fish	Cool	Salty, sweet
Chicken	Warm	Sweet
Eggs	Neutral	Salty
Yogurt	Cool	Sour, sweet
Milk	Cold	Sweet
Vegetables		
Cucumber	Cool	Salty
Celery	Cool	Salty
Kale	Warm	Bitter, salty
Lettuce	Cool	Bitter
Onion	Warm	Pungent
Tomato	Cold	Sweet, sour, salty
Carrot	Cool	Sweet
Potato	Neutral	Bland, sweet
Sweet peppers	Cool	Salty, sour
Hot peppers	Hot	Pungent
Corn	Cool	Sweet
Summer squash	Cool	Sweet
Winter squash	Warm	Sweet
Grains		
Wheat bread	Warm	Sweet
Millet	Cool	Sweet, salty
Buckwheat	Warm	Sweet
White rice	Neutral	Sweet
Brown rice	Warm	Sweet
Oats	Warm	Sweet
Barley	Neutral	Sweet
Rye	Neutral	Bitter
Fruits		
Apple	Cool	Sweet, sour
Pear	Cool	Sweet
Banana	Neutral	Sweet
Peach	Warm	Sweet, sour
Cherry	Warm	Sweet, sour
Watermelon	Cold	Sweet
Cantaloupe	Cool	Sweet
Blackberry	Cool	Sweet, sour
Blueberry	Neutral	Sweet, sour
Raspberry	Cool	Sweet, sour

tastes of a number of common beverages and foods. Table 3-12 (page 82) summarizes digestive herbs.

HERBS FOR RELAXING

Herbal teas and other preparations play a time-honored role in simple relaxation. The best known are valerian, hops, and chamomile, the sedative nervines or calmatives. Table 3-15 summarizes calming herbs.

RECOVERING FROM SUGAR ADDICTION

Addiction to sugar is very common but overlooked in our society. Overcoming such an addiction requires replacing present, harmful eating habits with healthy ones.

Increasing the fruits and vegetables we eat is important. By eating plants, we consume complex carbohydrates such as starch and cellulose. Cellulose cannot be digested by the body, but it serves as dietary fiber, important in promoting the movement of food through the intestines and protecting against diseases such as cancer and cardiovascular disease. Complex carbohydrates are slowly broken down by the body into the simple sugars that provide energy. Because of this, the body has a more consistent supply of energy available. Complex carbohydrates are found in fruits and vegetables.

Complex carbohydrates support and nourish the body in many additional, important ways. Certain soluble fibers, such as pectin, are known to reduce serum cholesterol (Sipple, 1974). Consumption of high-quality plant food and fiber lower the incidence of cardiovascular disease, colon cancer, and diabetes (Schneeman, 1994). Diets high in complex carbohydrates lower the risk of cardiovascular disease, diabetes, and obesity (Smith, 1994). Complex carbohydrates are a nonfattening energy source. The best dietary advice for weight maintenance and for controlling hunger is to consume a low-fat, high-complex-carbohydrate diet with plenty of fiber (Rolls, 1995).

As a first step to eliminating a sugar addiction, purchase products that contain natural sugars such as honey, molasses, maple syrup, or fruit juice. Minimize your use of processed foods. Remember that home-cooked meals contain less sugar than restaurant fare or packaged foods. Use noncaloric natural sweeteners, such as stevia and licorice extracts.

Purchase whole-grain breads instead of white, bleached-flour bread. When baking, reduce the sugar by a half or a third. Many people remark that this makes

Table 3-15. Anti-Anxiety Herbs

Herb	Temperature (TCM)	Action	Uses
California poppy	Cool	Antianxiety	Mild anxiety, insomnia, intestinal spasms
Reishi	Warm	Immune, adrenal tonic	Mild anxiety, chronic fatigue, immune disorders; calms spirit. Use 3 months or more for best results.
Kava-kava	Hot	Sedative, muscle relaxant	Muscle cramps, general tension
Hops	Warm	Antispasmodic, anxiolytic	Heart palpitation, mild anxiety, sleeplessness
Valerian	Warm	Antispasmodic, anxiolytic	Mild anxiety, sleeplessness, intestinal spasms

Note: Reishi is most suitable for people with long-standing immune or adrenal weakness. Some people may experience a stimulating rather than a calming effect from valerian (idiosyncratic reaction), depending on constitutional type and how the valerian is pre-pared. Generally, fresh valerian roots from the garden, or tinctures that are made from the fresh root, will provide the most useful sedative effect.

Tranquility Tea

3 parts linden flower, dried
2 parts lemon balm, dried
2 parts orange peel, dried
1 part chamomile, dried

1 part lavender, dried
1 part hops, dried
1 part oat straw, dried

Finely chop or crumble the herbs and mix them well. Store in a glass jar in a cool, dark place. To make tea, measure 1 heaping teaspoon (more or less to taste) per serving, plus one "for the pot" and add to water just off the boil. Cover and allow to steep for ten minutes. Serve this delicious-smelling tea blend after dinner to promote digestion and relaxation.

their homemade baked goods taste even better.

Keep a sugar-consumption chart and record your cravings for sugar. Find your own pattern of sugar use and sugar craving. When shopping, distinguish among different types of sugars and scrutinize labels. Euphemisms for sugar include corn syrup, modified corn starch, food starch, fruit juice, and ingredients ending in "ose".

IF YOU CHOOSE TO DRINK ALCOHOL

Excessive alcohol consumption increases one's risk of developing a number of serious diseases. But what is "excessive"? Each person has a unique constitutional make-up and ability to break down alcohol and deal with its toxic byproducts. Many researchers consider anything over two drinks per day on a consistent basis a possible threat to health.

If you do drink alcohol, drink three or four glasses of pure water after your last drink. This helps prevent dehydration and can allay some of the unpleasant symptoms of hangover, such as headaches. The following herbs, vitamins, and foods can also help protect your body against the effects of alcohol:

- Milk thistle: two to four tablets per day of a standardized extract helps protect the liver.
- Other liver protectors include ginger, turmeric, and artichokes. Use them in cooking, or take a supplement that contains the pure herbal extract.
- A daily nutritional supplement containing a carotenoid complex (with beta-carotene), B vitamins, and a complete array of essential vitamins and minerals is recommended.

Table 3-16. Substitutions for Foods Containing Sugars

Food	Substitute
Bottled fruit juices	Fresh vegetable or fruit juice mixed half and half with water or lemonade made with the juice of half a lemon in a quart of water with a teaspoon of honey or maple syrup
Dried fruits	A few pieces of dried fruit soaked overnight in water
Baked goods	Sweeten with barley malt syrup or brown rice syrup (cookies, cake, unsweetened crackers, etc.)
Ice cream	Frozen fresh fruit (bananas, berries, melon slices, etc.)
Frozen yogurt	Fresh fruit blended with almond milk and frozen

Confessions of a Sweet Guy

I once had a strong sweet tooth. For many years after I left my parents' home, I was fond of eating candy bars, baked goods, and soft drinks. At the age of 23, I eliminated all refined sugar except honey and maple syrup, but my sweet tooth remained. I still consumed fruit juice, dates, raisins, baked goods sweetened with juice, honey, and any other kind of natural sweet treat I could find. Slowly I was able to reduce the amount of natural refined sugars, depending mostly on fruit juice and dried fruits. Still, I craved them every day. In 1992, I eliminated all sugar from my diet except fresh fruit in season. After the first few weeks of no sugar, I not only didn't crave sugar, but I didn't even give it a second thought. For five years I have been sugar-free. Fresh fruit in season doesn't seem to stimulate a craving for sugar, and I find apples, pears, peaches, and figs to be healthful when eaten undried and in moderation. My symptoms of fatigue, heart palpitations, and weak lower back and knees, which are indications of adrenal stress, have disappeared.

For most people, a step-by-step process for eliminating sugar will work best. Make one change, then wait one month before taking the next step.

Week 1. Choose only foods with natural sugars and eliminate products that contain white, refined sugars. This leaves foods sweetened with honey, maple syrup, and fruit juice concentrate, as well as dried fruit and fruit juices. Remember that honey, maple syrup, and fruit juice are pure sugar.

Week 5. Begin to reduce the amount of processed foods that contain sugar of any kind, focusing instead on dried fruits and fruit juices and allowing some maple syrup or honey in drinks, on cereals, and so on.

Week 10. Slowly remove all simple sugars from the diet, using only barley malt syrup and brown rice syrup. Fresh fruit in season, fruit juices, and dried fruits soaked in water overnight are allowed.

Week 15. Finally, eliminate sugar in any form, including fruit juices and dried fruits. Fresh fruit in season are the only "sweets" to include in the diet. Bananas, apples, and pears are especially good, and they are available year-round. Try baking apples and pears for a natural dessert.

I recommend taking as much time as necessary with this process. Focus on the good foods that are added to the diet as sugar is eliminated, not on what is being lost. You may find that some nagging symptoms simply disappear several weeks or months after eliminating sugar from the diet. As a bonus, your sleep may improve, and you may gain a feeling of calmness and steadiness.

Calming Tea Blend

I part linden flowers, dried
I part hawthorn flowers and/or leaves, dried
2 parts chamomile flowers, dried
I part catnip, dried

I part lemon balm, dried
I part wintergreen, dried
1/4 part stevia herb

Blend the loose herbs, finely chopped and crumbled, and place in a quart jar. Store out of direct sunlight in a cool place. Make I quart of tea at a time, using 4 teaspoons of the mix and adding I extra teaspoon "for the pot." Add the herbs to the boiling water, cover, and remove from heat. Let steep for 20 minutes, strain, and store the tea in the quart jar in the refrigerator. The tea will keep for 3 days. Pour out I cup, warm it, and drink several times daily or before bedtime as needed

- Antioxidants such as vitamin E (400 to 800 units daily), vitamin C (one or two grams per day), and a good source of proanthocyanidins, such as grape-seed extract, will help.
- A diet rich in green vegetables and a variety of fruits contains naturally protective compounds.

Moderate amounts of naturally fermented beverages can promote relaxation and stimulate the digestive and assimilative processes of the body. Many cultures use "bitter tonics," preparations containing herbs like gentian, artichoke leaf, ginger, and cardamom, to enhance the digestive process.

Traditionally, beers and wines are fermented from natural grains and herbs. See *Foundations of Health* (Hobbs, 1992) for a complete discussion of these foods and practical recipes for making them.

CHAPTER 4:

A COMPLETE PLAN FOR HEALTH

MEDICINAL HERBS can relieve the symptoms of stress and support our bodies' healing, but can anything stop—or even slow—the constant intrusion of stress into our lives? Is there a way to protect ourselves from the constant barrage?

Yes! A complete plan for health must go beyond the wise and timely use of foods and medicinal herbs, although that foundation is tremendously beneficial. To achieve total health, we must carefully examine aspects of our lives that are often neglected and make changes that support healing and health. Controlling stress requires that we seek habits, relationships, and environments that nurture growth and good health.

GAINING EMOTIONAL MATURITY

Our personal relationships can be the source of serious emotional stress, especially when arguments, intense disagreements, and insults become regular elements in the relationship. The impact of intense emotional episodes depends on attitude and maturity. Some people carry grudges for years over real or imagined insults; others deal with them and go on living a healthy life. Like environmental influences such as cold and dampness, these strong feelings have the ability, if allowed, to become stressors.

Experience, emotional maturity, and wisdom are our best tools in dealing with emotional disruptions. As we grow in these areas, we realize the unwanted consequences of holding within us the negative feelings generated by emotional upsets. Attachment to negative feelings or thoughts brings them into the body where they form obstructions to the natural flow of energy in the organs, muscles, and other tissues. They may manifest as swellings or lumps. The longer these structures are retained, the harder they become. Eventually they disrupt the flow of energy, causing pain and disease. Relief is attained only through release of the negative thought-forms and emotions.

Natural healing methods offer numerous ways of releasing emotional tension. Meditation, massage, polarity therapy, and Rolfing have been developed to break up these negative-energy patterns. During or after an intense session designed to work tension out of the muscles, one often re-experiences negative emotions, yielding the opportunity to examine and then dismiss them. Yoga, tai ch'i, and qi gong are other ways of releasing negative energy while fostering internal harmony and balance.

Working For the Higher Good—A Way of Detachment

Karma Yoga is the ancient science of working for the higher good and learning to be whole. A journey of mind, body, and spirit, yoga is not associated with a particular religion. People of many beliefs, and from all walks of life, practice yoga daily. Each of the world's major religions, in their pure form, embrace and encourage principles similar to those of yoga.

Examining and changing our relationship with earthly goods is a central goal of Karma Yoga. Many today suffer great stress as

they seek to gain, retain, improve, and enlarge their array of possessions: buying the big house, filling it up with expensive goods, purchasing cars, buying a summer home, buying a boat, buying better cars, adding on to the house. The burden of stress that many endure as they pursue earthly goods is enormous.

Focusing on possessions and sacrificing to gain them fosters attachment to the ups and downs of the world. One who is in service to gaining and maintaining possessions finds the loss of a job or a promotion to be an incredibly painful, even shattering experi-

MENTAL HEALTH DAYS

A recent *Wall Street Journal* article suggests that mental health days may be invaluable for coping with the stress and challenge of the modern work environment. Time away for nurturing may enhance creativity and help prevent illness. After a bruising schedule, taking time for oneself may be important for preventing burnout and promoting optimal functioning. Many individuals only take time away from work for physical illness or for vacation; for some, however, an occasional mental health day may be revitalizing (Chase, 1996).

BODYWORK
By Marshall Reilly

In our fast-paced, stressful, mechanical world, massage (bodywork) offers a gentle reprieve. For thousands of years massage has been used to heal and soothe. The laying on of hands—touch—is so elemental that its profound necessity is often overlooked. Of all our senses, touch is the first to develop. Through touch our interpretation of the world begins. Touch is essential for healthy growth; it is also a foundation for our self-esteem. It is an instinctive language for expressing feelings and giving and receiving care and love. All too often, as adults we receive too little touch, which alone makes massage wonderful.

Secondly, our bodies rely on appropriate movement of fluids through our systems. Massage is a very effective means of promoting circulation; the proper flow of blood, lymph, breath, and fluids are vital to health. Nutrients, oxygen, hormones, and antibodies must reach every cell for survival, and toxic waste must be carried away. Increased efficiency comes from good circulation, which can be achieved in part by the vigorous stroke of massage. Over time and with repetitive movement, the muscles and connective tissues which hold us together often become shortened; this can inhibit our range of motion, distort our posture, and consequently lead to pain. Overuse, brain injury, or fatigue can also produce the same effects. Massage has been used in various cultures to relax muscles, diminish spasms, invigorate energy, and create a sense of well-being that frees the body from dis-ease. Exercise, in various forms, is of course excellent for minimizing the effects of stress on the body.

- Swimming is a superb strengthening and aerobic exercise that offers the additional benefit of cool water, which tonifies the circulation, digestion, and nerves.
- Walking is a great health tonic, and it does not place a great stress on any part of the body. Recent studies show that walking can be as effective as more vigorous activities in protecting the heart and blood vessels against disease, reducing weight, and releasing stress.
- Running or jogging is beneficial for all processes of the body, provided that a soft surface, such as sand or a path through the forest, is used. Avoid running or jogging on pavement.
- Dancing is an aerobic workout, increases flexibility, and helps release static energy stored in the muscles and emotions.

Marshall Reilly is a licensed acupuncturist and massage practitioner.

ence that can bring despair and anxiety. When self-worth and income are entwined, the job takes on excessive importance. While job success and its satisfactions are honorable, concern for success and income may arouse out-of-control pride, making failure doubly damaging to self-worth and exhausting to vital energy.

Giving up excess income, pride, and possessions to the higher good allows one to detach from the stressful, destructive cycle of personal gain. Renunciation yields a peaceful, serene inner feeling, allowing the development of inner poise. When stressful events are no longer considered personally threatening, and the adrenals are not being constantly activated, one's aging process slows. More energy can be devoted to the ful-

fillment of dreams and visions.

What would happen if we remove the big adrenaline rushes of intense competition, big rewards, increased power, and impressive social status? First, you could look for another job that doesn't send you home exhausted, take up your weekends, and interfere with your family life. Consider the value of working with a team of like-minded colleagues, each using innate talents to the fullest, loving work that is chosen for the value of doing it, not for the excessive money or prestige it confers on you. Consider the improvement of your personal and family life as love and joy replace stress and exhaustion, as weekends at the office are replaced by weekends of rest, interaction, exploration, and fulfillment. Whatever is lost

Table 4-1. Rating The Safeguards Against Stress

Stress-protector	Rating
Meditation and visualization	10
Stable family environment	9
Supportive network of friends	9
Good sense of humor	8
Regular practice of positive "spin"	8
Enjoyment of work	7
Healthy diet	6
Regular exercise	6
Conscious deep breathing	5
Regular stretching or yoga	5
Regular bodywork such as massage	5

Note: 10 is the highest protection rating.

by renouncing earthly goods is small compared to what can be gained.

Health and happiness are enriched as the attachment to other surface aspects of life are identified and loosened. Wisdom and maturity do not necessarily develop automatically with age; each person must choose ways of developing wisdom. Some people gain it early in life, some never.

SPIN

I invite you to consider that every human experience has a positive and negative aspect, depending on our perception of the experience. This is based on our constitution and previous experience. Whether we judge an event as uplifting, healing, and rejuvenating or depressing, enervating, and disease-promoting depends on the *spin* we put on it. Illnesses, emotional challenges, insults, and accidents all hold power for change, re-evaluation, and rejuvenation if only we let them.

A close friend of ours, European-trained naturopathic physician Svevo Brooks, tells this story: One morning he had to drive five miles into town to an appointment. He went out to his car and found it had two flat tires! His first reaction was to bemoan missing his appointment, but on further reflection, he decided to request that the meeting be postponed for an hour. Since it was a beautiful day, he packed a water bottle and some fruit and walked into town. When he arrived, he was feeling much more fit, relaxed, and centered. The time had given him a valuable break in the fresh air.

Coping

The concept of coping is important in learning how a stressful event will affect health. Coping combines the emotional, mental, and physical processes of adapting to the environment. It helps maintain equilibrium and protects health. If someone has suffered the death of a loved one, it may be said "It was a big loss, but he's coping." Some people are better at coping than others. But is the ability to cope with life's problems and ups-and-downs inherited or learned? Can poor copers learn the skill? The answer is a definite yes!

Many of the habits, qualities, and beliefs of those who successfully cope with life's stress can be learned and adopted by others. If a table of potential stressors can be constructed, why not a corresponding table of safeguards against stress? Table 4-1 reviews a number of habits, events, and situations that can reduce the impact of stress and protect health.

Many of the ideas in this book can help increase your "positive coping quotient." As one develops and matures, coping skills are learned from role models—both positive and negative. Parents are the first role models, and most important coping habits are learned from them. A good sense of humor, good communication skills, forthrightness, honesty, and a friendly manner may be considered positive coping skills, since they are tools for easily disarming potentially stressful relationship problems. Alcohol and drug abuse, overeating, lying, refusing to communicate (the "silent treatment"), and destructive emotional outbursts (violence of word and deed) are examples of negative coping skills.

Even negative means of coping with stress can help some people survive very difficult childhoods and cope with adult life. After extensive research into stress and human health, Elliott and Eisdorfer (1982) have written that "[f]or many years, certain types of psychological reactions such as denial and hostility were thought to be maladaptive. Although they may contribute to adverse consequences under some circumstances, they may be associated with positive outcomes under other conditions." Thus, people who are strong deniers are more likely to survive the acute phase of a heart attack, and cancer patients who manifest high levels of hostility may live longer than those expressing less hostility.

Researchers point out that denial can be useful for parents caring for a child with a serious illness, because it helps them provide emotional and physical support to each other and the child during the illness. However, if the child dies, continued denial can affect the long-term health of the parents and their relationship. A number of studies show that short-term denial is associated with increased survival rates among heart-attack patients, but extended denial can interfere with their ability to develop healthier habits and avoid future episodes of heart trouble (Breznits, 1988; Kaufmann, 1985–86).

The specific protective effects of coping mechanisms on a given individual, as measured by physical changes in the body, are still under study. In the future, use of this knowledge may enable further reduction of the physical impact of stress.

Coping with Relationship Stress

The development of good communication is essential for family harmony and, in fact, for improving the quality of any relationship. People should learn to respect everyone's freedom, including their own, and to truly love and give without expecting return.

Good communication is built on listening. Deeply listening to others, with complete attention and love, and without judgment, inspires trust. This skill takes time to develop. Active listening alone can heal relationships because this act, more than any other, says to the other person, "I care about you, and I am here for you."

In the more typical style of communication, each participant seeks to be heard, and listening is not so important. Thus, there is little space for the other person to communicate, because both place their ideas, needs, and desires first. True communication fails, whereupon some may be driven to shouting or even hitting. The frustration level increases rapidly because each person demands, "Listen to me, listen to me," but no one is hearing. Feelings build to the breaking point and explosion.

Conversely, a person who listens actively says, "I am listening, I am listening." The stress level of the conversation goes down instead of up, and many emotions, including fear and appreciation, can be released. Relationships are healed when the participants learn how to respect each other's freedom, as well as their own, and to love truly, without expecting return.

Working with a local psychologist, psychiatrist, or counselor who practices and teaches active listening skills is often a necessary step in healing relationships. The tapes and books of Thich Nhat-Hanh offer a powerful guide to developing this vital skill (see Resource Directory).

Visualization and meditation help in healing relationships, too. We may step back from the situ-

Table 4-2. Effective Tools for Managing Stress

1. Develop positive coping skills

2. Keep a journal

3. Develop a personalized diet and herbal program

4. Practice meditation and visualization

5. Release physical tension regularly by stretching, yoga, receiving massage, deep breathing.

6. Work with a counselor or group for resolving inner conflicts

7. Exercise regularly

8. Release addictions naturally, finding a balance with caffeine, sugar, and other substances used to cope with stress

9. Maintain a regular spiritual practice

ation and take some deep breaths, focusing on a peaceful hideaway. We have the unique ability to mentally detach from our crowded surroundings, from unhealthy situations, and focus on an imaginary place that is quiet and untroubled. Through meditation and visualization, we can create for ourselves a comforting and calming peace that may not exist, at the moment, in our lives.

Each individual is affected by stress in different ways and develops different symptoms. Our individual components such as genetic predisposition, constitution, diet, responses to herbal medicines, and present condition require an individual, practical plan to support inner work and wellness. Understanding these components and their interactions is essential to using herbs and foods wisely for health.

MEDITATION

Over the centuries, numerous forms of meditation have been developed. Although they differ in approach and technique, all share the following objectives:
- quieting the mind
- breaking attachment to personal identity
- becoming receptive to the influence of a higher purpose or wisdom.

By practicing meditation diligently, one may develop an increasingly powerful connection with higher wisdom while diminishing attachment to the vicissitudes of life. This detachment dramatically decreases stress levels. Although this book is not a complete meditation guide (see the Resource Directory for suggested sources), we include a discussion of basic approaches.

The primary tool of meditation is awareness. When one sits quietly and comfortably, free from distractions, our busy neurons continuously generate streams of thoughts through the mind. We identify with these thoughts; in fact, many of us believe that we *are* our thoughts—that these thoughts precisely reflect our real, soulful selves. We firmly fix our attention on this stream, identifying completely with it.

Yet we are not our thoughts, and our thoughts do not reflect our true being. We are, in fact, the unlimited breath of love that permeates every thought and atom of the universe. We are every flower, drop of rain, and speck of comet dust. This truth is lost to us until we begin to turn our awareness from the stream of thoughts.

The mind, however, is a jealous, demanding master of awareness, not a servant. Attempts to shift awareness away from the thought stream can be exasperating. Many systems have been devised to distract the mind, including focusing on objects (perhaps on the breath), or on repetition of a particular word or phrase (a mantra). With practice and the use of a focus or mantra, a trance-like state can be achieved. Thus we reclaim our awareness.

The following practice is recommended for the beginner who has never meditated. Begin by concentrating on the breath. Sitting quietly, and breathing in and out slowly, listen for the subtle sound of the breath through the nasal passages and bronchi. Focus on the inflow and outflow of the breath while repeating a phrase such as "I breathe in, I breathe out." The words distract the mind while the sound and experience of the breath going in and out provide a calm, deep, steady focal point. When the mind seeks return to the stream of everyday thoughts, gently but firmly refocus on the breathing process. The mind is stubborn and will not easily give in, so the process must be repeated over and over again, like drops of water wearing away rock.

The beginning and end of each day are the best times to meditate. At these times, we are "between the worlds" of unconsciousness and everyday life. The mind is

slightly befuddled (sometimes very much so) and will more easily slip into the peaceful state of serenity conducive to meditation.

No particular posture is required when meditating, but it is important to be comfortable. A quiet place away from the tumult of daily traffic and noise helps, and you must keep your spine as straight as possible. You can sit in a chair, on the floor, on pillows, or even lie in bed. The main point is to be comfortable.

Consistent practice of meditation is essential to optimum results. Start with ten to twenty minutes upon awakening, before the everyday world intrudes. The end of the day, after work or before bedtime, is also an excellent time for meditation practice. If twenty minutes a day is difficult to manage, take time for ten. Even this amount of meditation time, if practiced daily, can help nurture the habit. Eventually it may be easy to extend the time to thirty or even sixty minutes daily, as meditation becomes an essential part of life.

Meditation reduces stress directly by giving the mind a much-needed rest, relaxing muscle tension, slowing the heart rate, and lowering blood pressure. The body's stress-fighting activities increase when this state of deep rest is reached. The process of focusing on breathing during meditation strengthens awareness of the breath and increases its quality. Ayurvedic traditions teach that energy, *prana*, is extracted from the air, so it is vital to breathe deeply and fully. Thus, besides learning to meditate, one develops the practice of breathing fully. Stress often results in shallow, irregular breathing, and meditation counteracts this to increase our energy level and vitality.

Meditation also relieves the psychological symptoms of stress such as anxiety and irritability. Those who meditate report improved moods and increasingly positive outlooks. The feeling of being spiritually centered and touched by the higher wisdom gives us the calm and courage to face life without becoming overwhelmed by the stress that awaits us daily.

VISUALIZATION

Visualization is defined as forming "a mental image or picture of . . . something not visible or present to the sight" according to the *Oxford English Dictionary*. The term has been in common use for nearly two centuries but more recently has been associated with processes used to unlock the healing potential of the mind and vital inner forces. We each hold the innate wisdom and skills to heal ourselves, but we have forgotten how to access this power. The process allows us to create a new vision of life, and opens the way for us to achieve that vision.

The first step in visualization is meditation, which clears both the body and the mind of turbulence, distractions, and pain. From this peaceful state, connecting with higher wisdom becomes possible. Then, far away from the daily uproar, we can visualize a pure, positive way of life.

Visualization is based on the belief that if we think about something enough—if we imagine it happening—it nearly always manifests. If something can be dreamed, both night and day, it will often come in physical form. The vision may not be realized in the expected form; in fact, it often appears in a better form than we visualized, even if we don't recognize it immediately.

The most important step in visualization is achieving clarity about what is wanted, and, even more important, what is needed for the higher good of all involved. This clear inner vision usually does not come immediately; it must be worked for and refined.

For instance, suppose I wish for a million dollars and meditate and visualize continually that the money appears on my doorstep. Despite my effort—I visualize intensely to get this million bucks —my wish is highly unlikely to manifest. It reflects a desire for pleasure and dominance that is unrelated to higher wisdom; I know, and the higher wisdom knows, that I want that money for myself.

Suppose, however, that I wish for a million dollars so that I can help the homeless by handing out twenty-dollar bills. As I meditate and visualize and the money does not appear, I nonetheless begin to learn a little about homelessness and how best to help those who have no place to live. While waiting for the money, I volunteer a couple of hours a week distributing food on the streets. Then I become a bit more involved, and I'm really looking forward to getting the million bucks so I can actually make a difference.

Suddenly, as I work my volunteer hours and place a chicken sandwich and a carton of milk into a homeless child's hand, I am stunned by my original vision of handing out a million dollars, one twenty at a time. My vision has manifested, but not in the way I imagined it. The money isn't on the way; instead, I myself must work, day by day, to make a difference. My heart and the child's smile tell me that I am in the right place; that my hope for the benefit and uplifting of the higher good has been realized, and that much can evolve.

The Vision Quest

In some cultures, seekers of visions travel alone to wild, isolated places in order to connect to the higher wisdom. These retreats are sometimes called vision quests or walkabouts. Native American Indians, primarily the males, went on vision quests as a rite of passage into puberty, or at times of life when facing important decisions.

The quester sought a pure vision that held power and meaning. Sometimes he fasted for several days to a week, used the sweat lodge, and otherwise sought purification to remove negative influences and help break the chains of attachment to the physical world. If the vision was granted by the higher wisdom, it frequently appeared in a language of symbols that required intense scrutiny and interpretation by the elders of the village. The vision of a war horse, for instance, could be interpreted in numerous ways, depending on the action of the horse, how it was painted and dressed, and from which direction it appeared.

Today, few take time for vision quests. We have rare moments, sometimes stolen moments, when we may sit at night looking at the moon's reflection on a lake, or walk under the stars with the breeze ruffling the trees. During these times, we may feel connected with our higher wisdom and perceive answers to our questions, find inspiration to strike out in a new direction, or reach a higher level of awareness or health. Or we may simply find ourselves welling with new questions. These are precious moments but often infrequent ones.

Taking a few days out of a busy life and spending time alone, without distractions, can foster new beginnings. Even more valuable is taking time every day to create mini-vision quests: a walk in the park, even in our own backyard, or half an hour alone in meditation or prayer. These moments hold great power when practiced consistently. Dr. Martin Luther King, Jr., in his best-known and moving speech, said "I just want to do God's will. And He's allowed me to go up to the mountain." King expressed the power, clarity, and spiritual wisdom he had found when he "went up to the mountain," whether his journey was literal or metaphorical.

Visualization for Healing

Visualization is a powerful weapon against stress. The moment we breathe deeply and step back from a stressful situation, visualizing power and serenity, stress is reduced. Visualize a quiet place by a lake or on a mountain top, and stay there for a few moments. Equilibrium and poise replace the stress and anxiety. With persistence, this habit becomes an integral characteristic, helping define and shape us. Over time, we evolve from the stressed-out, harried, tense, sick individual to one who maintains inner serenity, even in times of stress and external chaos, and we speak and act with power and wisdom.

Visualization has amazing potential for healing. If a cold is imminent, imagine the immune system being activated and working together with the liver, bowels, kidneys, and skin to eliminate toxins and waste products. Imagine toxins pouring out of your body in droplets and rivulets; as they pass from the body, visualize their transformation into pure light energy and powerful healing forces. If facing a chronic illness such as cancer, envision the immune system eliminating the cancer cells. Imagine the cancerous cells becoming normal and cooperating with the body to work for the good of all. Such visualization can support the body's efforts to heal itself.

MEDITATION AND RELAXATION
By Shanti Coble

Relaxation implies something much deeper than the commonly assumed meaning of a pleasant interlude, a change of scene or pace, a getting away from a too-intense work schedule, or a smoothing of muscles. All these are to be recommended and can be temporarily beneficial; but more depth is implied.

The word relaxation itself is constituted of *re* = back and *laxare* = to loosen or open. No doubt it is good to apply this process to the body through a program of physical exercises that alternate with muscular relaxation, such as yoga. For the intestinal tract, a change to a more consciously chosen, suitable diet, or a short fast, or a live-foods regimen can have very favorably relaxing effects. Again, a better organization of our time and scheduling can reduce tensions and make our overall functioning much more relaxed. Ordering our affairs, our desks and drawers, as well as our relationships and attitudes, can contribute to a more harmonious and, therefore, relaxed lifestyle. But yet more depth is still implied.

On a mental level, we can discover through self-help books, autobiographies, or biographies a way of transcendent and victorious living that includes the loosening of tensions, a rising above myriad stresses, and the discovery of our inherent center: an awareness of that in us which is not subject to a hectic pace, superficial sensory thrills, nor even the major ups and downs of "modern" life.

So become quietly familiar with your own Being and also the operation of your mind by regular silent times—just for you. Read some inspiring words, reflect on them. Better yet, ask yourself directly, "Who am I, anyway?" Your functioning in the world will never answer this question; it will only add names or titles for the roles you play. Are you not curious as to who you are for yourself and your very own business—which is to Be exactly as you really and lastingly are?

Deep interior relaxation is a letting go at the core of our being, a loosening and releasing of ego-centered limitations that needlessly cramp us into stressful, unfulfilling situations. Sincere, modern researchers have pointed the way; current and past masters of wisdom have clearly revealed their direct experience; thus, genuine guidance is accessible. When we are earnestly looking within ourselves in meditation to uncover the wisdom of life and love as it flows within us, a profound sense of loosening, widening, and opening inwardly may arise, leading to deep, real relaxation. Light will begin to shine through our being from an innermost center where true wholeness, sanity, harmony, and peace abide.

Shanti Coble is a medical translator.

THE JOYS OF NAPPING

Napping is a time-honored way of allowing the body the rest it needs during the day. As the day progresses, the demands of work, especially intense mental effort, can easily create an inner tension that impairs the smooth movement of blood, nutrients, and vital energy to all parts of the body. Napping can help release this inner tension in a thoroughly enjoyable way.

Napping is not a new idea. In many cultures, napping is an integral part of the work day. For instance, in most European countries, napping is an afternoon ritual, viewed as the best way to keep the body rested (Theodora-copulos, 1995). Latin cultures have "siestas," a time set aside for afternoon napping. In the United States, however, napping is not accepted. Perhaps with new medical findings and increased integration of the world's cultural traditions into our own, napping may become a worthwhile part of the daily routine.

Although finding a quiet place to stretch out is ideal, one can nap anywhere, even in a chair. The Surrealist painter, Salvador Dali, had a particularly interesting way to nap. He writes that his practice was to sit in a comfortable chair with his arm resting on the arm-rest. In his hand he held a spoon, and on the floor directly under his hand he placed a metal plate. In a few minutes, he began to feel drowsy and soon fell asleep. At that instant, his hand opened and the spoon dropped to the floor, hitting the metal plate. The noise awakened Dali immediately, but in that one moment of sleep he received all the rest he needed. He returned to work, fully refreshed (Etherington-Smith, 1992). It is a rare person who can benefit from so little rest, but a five- to thirty-minute nap will often provide excellent results. Although individuals vary greatly, naps longer than an hour often leave one feeling tired and "dopey."

Here are some facts about the benefits of napping. Babies spend more than eighty-five percent of the time sleeping, most of it in deep rapid-eye-movement sleep, a phase crucial for the development of the mind, body, and spirit. With maturity, the amount of time spent sleeping declines sharply, but sleep is as important for adults as it is for children. For many adults, seven hours of sleep per night is considered a blessing, although an average of eight hours is recommended (Robinson, 1989). Naps are one of the best ways to compensate for lack of sleep, for they not only reenergize the individual but provide a wide range of health benefits as well.

A variety of studies have demonstrated that napping can prevent illness and relieve stress and tension. One biological mechanism known to support this claim is the secretion of HGH, or human growth hormone, during napping (Carey & Lee, 1996). The biochemical effects of HGH on the body are complex, but generally it helps the body adjust to stress, boosts immunity, restores depleted energy, and enhances the action and efficiency of other neurotransmitters like serotonin, which has an uplifting effect on mood. Other studies show that napping can help ease migraine and stomach-related distress (Delaney et al. 1993). Workplace-health advocates claim that a fifteen-minute nap can boost the performance and productivity of employees (Gould, 1995; Bohner, 1994).

It is best to take naps in the mid-afternoon, between 1 P.M. and 4 P.M., because later napping can cause sleeplessness at night. Researchers recommend that people nap between fifteen and twenty-five minutes daily. Naps lasting longer than thirty minutes may cause sleepiness throughout the rest of the day or produce sleeplessness similar to the effects

of napping past four (Bohner, 1994).

RELAXATION TECHNIQUES

Although relaxation methods have been practiced worldwide for thousands of years, Edmund Jacobson in the 1920s was the first to introduce these methods to Western medical culture, which emphasizes pharmaceutical methods rather than natural methods of healing. Now, health practitioners use a number of approaches to relaxation, some of which resemble the ancient religious practices of meditation and contemplation.

Progressive muscle relaxation is based on controlling each muscle. Tense and hold a muscle or muscle group for five or ten seconds until you can easily identify it by slight discomfort. Slowly release the muscle or group of muscles. Repeat the process to reach total body relaxation.

Biofeedback machines monitor muscle tension, allowing the patient to practice relaxation techniques effectively. Some also measure physiological systems such as heart, respiration, and skin resistance, identifying stress symptoms and pinpointing where and when the stress is reduced.

Patients who have received **autogenic therapy** can relax by suggesting to themselves warmth and heaviness in their limbs. Developed by Wolfgang Luthe, this therapy releases forces in the brain that remove disturbing influences and restore functional harmony to body and mind. It involves biofeedback techniques and is particularly effective in helping insomnia.

Guided relaxation uses inspirational audio tapes that lead the patient toward relaxation. This method often employs soothing sounds of nature, such as water flowing, ocean waves, and so on. Some have found success in overcoming insomnia by using portable water fountains at home and when traveling.

IMMUNE-SHOCK THERAPY

In part, allopathic medicine is based on the principle that sudden stress, such as a fever or a cold, shifts the body's function in order to deal with and overcome the infection. Since we are large-

SHIATSU AND RELAXATION
By Shinzo Fujimake

When you have a pain or stress in a part of your body, you naturally touch it with your hands and rub it to release the pain. Shiatsu practitioners apply their hands to their patients' bodies and listen to the whole body's energy flow to understand the real causes of the pain or stress.

The body is like a baby—when there is some stress, it starts to cry without any words as a means of letting us know there is a blockage of energy flow. Just as a mother does not shut the baby's mouth to stop her cry but tries to patiently listen and feel the needs of the baby, so shiatsu practitioners are trained to acquire an ability to understand and diagnose the real blockage and try to release it through acupressure.

Once that blockage is released, the patient's energy begins to flow smoothly again throughout the entire body. When body stress is released, our whole body gets relaxed, and we can sleep restfully and deeply because the smooth flow of energy is healing our entire body naturally. Shiatsu wakes up your own healing energy to naturally soothe and heal your physical, as well as your emotional body.

Shinzo Fujimake is a certified massage practitioner.

ly creatures of habit, is it possible that the body develops a way of co-existing with a pathogen, syndrome, or disease so that it is not overcome by illness? An example is a nagging abscessed tooth. The abscess is a pocket of organisms feeding on living tissue deep inside the tooth, slowly eroding its integrity. Going to the dentist and having a root canal removes the symptoms of the infection, although sometimes the infection itself remains. However, by shocking the immune system with the herb echinacea, for example, the body's defenses might take a "second look" at the infection, stop living with it, and eliminate it.

The idea of shocking the immune system into action is not a new one; diluted snake, bee, and spider venom have been used for this purpose. The healing potential of venom has been understood for hundreds, if not thousands, of years; venom is currently used in a number of countries to activate immune function and eliminate various infections. Bee-venom therapy for alleviating the symptoms of arthritis is popular in Eastern Europe and is practiced in North America. A famous European immune-stimulating preparation, Esberitox, originally contained diluted snake and spider venom, and many believe that these ingredients helped

eliminate infections and stimulate immune function. The product has been reformulated and now contains extracts of three herbs—echinacea, wild indigo, and eastern white cedar—rather than the venoms, because the German government became concerned about allergic reactions as the popularity of the commercial formulas grew.

Other forms of immune-shock therapy are practiced in many parts of the world. For instance, even sudden exposure to cold water or hot steam in the form of a sauna or steam-bath can have the effect of retuning or refocusing the body's vital energy toward healing.

The skillful application of stressful agents to the body can be part of a healing program. If the substance (or event) is used for short periods of time with extended rest periods between, and at the proper dose, it has a much greater potential for stimulating the healing process and shocking the body out of its disease "rut" than if it is used continuously. For instance, a short course of strong antibiotics can cure an infection, for example, especially if the immune system is simultaneously supported by an herbal preparation, rest, appropriate diet, and other healthy habits. But if this antibiotic is taken day after day for years, it can lead to severe immune suppression and eventually play a role in such ailments as candidiasis and liver disease. Even with echinacea, one of nature's best immune remedies, scientists are clear that intermittent use creates immune stimulation, but continual use results in immune suppression.

We can use the immune-shock principle for everyday health by varying our diet, activities, and medicines. In my clinic, I focus on activities or habits that patients have carried on for years, ones that might play a role in creating the symptoms for which they seek relief. For instance, several months ago a young woman came in for a chronic sore throat. No matter what herbs or drugs she tried, including antibiotics, it persisted.

After we had thoroughly reviewed her health history, work, pastimes and daily habits, the patient mentioned chewing gum for the last five years—all day, every day. She didn't think this habit had anything to do with her symptoms. But after two weeks without chewing gum, her symptoms improved. Perhaps she had developed a reaction to an ingredient in the gum. Who knows? But her case illustrates that the body can react to any habit or substance, no matter how innocuous.

OVERCOMING PHYSICAL STRESS

Physical stress usually results from overuse of one part of the body, but the pain, soreness, and nerve damage that may be included eventually cause difficulties throughout the body. It's important to deal with overuse injuries promptly.

One way to minimize physical stress from overuse is to change activities or body position as often as possible. For instance, avoid eyestrain by frequently looking away from the computer screen to focus on a distant point. Stand up periodically and stretch or walk about a little when reading or writing. Learn proper body mechanics for lifting and bending, and if you must stand for long periods of time, shift your weight frequently and move around as much as you can. At break times, stretch your muscles well and walk vigorously to stimulate your circulation. Tension decreases while your alertness and physical comfort increase.

If an injury occurs, natural healing offers many alternatives. Icing the injury, massage, and acupuncture are a few of the possibilities for helping these stress-related injuries. Above all, injured bodies need appropriate rest and relaxation for healing.

CHAPTER 5:

NATURAL HEALING OF SELECTED STRESS-RELATED DISORDERS

EXCEEDING OUR natural capacities seems to be the American way of life today. When we fail to manage our money and run out, we reach for our credit cards and cry, "Charge it!" Sacrificing peace of mind to the object of momentary desire, we spend the resources of the future. Some use credit-card cash advances to pay credit-card debt—with the minimum payments on the many cards eventually surpassing monthly income—and the number of personal bankruptcies spirals upward every year.

Bankruptcies of personal energy are increasing, too, for we often mismanage this resource. Most of us work long hours daily, whether in the home or workplace, driven to succeed and acquire. Household chores and personal business are crammed into lunch hours or evenings; weekends are dominated by chores and errands. Even our children are hurried and worried, subjected to complicated schedules of sports, lessons, and homework. "Time to relax" seems to be interpreted only as vigorous activities like skiing or sailing. Whether we sleep well or fitfully, we don't sleep enough. Faced with fatigue and exhaustion, we once again cry, "Charge it!" and spend future resources of personal energy by reaching for caffeinated drinks and refined-sugar products or, better yet, foods and drinks that contain both.

These foods certainly provide an energy jump-start. Refined sugar is rich fuel for the body. It burns quickly, releasing heat and energy, and helps get millions of people going in the morning. Caffeine stimulates the central nervous system. A popular American breakfast consists of a glass of orange juice, coffee with sugar, and sweet rolls or pancakes smothered with sugary syrup. The most popular prepared breakfast cereals contain sugar, and many people add more. Candy bars and soda pop are commonly used throughout the day for "quick energy," although folks with a "natural" bent may choose sweet fruit juice instead.

Many people are unaware that stimulating the body with these foods and drinks may rob them of their future, but it is true. Old age can be a wonderful time of life if one is healthy and has sufficient energy to enjoy it. Sadly, however, this is often not the case. Years of overstimulation cause the body systems to weaken, malfunction, and perhaps fail in a bankruptcy of vital energy that was long ago overspent and cannot be refunded.

PAINFUL DIGESTION: DYSPEPSIA, INDIGESTION, IRRITABLE BOWEL SYNDROME

Dyspepsia, also called indigestion, is a general term referring to painful and imperfect digestion. It involves abdominal discomfort, a sense of fullness after eating, heartburn, and nausea. It can be caused by poor diet, stress, drug reactions, pregnancy, lactose intolerance, or a variety of diseases, including infection, ulcers, and cancer. More than half of dyspepsia patients suffer from multifactorial dyspepsia, meaning that symptoms arise from a complex interaction of factors. If abdominal pain or discomfort continues for more than several weeks without relief from simple natural remedies such as self-massage, switching to a light and simple diet, and herbal teas, seek the aid of a qualified health practitioner.

Functional dyspepsia means that the function of the digestive tract is affected, but there is no serious underlying disease such as diabetes or cancer. Associated psychological symptoms of functional dyspepsia may include depression, anxiety, and hypochondria.

What a Doctor Will Do

A doctor will generally order tests based on a person's symptoms. The two most common are a test that can identify hidden blood in the stool; and a colonoscopy and/or esophagogastroduodenoscopy (EGD). These tests involve the use of an optical system on a tube (endoscope) that is used to observe the upper and lower gastrointestinal tract for lesions, tumors, or other structural abnormalities that may be present.

Treatment for dyspepsia generally focuses on symptomatic relief because the specific source of irritation is often elusive. Typically, the most important aspect of therapy is the physician's reassurance that the patient's condition is not serious or life-threatening. Some patients with dyspepsia find relief with placebo therapy, indicating the importance of the sociological and emotional factors involved in dyspepsia. The role of physician-patient interaction in treatment success is especially important in these cases.

The doctor is likely to recommend that the patient avoid alcohol and caffeine, as these irritate the digestive system in numerous ways. The two most common causes of allergies that manifest in dyspepsia are to dairy and wheat products, so the doctor may recommend a lactose-free diet and/or avoidance of wheat products for several weeks. If the patient feels better, allergies may be involved.

Two categories of drugs can supply symptomatic relief. The first, antisecretory therapy, reduces the secretion of digestive juices and thus the irritation of the stomach as well as irritation from ulcers of the esophagus, stomach, or duodenum. The prokinetic agents (e.g., cisapride and metoclopramide) enhance emptying of the gastric tract to prevent build up of caustic gastric juices.

Natural Healing and Painful Digestion

Releasing stress in a positive way and resisting stressful situations is of vital importance in healing painful digestion. When these unpleasant digestive symptoms become chronic, the indi-

---

Kitcharee

1/4 teaspoon turmeric	1/2 cup mung beans
1/4 teaspoon cumin	1/2 cup brown rice
1/4 teaspoon coriander	4 cups water
3 tablespoons sesame oil	

Sauté turmeric, cumin, and coriander in sesame oil for two minutes. Add mung beans and rice and sauté another five minutes. Add water and simmer for 30 minutes

---

vidual must carefully evaluate his or her stress level, the ways of dealing with it, and the parts of the body that suffer particularly. Only with such an honest evaluation can natural healing succeed. General recommendations include:

- Eating with moderation; getting up from the table before feeling fully satisfied;
- Combining foods with care, for instance avoiding meals that combine fruit and sweets with beans or meats, or fruits and vegetables together;
- Practicing ease and relaxation when eating; do not eat while feeling stressed. Make the dinner table attractive and the conversation pleasant. Difficult topics should be discussed in another setting.
- Try adding kitcharee to the diet for a few days to calm the digestive tract.

Massage and Self-Massage

Keeping the abdomen free of tension is an important part of a total program for pain-free digestion. If possible, have a professional massage that includes the abdomen once a week or as often as you can. If your budget will not allow even monthly massage, learn to give a massage and trade every week with someone you feel good about—a friend or loved one.

Another alternative is to do your own abdominal massage. The best times are first thing in the morning or before bedtime. Find a warm, firm, yet slightly soft place to lie on your back; a carpet is usually fine. Try placing a folded pillow or bolster under your knees. You might want to use a warming, fragrant essential oil; I particularly like an almond-oil formula and use it often.

With the hands side-by-side and the finger tips close together, begin at the lower right quadrant

MASSAGE

Do you know where in your body you hold tension? Bodywork from another will identify the tense areas, although we alone often cannot. Gentle, firm massage frees tension from the body and relaxes areas that may have been congested from stress for a long time. Bodywork such as Swedish massage or shiatsu is an important part of my life and an excellent way to invest in something I find extremely worthwhile: Myself. When I am feeling good and relaxed, I am more effective in my job and in all other aspects of life. I believe that we cannot afford *not* to invest the time and money in our own well-being.

of the abdomen, near the hip bone. Work in three-inch circular movements, pressing rather firmly. Try to find sore spots as you slowly circle up toward the ribs, then along the bottom of the rib cage above the belly button and down on the left side of the abdomen to the opposite hip bone.

Linger on spots that seem especially sore, working them out by placing as much fingertip pressure on them as feels comfortable. Press more deeply if this releases tension without hurting too much.

This circle will cover the ileocecal valve, the large valve between the small intestine and large intestine, and the ascending, transverse, and descending colon. After working around this large circle, concentrate on the area around the belly button, where the small intestine is situated. If you feel a strong pulse pushing back at your fingers even when very little pressure is applied, you have found congestion. When these areas are worked thoroughly each day, soreness and congestion will ease.

Herbal Treatments for Dyspepsia

Use antispasmodic herbs to relax the smooth muscles in the body, particularly those in the intestines. These muscles also occur in the bladder, bronchial airways, and uterus. These herbs can effectively relax a knotted digestive tract and regulate the movement of food through the intestines (peristaltic movement), re-establishing the proper rate for food and wastes to move through the intestine. Teas are simple to prepare and effective for this purpose:

Chamomile tea, one strong cup three times daily, or as needed.

Peppermint tea, one strong cup three times daily, or as needed; or peppermint oil in enteric-coated capsules. Follow instructions on the product.

Wild yam root tincture, three droppersful in a little water or chamomile tea or peppermint tea, several times daily.

Valerian, up to three droppersful of the fresh root and rhizome tincture added to tea or a little water, up to four times daily.

PEPTIC ULCERS OF THE STOMACH AND SMALL INTESTINE

A peptic ulcer is a break in the inner lining of the digestive tract that results in burning abdominal pain. Ulcers occur when normal mucosal defense factors are impaired and then overwhelmed by corrosive digestive chemicals—such as hydrochloric acid and pepsin—that can harm the intestinal lining.

Severe Conditions Often Mistaken for Dyspepsia

Heart disease: Heart pain may be identified by the patient as gas or stomach pain. Sure signs of cardiac difficulty are pain radiating down the inside of the left arm or chest pain or pressure that intensifies after exertion. If cardiac signs, symptoms, or risk factors are present, consult a qualified expert for a proper diagnosis.

Ulcer: If burning or gnawing pains in the stomach or upper intestinal area recur at regular intervals—two to three hours after rising and after meals—for weeks or months, suspect an ulcer. Severe or persistent symptoms may indicate a perforated ulcer, and medical emergency.

Cholecystitis: Gallbladder inflammation is signaled by localized pain in the liver area and nausea after eating, particularly when fried or fatty foods are involved. Predisposing factors include a high-fat diet rich in red meat and other animal products, as well as regular consumption of spicy foods and coffee. It is important to seek medical help for gallbladder conditions.

Appendicitis: If moderate to severe pain is felt on the lower right abdominal quadrant or around the navel, seek medical attention for possible appendicitis, a life-threatening inflammation. If marked tenderness around these areas has persisted or increased over several days and is accompanied by nausea, fever, a fast pulse, and general weakness, seek the aid of a physician immediately, especially if the pain is more or less constant.

Bacterial, viral, or parasitic infection: The pathogens that cause food poisoning, such as salmonella or *E. coli*, can cause symptoms that are similar to dyspepsia. Giardia, a parasite that is increasingly common in water supplies, also causes similar upset.

Cancer: Cancerous lesions of the stomach, esophagus, bowel, or other abdominal areas may cause pain, bloating, or other symptoms.

OVERVIEW OF PHARMACEUTICAL AGENTS FOR ULCERS

Antisecretory agents. The most popular antisecretory agents used against ulcers are H2-receptor antagonists such as Tagamet (cimetidine) and Zantac (ranitidine). By reducing the amount of acid secretion in the stomach, these medications allow the ulcer lesion to heal, usually in four to six weeks. Eighty-five to ninety percent of duodenal ulcers are healed within four to eight weeks, and the same percentage of stomach ulcers within ten to twelve weeks. Minor side effects, such as headache, confusion, and lethargy, occur in fewer than three percent of patients.

Standard over-the-counter (OTC) oral antacids and mucosal protective agents—antacids such as Maalox, Tums, Alka-Seltzer, Rolaids, and Phillips Milk of Magnesia, are also very popular. Many people take these products for relief of intestinal upset, and these products also may be prescribed for mild ulcers. Other types of mucosal protective agents include bismuth (Pepto-Bismol) and sucralfate.

People often resort to OTC antacids and Pepto-Bismol in the early stages of an ulcer or between recurrences. There is evidence that both drugs can be as effective as H2 antagonists in ulcer healing, but high doses of oral antacids have side effects of diarrhea and elevated levels of phosphate, aluminum, and magnesium (Tierney et al, 1996). These agents might play a role in nutritional imbalances or even Alzheimer's disease (Zapatero, 1995).

Antibiotic Treatment of Duodenal Ulcers. Recommended antibiotics for eradication of *H. pylori* include ranitidine, metronidazole, clarithromycin, and tetracycline. The eradication of these bacteria can be difficult, but with a triple therapy combining two antibiotics and Pepto-Bismol, the bacteria can usually be destroyed. Side effects depend upon the choice of antibiotics, and certain combinations may cause nausea, vomiting, and diarrhea in as many as ten to twenty-five percent of patients.

Half a million new cases of peptic ulcer are reported annually. Most patients are between the ages of 30 and 55, and 62 percent are men. At one time or another, 10 percent of the adult population have ulcers.

Ulcers are most commonly caused by a combination of stress, genetic factors, food allergies, immune-system dysfunction, side effects of over-the-counter pain relievers like ibuprofen, and possibly corticosteroids. Recent research implicates the *Helicobacter pylori* bacteria in up to ninety percent of cases of ulcers (Tierney et al, 1996).

While stress is widely held to be a contributing factor in the development of peptic ulcers, research is inconclusive. Alcohol and dietary factors do not appear to cause ulcer disease (Tierney et al, 1996). Traditional Chinese Medicine holds that ulcers are caused by too much heat in the body; so to prevent or heal ulcers, foods that create body heat (stimulant beverages like coffee and cola drinks, red meat, and spicy foods) are to be avoided.

Anatomy of Ulcers

Ulcers are defined as a sore or lesion that is at least five millimeters in diameter. They are most common in the duodenum, especially at the source of the pyloric channel where acid is released. Ulcerations of the esophagus, stomach, or duodenum are more common early in life.

The principal symptom of ulcer is burning, gnawing pain in the abdomen. Up to ninety percent of patients complain of sensations of indigestion. The symptoms may be rhythmic and periodic.

In cases of both gastric and duodenal ulcers, patients typically awaken with pain at 1 or 2 A.M. Duodenal ulcer pain is often absent when the patient awakens at the usual hour, begins around midmorning, is often relieved by food, and then recurs two or three hours after a meal. Gastric ulcer pain, on the other hand, is often aggravated by eating. Esophageal ulcer pain typically occurs when one is lying down or after swallowing food.

Change of symptoms from periodic or rhythmic occurrence to constant or radiating pain may indicate ulcer penetration or perforation, each an extremely dangerous condition. Other severe conditions can be mimicked by peptic ulcer as well. If there is any doubt, consult a medical doctor for a proper diagnosis.

What a Doctor Will Do about Peptic Ulcers

Five classes of drugs are used to treat ulcers: antacids, antisecretory agents, mucosal protective agents, and antibiotics. Some provide only temporary relief. Antacids, available over the counter, decrease the stomach acidity and reduce the activity of gastric secretions. These drugs include magnesium or aluminum combined with sodium bicarbonate or a calcium salt. The antisecretory agents are antihistamines that reduce the amount of stomach acid that is secreted. They include Zantac, Tagamet, and Pepcid.

The mucosal protective agents seem to be able to bind directly to the injured site or ulcer, protecting it from digestive juices, or they can increase the secretion of mucus in the stomach. These include sucralfate, bismuth, and carbenoxolone (derived from licorice). Since many ulcers are thought to be caused by the bacteria *H. pylori*, antibiotics such as tetracycline, amoxicillin, and metronidazole are used in some cases. Buffering agents offer very temporary results; they work by neutralizing stomach acid and have no effect on the cause of the pain. If psychological symptoms such as anxiety or depression accompany an ulcer, benzodiazepines or other sedatives and/or antidepressants may be prescribed.

Although research is unclear on the relationship of stress and diet to the formation of ulcers, most practitioners do prescribe diet restrictions and relaxation therapy in their comprehensive ulcer-treatment plan. Common dietary restrictions forbid coffee, tea, soda, alcoholic beverages, hot spices, fruit juices, and fatty foods. A low-protein diet is sometimes indicated as well.

Within two years of stopping drug therapy, at least half of all ulcer patients suffer recurrences brought about by stress or overwork. In fact, most people will experience at least some recurring difficulty in the ten-year period following initial treatment (Berkow, 1992). Perhaps new treatments that combine long-term prevention with stress management will help decrease the incidence of ulcers.

Natural Healing and Ulcers

The organic or functional cause of indigestion is very difficult to determine, but it is likely that seventy percent or more of cases are due to eating too much and/or too fast, eating irritating foods, eating while stressed, and/or eating poor food combinations. Good foods for ulcers include coleslaw, cabbage juice, basmati or organic white rice, and other low-fat, low-protein foods. It is important to remember that the digestion of proteins begins in the stomach, so stomach acids and other enzymes are increased after a high-protein meal. Vegetarian fare usually poses fewer digestive challenges than a meat-filled diet because the proteins in legumes are mixed with starches and polysaccharides, which may help soothe the intestinal mucosa.

Keep foods that are spicy (mustard, black pepper, hot peppers), highly sour (pickles), and very salty (chips, salted nuts) to a minimum, and eat foods mainly at room temperature, not too hot or too cold. Avoid stimulants such as coffee, tea, cola drinks, cocoa, and chocolate.

It is particularly important when dealing with ulcers to practice relaxation techniques and minimize stress by following a good exercise program and remembering the two laws of stress reduction, the first one being, "Don't sweat the small stuff," and the second, "It's all small stuff" (Ferguson, 1990).

Herbal Therapies

Two of the best-known natural remedies for ulcers are licorice tea and cabbage juice. When taking licorice over a long period of time, use it in the form of deglycyrrhizinated (DGL) tablets. Those with high blood pressure or water retention should use this form only; it is available in tablets or capsules. Recommended dosage is two 300-milligram tablets, four times daily. Try one or two cups of strong licorice tea both morning and evening. It is best to strictly avoid salt and supplement the diet with extra potassium, which can be lost during the treatment. After taking the tea for about two weeks, many of the ulcer symptoms may disappear. When employing this therapy to heal ulcers it is best to be under the supervision of a qualified herbalist.

Another approach is to take a quart of cabbage juice daily for three to four weeks. For best results, juice fresh organic cabbage. In addition, drinking a cup of chamomile tea on an empty stomach three or four times per day may be extremely beneficial. Because of its demulcent and emollient properties, one cup of marshmallow-root tea taken three times daily or three "00" capsules of the powdered form, taken three times daily, are also recommended for ulcers.

ANXIETY, NERVOUSNESS, AND DEPRESSION

Everyone has felt anxious at one time or another. Mild anxiety, or nervousness, typically occurs during times of stress like

Soothing Digestive Tea

1 part chamomile	1 part marshmallow root
1 part plantain	10 parts water
1 part licorice root	

Mix herbs together, simmer in water for 15 minutes. Turn off the heat and let steep for another 15 minutes. Strain and store the tea in the refrigerator. Drink throughout the day in small amounts, about half a cup at a time.

taking a test or visiting the doctor; it's usually a brief but uncomfortable experience that might involve increased heart rate, sweaty palms and face, rapid breathing, and a feeling of tightness in the chest.

Anxiety is excessive worry accompanied by physical symptoms such as tightening of the chest, upset stomach, diarrhea, perspiration, dry mouth, dizziness, increased heart rate, rapid breathing, and muscle tension. Most people feel distressing levels of anxiety at some point in their lives; for fewer than five percent (Berkow, 1982), persistent anxiety progresses to a moderate or severe level, prompting the individual to seek relief. In extreme cases, anxiety can grow to include constant feelings of dread or peril, making life a terrible walk through an endless corridor of doom.

For treatment, anxiety must be distinguished from nervousness. "Situational anxiety" is usually a mild response to a specific stress such as a public-speaking engagement. In contrast, anxiety sufferers typically report the physical and emotional symptoms of fear but cannot identify the source. Untreated anxiety can lead to chronic problems such as insomnia, addiction to alcohol and drugs, and high blood pressure.

Serious anxiety manifests in many ways. The anxious patient may be chronically impatient and irritable, have difficulty sleeping and concentrating, and feel fearful. Depression and anxiety may intermix, producing symptoms that include insomnia, loss of sexual drive, guilt, indecisiveness, and thoughts of suicide. Acute anxiety attacks can be among the most painful experiences in life, but they are usually self-limiting and short. Although an accident, imminent change, or bad news may trigger an anxiety attack, although some occur for no apparent reason.

Depression is an organic disease—an imbalance of brain chemicals—characterized by deep sadness and hopelessness, irritability, change in sleeping and eating patterns, and feelings of worthlessness. Although an experience may trigger a severe depression, most depression is unrelated to life's events. Adolescents and the elderly most frequently have unrecognized depression, but the illness is pervasive throughout society. Although treatments are often successful, because of the ancient stigma of mental illness many do not seek help.

Anxiety and depression cannot always be cured, but they can be eased. Understanding the nature of these disorders enables many to overcome it. Effective treatments can help people who have suffered severe anxiety and depression to find a level of peace and joy they never dreamed possible.

The Anatomy of Anxiety and Depression

The causes of anxiety and depression are varied and sometimes obscure. Some individuals seem to be predisposed, perhaps due to genetic heritage or behavioral habits. In small doses, anxiety can be helpful in coping with difficult transitions (Rakel, 1996) because it is usually accompanied by an increase in energy concentration and ability to adapt to change.

Conversely, serious depression more typically saps energy, slows and confuses the thinking process, and limits the sufferer's ability to respond. The individual seeks to withdraw and limit stimuli, although isolation exacerbates the symptoms of depression.

Clearly, both anxiety and depression have physical components and may arise from continued stimulation of the sympathetic nervous system. When one feels stress, which activates the fight-or-flight response, a rush of hormones and neurotransmitters circulate in the body. Occasional incidents are harmless, but sustained activation of the system leads to ongoing anxiety and eventually, perhaps, to depression. Conversely, various degrees of anxiety can result in chronic fatigue and adrenal weakness; insufficient energy weakens one's self-control.

Our foods and environment may also generate feelings of anxiety. Stimulants such as coffee, cola drinks, and products containing ephedra and/or excessive refined sugar can raise one's responsiveness to stimuli. Such products stimulate the metabolism as well, precipitating an anxiety attack or at least predisposing one to a feeling of uneasiness. Environmental toxins such as mercury, lead, and pesticide residues can irritate the nervous system and perhaps contribute to the chemical imbalances that result in symptoms of anxiety and depression.

A weakened Heart system, according to Traditional Chinese Medicine, generates anxiety. Treatment, however, addresses the Liver system in addition to the Heart, because the Liver, associated with the Wood element, is said to be the "mother" of the Heart. Thus, relief can be sought by supplementing the diet with liver-soothing herbs such as dandelion and burdock root, and taking calming nervines such as California poppy and valerian root.

Many who suffer from anxiety and depression are simultaneously undergoing emotional difficulty or life transitions. Emotional stress, such as a change in an important relationship, often provokes episodes of anxiety or depression. Underlying emotional upset may be evident only in specific circumstances, such as being alone in the dark. Without much sensory stimulation from the outside world, an inner fear may leap into focus, triggering anxiety. Such frightening experiences can be converted into positive ones by facing the fear directly, perhaps with the help of a friend or professional therapist.

Psychological conflicts, however, can result in more intense anxieties. Anxiety is a major symptom of severe phobias such as fear of public speaking or fear of heights; in panic disorder, a sudden and severe onset of anxiety; in post-traumatic stress disorder (PTSD) suffered by Vietnam war veterans and rape victims; and in obsessive-compulsive disorder. Inner drives that race out of control or grow inappropriate to a situation create anxiety, as when powerful sexual desires conflict with society's demands. When anxiety becomes a constant factor in life, depression may rapidly follow, or alternate with the anxiety.

Fortunately, about one-third of people suffering from anxiety disorders recover completely. Most others find significant relief through psychotherapy and drug therapy. Men have a higher recovery rate than women, and recovery is much more certain among the middle-aged and the elderly (Berkow, 1982), indicating that life experience is important when dealing with anxiety.

What a Doctor Will Do About Anxiety, Nervousness and Depression

Nervousness, or mild anxiety, typically requires no particular medical treatment. Exercise is sometimes recommended to release excess energy that may contribute to the nervousness. Psychotherapy or behavioral relaxation techniques, such as meditation and biofeedback, may be recommended for some patients.

In cases of more troublesome anxiety, the physician will seek the cause of the patient's complaint by conducting a complete medical history and physical evaluation. Anxiety caused by a physical problem such as thyroid imbalance or alcohol withdrawal may respond to treatment of the physical condition. Counseling alone sometimes alleviates anxiety arising from work-related, financial, or relationship difficulties, but in cases of severe anxiety the doctor may recommend psychotherapy, relaxation training, medication, or a combination. I have observed that anxiety and depression often occur together when individuals suffer depleted and overtaxed nervous systems.

HYPERVENTILATION SYNDROME AND BIOFEEDBACK

Hyperventilation is rapid, light breathing that results in more carbon dioxide leaving the lungs than oxygen entering the lungs. Because the blood level of carbon dioxide increases, this also causes the pH of the blood to increase, resulting in alkalosis. This build-up of carbon dioxide can also cause dizziness, lightheadedness, and increased cardiac output. Hyperventilation, "overbreathing", can occur in states of anxiety or neurosis brought on by a variety of situations. The easiest way to treat hyperventilation is by breathing into a paper bag for a few minutes. This increases the carbon dioxide that enters the lungs, balances the biochemistry, and stimulates normal breathing patterns again.

The solution to chronic hyperventilation is relearning slow, deep, easy breathing habits that change one's biochemistry and ultimately one's response to the world. Biofeedback is a good start because it provides an objective report of breathing and muscle-tension patterns. A biofeedback therapist skilled in teaching breathing techniques can be extremely helpful.

Beyond this, learning meditation and deep breathing is recommended. Meditators have said for thousands of years that the breath is the key to calming the mind and emotions.

In cases of depression, a physician is likely to prescribe an antidepressant medication and recommend that the patient work with a psychiatrist or psychologist to overcome personal difficulties and concerns that may be contributing to the depression. Usually, the patient and doctor must work together over a period of time to monitor the dosage and side effects of the antidepressants, making adjustments from time to time. A regular exercise program is often recommended to the patient as well.

Psychotherapy, given time and commitment, is very effective in helping patients cope with anxiety and depression. Some forms of psychotherapy encourage patients to explore and resolve inner conflicts. Becoming aware of unhealthy thoughts and replacing them with positive ones is often an important part of the process. Behavioral therapy, another effective approach, uses increased awareness and rewards to reinforce newly learned healthy behavior.

Relaxation training helps both anxiety and depression patients by using a range of techniques. Progressive muscle relaxation, biofeedback training, guided imagery, visualization, yoga, or meditation are effective for relaxing.

For more rapid results in treating severe anxiety and depression, some doctors prescribe selective serotonin reuptake inhibitors (SSRIs) like Prozac and Paxil; sedative benzodiazepines such as Xanax, Ativan, Librium, and Valium; and buspirone (Buspar). Buspar is an antianxiety agent that is not habit-forming, and it lacks the anticonvulsant and muscle-relaxing properties of the benzodiazepines. Buspar's exact action is unknown, but it aids in bringing on sleep. Patients sometimes recover more quickly when these drugs are used in conjunction with appropriate psychotherapy.

While these medications are useful for helping patients "get over the hump" during particularly difficult times, in the long run, SSRIs drain the deep reservoirs of the nervous system and precious ancestral vitality. They should be used cautiously and briefly as part of a total program for health that includes tonic herbs, a strengthening diet, digestive enhancement, plenty of rest and relaxation, meditation, stress release, and proper breathing. In addition, the patient benefits from a conscious effort to learn why the drugs were needed in the first place.

When anxiolytic therapy is no longer needed, gradual withdrawal from these drugs reduces symptoms of restlessness, irritability, depression, insomnia, nightmares, and even seizures. Use of the smallest effective dose for only a two- to four-week period is considered safe.

All healthy life includes a balance of yin and yang, the Chinese cultural and medical expression of opposing forces both physical and spiritual. In our modern societies, we are frequently out of balance because of hyperfocusing—fixating on work or other activities—or emotional hyperactivity, the constant experience of very strong emotions like anger, joy, fear, grief, and worry. These states do not allow ample time for the relaxation phase of life, which gives balance to the other phases that include concentration, activity, and strong emotion.

Natural Healing and Anxiety Disorders

A holistic approach to treating anxiety and depression may include herbal treatments, practicing stress-management principles, psychotherapy, and behavioral therapy. Dietary and nutritional changes may be necessary, too. A progressive program begins with simple, mild methods and moves on to more drastic measures only if symptoms continue.

Mild anxiety and depression may respond to simple remedies such as friendly assurances, a soothing touch, and a safe environment. Removing stimulants from the diet such as coffee, chocolate, cola drinks, and refined sugar also helps, as does discontinuing any drugs that are not absolutely needed to preserve health or sustain life. Review these with a holistic practitioner if possible.

California poppy tincture is one of the most effective herbs in relieving mild anxiety. Unlike opium poppy, it does not contain habit-forming narcotic alkaloids. It is available in tincture form as a single herb or in combination with other herbs. Take four droppersful, up to a teaspoonful, three or four times daily as needed.

The health of the liver influences the emotions. If the liver becomes hyperactive from the use of stimulants or a continued state of overexcitement, it can allow one to indulge in a continual outpouring of strong emotions. This destroys the body's yin—hormones, neurotransmitters, and fluids—and opens the door to declining health. Grains such as basmati or brown rice and millet over a period of several weeks or months soothe the liver and support its function.

For more persistent anxiety and depression, add to the healing program relaxation techniques such as biofeedback, meditation, deep breathing, and walking.

VALIUM VS. CALIFORNIA POPPY AND VALERIAN

Several years ago, my mother was severely ill with emphysema and congestive heart failure brought on by over fifty years of smoking. She had a tremendous spirit, an uplifting sense of humor, and a pixie-like delight in the follies of humans. I give many thanks that she passed on to me her sense of humor about the human condition—a wonderful gift!

When I arrived to stay with her—it turned out to be the last month of her life—Mother was very anxious and had great difficulty breathing. She was addicted to Valium as well. I watched her memory fail until she had trouble remembering the names of her closest friends. I observed that while the Valium sometimes sedated her, at other times it precipitated acute episodes of anxiety and hyperventilation.

I set out to help Mother reduce and perhaps eliminate the Valium. I used an herbal preparation of California poppy and fresh valerian root—she called it "the poppy"—and soon it became her mainstay against the anxiety attacks and hyperventilation. We were both deeply relieved when, after two weeks, Mother's memory had improved remarkably. She was delighted to have some measure of clarity; for her, fading into darkness and isolation was the most terrible part of her illness. If Mother were alive today, I know that she would be happy to talk about the benefit she received from these simple but effective natural remedies.

A very ill person, especially one who is elderly and intolerant to powerful drugs, often benefits from simple and supportive measures that place little stress on the body and spirit. Shifting dependence away from drugs and toward nourishing foods and restorative herbs can bring great relief. Reducing the use of powerful medications, however, requires the guidance of a qualified health-care practitioner.

Soothing herbs can bring further relief. Valerian, an excellent herbal sedative that has none of the side effects of Valium, is especially effective in combination with passion flower, hops, California poppy, or St. John's wort.

Some patients who take antidepressants such as Zoloft, Paxil, and Prozac, or the benzodiazepines like Xanax or Valium, experience difficulty in discontinuing the drugs. These drugs alter serotonin metabolism in the brain and can help lift depression and ease anxiety and insomnia. Herbs can be used to support the process of discontinuation, but it is vital to work with a health-care practitioner or doctor trained in herbal medicine when attempting to replace psychoactive pharmaceuticals. I have found that it is best to take from three to six months to make this transition, and that many benefit from following a three-step program.

Step 1. Begin by establishing a total program for health with an experienced herbalist, practitioner of Traditional Chinese Medicine, naturopathic doctor, holistic physician, or other health-care practitioner. The program should include stress release, self-massage, receiving bodywork, an herbal program to eliminate any deficiencies such as adrenal weakness, conscious breathing, medi-

tation, visualization, and an exercise program. This will lay the foundation for eliminating pharmaceutical drugs. After you have established this program firmly, make plans with your practitioner to phase out psychiatric drugs.

Step 2. Begin a herbal supplement that can help support the nervous and hormonal system. This supplement can help smooth the transition when eliminating the pharmaceutical.

For any SSRI-family drug, such as Paxil, Prozac, or Zoloft, begin with half a teaspoon of St. John's wort tincture in a little water, three times daily between meals, or one tablet of standardized extract (0.3% hypericin) twice daily, morning and evening.

For pharmaceuticals from the benzodiazepine family, such as Valium, Xanax, or Ativan, follow the program above but add half a teaspoon of California poppy liquid extract, taken three times daily with the St. John's wort extract. Also use any of the calming herb formulas in this book for extra support.

Step 3. After one month of taking the St. John's wort and calming herbs, increase the dosage of the herbs by one-third and reduce the dose of the pharmaceutical by one-third. Wait another month and decrease the dosage of the drug by another third, and increase the herbs by one-third. The entire process should take three or four months. If you experience an increase of unpleasant symptoms such as depression, anxiety, or insomnia, consult your practitioner and readjust your medications or herbs according to recommendations.

It is absolutely necessary to work with a practitioner to oversee this process. The information given here is not meant to substitute for the guidance and care of a professional health-care practitioner; instead, it is information that may assist you and your practitioner in the process of withdrawing from pharmaceuticals. Especially when reducing the dosage of benzodiazepines, which are highly addictive, rapid withdrawal can cause a variety of intense or even dangerous symptoms.

Having said this, I support your quest to eliminate pharmaceuticals, which can have a serious impact on mental, emotional, and physical health when used over a long period. A total health program as outlined in this book can support joyous and vital health throughout life.

The popularity of St. John's wort is increasing at a remarkable rate. After major news stories in the United States aired on television and in magazines such as *Newsweek*, demand has outpaced availability in some markets. The reason for this is simple. There are many, many people who use pharmaceutical drugs for anxiety, depression, and insomnia. They might benefit from herbs.

FATIGUE ILLNESSES

As stressful patterns of life become the norm, people increasingly suffer from illnesses related to unhealthy living. These are disruptive illnesses that burden the patient with numerous symptoms, and the outstanding one is overwhelming tiredness that does not respond to rest. Health practitioners of all traditions are prescribing more and more remedies for such illnesses.

Chronic Fatigue Syndrome and Related Disorders

"Going through each day is like trying to swim upstream. . . . It's like sleepwalking through life, and you can't wake up. . . . It's like having a hangover that you can't sleep off. . . . Mostly it's the fatigue, the endless exhaustion from which there is no relief. It's like living your worst nightmare" (www.nmia.com).

Epidemiologists of the future may note the 1990s as the decade of exploding rates of fatigue illnesses such as chronic fatigue syndrome (CFS). An astonishingly high rate of fatigue afflicts our society. A 1993 clinical study of the prevalence of fatigue syndromes in Western medical primary-care clinics reported that 32 percent of 1,000 consecutive patients complained of at least six months of unusual fatigue that disrupted normal routines (Bates, 1993). Another study of 14,000 randomly selected individuals showed that lifetime prevalence of significant fatigue (present for at least two weeks) was 24 percent (Fukuda et al, 1994). What was first generally noticed in the 1970s and termed the "yuppie disease" has now spread throughout the population.

What, exactly, is chronic fatigue syndrome? Despite statistics and studies, very little is known about the illness or agreed upon by leading researchers and physicians. Neither the cause nor source of CFS has been discovered. Conflicting theories remain unproven. The illness cannot be positively diagnosed through testing; consequently, some physicians deny the reality of CFS. Researchers don't know how to prevent the disease or treat it effectively. They do agree that CFS is not contagious, and patients do not die from it—CFS is not a terminal illness.

Chronic fatigue syndrome is also known as chronic fatigue immune dysfunction syndrome (CFIDS) and chronic Epstein-Barr virus (CEBV). These variants reflect the confusion about the origin, workings, and symptoms of chronic fatigue syndrome.

Two other maladies sometimes mimic the symptoms of CFS and may be indistinguishable from it (Buchwald & Garrity, 1994). Fibromyalgia syndrome (FMS), like CFS, may involve fatigue, headaches, sleep problems, and digestive difficulties. It is thought to be an autoimmune disorder also characterized by pain and tender spots in the muscles, ligaments, and tendons. The symptoms of multiple chemical sensitivities (MCS) are also similar to those of CFS.

Those who suffer from CFS and related illnesses sometimes face daunting odds finding helpful health care. Diagnosis is uncertain. Medical personnel who fail to acknowledge the illness add to the patient's stress and discomfort, and ineffective treatments sap both energy and finances. The long-term outlook for resolving questions about CFS are not good, either, and frustrated support organizations for CFS and related illnesses have accused the United States government of trivializing the disease and failing to fund research (Tierney et al, 1996). Substantial progress in treatment and cure through drugs may be distant.

In 1988, the Federal Center for Disease Control and Prevention stated that the source of CFS is unknown and undefined. In other words, no known virus, infectious bacteria, or toxic agent causes CFS. No laboratory test or panel of tests can positively diagnose it (Tierney et al, 1996). Clearly, CFS is a poorly understood and probably misclassified disease.

The official diagnosis of CFS relies solely on the patient's health history and symptoms. Persistent relapses or continuous symptoms of chronic fatigue for at least six months are essential to a CFS diagnosis. In addition, the patient must experience at least four of the following symptoms:

1. impaired memory or concentration

2. sore throat and/or tender lymph nodes

3. muscle pain

4. pain in multiple joints

5. new headaches

6. unrefreshing sleep

7. post-exertion malaise.

Finally, cancer, hepatitis, diabetes, and autoimmune illnesses share symptoms with CFS and must be eliminated through a large battery of tests as possible sources of the illness (Tierney et al, 1996). For example, fatigue is a prominent symptom in liver disease because the liver stores glycogen, which is broken down into the glucose the body uses for fuel. When this process is disrupted, fatigue results; so liver function should be evaluated. Hyperthyroidism and hypothyroidism, heart disease, anemia, and alcoholism may also confuse the diagnosis of CFS, as can emotional disturbances such as depression. Finally, extensive testing is important because some pharmaceutical drugs, such as sedatives and beta-blockers, typically prescribed for conditions that share symptoms with CFS, can aggravate fatigue symptoms for some people and should be avoided.

Although there is no one definitive test to diagnose CFS, a recent study suggests the nature of the illness. Immunological blood tests from 579 CFS patients and those from 147 controls who denied experiencing chronic fatigue were shown to differ. The CFS patients' blood contained more immune complexes and greater white-blood-cell counts than did the blood of the controls. Significantly, the CFS patients were drawn from two widely separated United States cities, Seattle and Boston, thus eliminating the possibility of regional consistency of results (Bates et al, 1995).

These findings point to the likelihood that CFS is related to abnormal immune function. Perhaps the immune system is activated by chronic viral infection or environmental factors to foster the disease. Patients experiencing persistent chronic fatigue may find it useful to request an immune panel from a physician and work with a natural health practitioner to develop a total health program.

Hypotension, or low blood pressure, has also been implicated in chronic fatigue syndrome. Some researchers have concluded that "neurally mediated hypotension should be considered a treatable cause of chronic fatigue, especially in patients with recurrent light-headedness, post-exertional fatigue, or fainting" (Rowe et al, 1995).

Given the scientific evidence available, CFS is probably caused by a combination of factors. It makes sense that exposure to a wide variety of stressors fatigues the body. How else can it respond when continuously bombarded by the thousands of toxic chemicals present in the air, water, food, home, and workplace? The body must resist severe attacks from toxins while the mind and spirit are taxed by overwork, financial burden, and lack of relaxation.

Our contemporary environment is completely unlike the one in which our immune systems evolved. The complex soup of synthetic chemical compounds in which many must live today confounds bodily ability to resist illness. Further, most people favor excitement and striving rather than an atmosphere of rest, relaxation, and rejuvenation needed for effective mental performance. The body is thus denied what it needs to function in a healthy and optimum manner. Stress, worry, overwork, and other harmful lifestyle choices, along with constant exposure to environmental toxins, likely contribute to the development of this mysterious illness.

Signs and Symptoms

The typical CFS patient is a 30- to 50-year-old individual who tends to be in poor physical condition, overweight, undernourished, stressed, emotionally drained, and exhausted from inadequate rest. The illness is more common in women and in the affluent sector of the population. Children and teenagers may also suffer the persistent lethargy that characterizes CFS.

The onset of CFS is usually sudden, and most patients think they have the flu. They typically describe flu-like symptoms such as debilitating fatigue, mental fogginess, depression, and gastrointestinal problems. Some patients report headaches, sore throat, sleep disorders, abnormal temperature, neurological problems, weakness, weight loss, and the inability to focus attention. The symptoms persist well beyond the seven- or ten-day limit of viral infection. Many note that a very stressful event preceded the onset of the illness (www.alternatives.com/cfs-news/faq.htm).

As the illness continues, patients may experience widely differing levels of severity. One who is totally bedridden for a time may at other times feel normal except for a little tiredness. Symptoms may come and go for reasons that are obscure, frustrating both health-care practitioners and patients alike.

The duration of CFS varies greatly. Some patients recover after a year or two, but more often they improve over three to six years. Some remain ill a decade or more, others never fully recover. In one study, 498 patients with either simple, ongoing fatigue or diagnosed CFS were followed for eighteen months. Sixty-four percent of the patients reported an improvement in their symptoms, but only two percent reported complete recovery. Those diagnosed with CFS had less improvement and more severe symptoms than those with simple fatigue (Bombardier & Buchwald, 1995).

In another study of seventy-eight patients reporting chronic fatigue for more than six months, five unrelated factors strongly predicted which patients would continue to experience chronic fatigue after two and a half years:

1. More than eight medically unexplained physical symptoms separate from those associated with the official CFS case definition;

2. A lifetime history of mild depression

3. Duration of chronic fatigue symptoms greater than eighteen months

4. Fewer than sixteen years of formal education

5. Age older than 38 years (Clark et al, 1995).

What a Doctor Will Do about Chronic Fatigue Syndrome

Little success has been achieved with medical treatments for CFS. Most antiviral, antibacterial, and immunosuppressive drugs are of no use, and the FDA has been slow to approve new, radical drug therapies for CFS patients.

Medication prescribed to address specific symptoms may yield limited success. CFS patients are so sensitive to drugs that they must be limited to doses that are one-fourth or less of the standard. Commonly prescribed drugs include SSRIs, or selective serotonin reuptake inhibitors such as Prozac and Zoloft, typically prescribed to treat depression. Likewise, medical doctors may prescribe low doses of tricyclic antidepressants. Recent studies have demonstrated that antidepressants, especially SSRIs, can restrict the symptoms of CFS and for some patients bring about remission (Tierney et al, 1996).

The physician may also prescribe nonsteroidal anti-inflammatory drugs like Advil and Tylenol, intramuscular gamma globulin, antivirals, interferon, and nutritional supplements such as antioxidants. These medication strategies may also succeed in relieving the patient's discomfort.

With no cure and no official treatment protocol for CFS, medical doctors have used a wide variety of alternative techniques to treat the illness. For example, one current medical manual suggests that continuation of a normal lifestyle, including exercise, is crucial for full recovery (Tierney et al, 1996). Other recommendations include healthy dietary changes, avoiding stress, and relaxation therapy such as biofeedback or meditation to promote recovery (Blonde-Hill & Sharfan, 1993). Psychotherapy or counseling may be recommended to help sufferers learn to cope with reduced abilities and other unpleasant symptoms.

Healing Chronic Fatigue Naturally

Nearly everyone suffering from chronic fatigue syndrome can improve by following a total program for health. Because the illness is related to overspending vital energy, learning about conserving that energy and following healthy habits can lead many with severe chronic fatigue to recovery.

Consider the case of a 45-year-old woman named Marge, a successful attorney who began to experience debilitating fatigue. Highly self-motivated, Marge had graduated at the top of her class and joined a major law firm. When she wasn't working, Marge was rearing her two children or training for running competitions.

Marge's illness progressed gradually, and she tried to cope with it in typical, modern ways. Noticing some tiredness in the late afternoons, Marge began to drink one or two cans of cola to get going again. Then, upon waking up tired in the morning, she drank her customary single cup of coffee plus one or two more. This helped for a while, but within six months Marge's fatigue became worse, and the coffee and soft drinks no longer helped.

Marge became depressed and slept poorly, developments that aggravated the fatigue. After several months, anxiety attacks began to alternate with her depression. Marge's family doctor administered a series of tests and concluded that she was overstressed and overworked but without identifiable disease. The physician referred Marge to a psychiatrist, who prescribed drugs to help her sleep and relieve the anxiety and depression. Neither doctor could offer Marge an effective treatment for the fatigue.

After one year of these drugs, Marge was unable to work. Her body ached all over, and her digestion was weak. She felt used up; sometimes life seemed not worth living.

At this point, Marge decided she had nothing to lose and visited a practitioner of Traditional Chinese Medicine (TCM). The practitioner's acupuncture treatments were designed to regulate the vital energy of Marge's internal organs. She also prescribed an herbal formula to strengthen Marge's digestive functions, regulate her liver, and supplement her vital energy. Dietary recom-

mendations, positive methods of releasing stress, and encouragement to walk regularly were also part of the practitioner's treatments for Marge.

After several months, Marge felt a positive difference in her condition. She conscientiously continued the regimen and treatments recommended by the TCM practitioner, and eventually stopped taking the antidepressants and sleep aids. The natural program for health became a commitment that she upholds today. Although Marge continued treatment for more than a year before she felt most of her energy and enthusiasm for life return, she considers herself recovered today.

Marge has much in common with others who make rapid and complete recovery from CFS. The most successful patients learn to balance energy resources with energy expenditures and seek to create and maintain an inner poise, steadiness, and calm. They exercise consistently but moderately, in keeping with personal ability. Those who recover quickly are also likely to develop a conscious eating plan based on individual needs and providing easily digested, high-energy, nutritious foods. They supplement the diet with a complete nutritional system that contains all known vitamins, minerals and co-factors to help reduce the possibility of nutritional deficiencies. Finally, the successful patient learns to breathe properly and develops and practices healthy sleep patterns.

A Health Practitioner Considers CFS

Specific nutritional deficiencies are associated with fatigue. Elin (1994) identified magnesium deficiency as a possible factor in CFS. Other studies have shown that magnesium intake among people living in many industrial countries may be deficient. Magnesium is a cofactor of more than 300 enzymatic reactions involving energy metabolism, so its lack may have negative implications for CFS patients. Zinc deficiency, shown to be a factor in muscle fatigue (Cordova & Alvarez-Mon, 1995), may have a similar impact on those afflicted with CFS.

Fatigue has been noted in women with silicone breast implants (Bar-Meir et al, 1995). Introducing a foreign substance into the body, and doing so in a way that frustrates the immune system's ability to attack and eliminate it, may cause serious overstimulation and imbalance to the body. This may also have serious consequences for those with CFS.

Chronic fatigue syndrome may be exacerbated, even caused, by environmental factors. Heavy-metal toxicity masquerades as chronic fatigue in some cases. Lead can be absorbed from paint, solder in hot-water heaters, and, after years of exposure, leaded fuel. Mercury is absorbed from paint and silver-mercury fillings in teeth (Mesch et al, 1996). Those with such fillings may consider having them removed by a dentist who has experience with the procedure. High levels of toxic chlorinated hydrocarbons, such as those found in industrial solvents, pesticides, and herbicides, are more prevalent in the tissues of chronic fatigue patients than in those of normal volunteers (Dunstan et al, 1995). Such toxins can be cleansed from the body with a comprehensive program designed by a qualified natural health-care practitioner.

Allergens that induce a generalized immune response can be a factor in up to eighty percent of chronic fatigue patients (Prince et al, 1995). For instance, certain food allergies can trigger migraine headaches or respiratory distress in addition to the more-common hives and skin problems. The resulting immune-system response can contribute to chronic fatigue. If a food allergy is suspected in CFS, try excluding one food at a time from the diet for at least one month to determine if improvement occurs. Allergies to such airborne factors as pollen, mold spores, and dust mites are more difficult to control, for they are pervasive throughout homes and places of work.

Eliminating these factors from the environment or determining the role they may play in chronic fatigue syndrome is difficult. Fortunately, Debra Dadd's book, *Non-Toxic, Natural and Earthwise*, contains excellent information about ways to eliminate environmental allergens.

High-quality air is extremely important for maintaining health and vigor. As mentioned previously, the practice of correct breathing is an essential component of health, but it does little good if the quality of the air is poor. Working in a building with "sick" air or living in a badly polluted city affects one's energy dramatically. Fatigue is a common symptom when people are con-

tinually exposed to poor-quality air (Ratner & Carey, 1995). Table 5-1 shows factors that contribute to fatigue illnesses and factors that are healing.

HEALING PRINCIPLES FOR CHRONIC FATIGUE

Wise management and conservation of vital energy are two key concepts for relieving the symptoms of chronic fatigue and ensuring that one retains enough vital energy to enjoy middle and old age. Objective self-observation reveals exactly where vital energy is being wasted and which areas of life are causing needless energy expenditures.

To begin your self-examination, consider your mental habits. Excessive mental activity such as continuous thinking, worrying, and studying for long hours uses up tremendous amounts of vital

Table 5-1. Contributing and Healing Factors for Chronic Fatigue Syndrome

Contributing Factors	Helpful Alternatives
Overextending, hyperfocusing	Rest, meditation, scheduling time for oneself
Worry and stress, holding tension	"Not-doing," meditation, stretching, yoga, massage, acupuncture
Addiction to stimulants (coffee, cola drinks, sugar)	Herbal energizers, regular exercise
Over 40 years old	Healthy habits, positive outlook, herbal supplementation
Diet high in processed foods leading to nutritional deficiencies	Whole, natural foods; grow your own!

SUPPORTIVE THINGS TO DO
WHEN DEALING WITH CHRONIC FATIGUE

First, conserve your vital energy by giving yourself a break: Lower your expectations and find an equilibrium point at which you function comfortably. Accepting decreased capabilities is difficult, but it will help you adjust to the reality of your illness. If necessary, set aside a time to grieve the loss of your normal, healthy self. Then take a positive, hopeful attitude toward daily life and eventual recovery from your illness.

Work toward healing by incorporating relaxation and stress-releasing techniques into your daily life. Educate yourself, work with others, and practice these techniques.

Pay careful attention to diet and proper deep breathing; eat according to the seasons and your constitutional makeup. Restoring your vital energy through vital food and adequate oxygen intake is very important.

Search out a CFS support group. Everyone suffering from this illness benefits from positive and healthy support structures. Vast resources, including support groups, can be found on the World Wide Web. Ironically, however, it seems that some workaholic CFS patients have continued their stressful work habits by over-involving themselves in CFS-related support groups and organizations. Check the Resource Directory of this book for on-line references as well as for books and articles.

Practice the development of inner poise. Through meditation and visualization, make a calm inner place for yourself that is unshakable and will provide you a safe retreat during times of stress.

Take time to create a new self-image and explore the truth that physical limitations do not necessarily limit a person's heart and spirit.

Because your work will likely be affected, educate your supervisors and colleagues about your condition.

On a regular basis, use immune-strengthening tonic herbs and hormone-balancing herbs (adaptogens) and foods. Continue this regimen as long as necessary—for years, if needed.

energy. The brain and nervous system burn a constant supply of energy in the form of glucose, and almost any constant mental activity depletes vital energy. One remedy is daily meditation.

A related issue is negative or unproductive attachment. Mulling over an unsuccessful relationship, a lost possession such as money, or a threatened notion of self-worth is draining. Vital energy is wasted by indulging in prolonged periods of such emotions as regret and anger. Consciously identifying such potentially wasteful emotions and letting them go saves precious energy. The ritual of grieving produces relief for many who seek release from old attachments.

Relaxing and releasing stress are also essential to recovery from CFS. In the process of living, vital energy is directed towards the muscles, both the motion-producing skeletal muscles and the internal muscles like the diaphragm and heart. When vital energy is continuously directed to the muscles but cannot be used, the muscles become tense, stiff, and painful. The tension can be released by stretching, napping, bodywork such as acupuncture and massage, exercise like walking and dancing, and hot or cold hydrotherapy. Conversely, when these muscles cannot burn energy in activity, it becomes congested and inhibits the flow of blood, nutrients, and vitality. Stagnation or disease may eventually follow.

Effective breathing, another principle of healing, must be relearned by adults. Children know how to breathe effectively, but as they take on stress and develop the defense mechanisms necessary for modern life, they quickly lose this ability. Correct breathing originates beneath the navel, proceeds with a conscious effort to expand the lower abdomen, and expands the middle and upper lungs and chest in one fluid movement. Held for a few seconds, the breath is then fully released.

Proper digestion has been recognized since ancient times as an essential factor in healing and producing energy. Strong digestion extracts maximum vital energy from food, especially when the food is fresh and full of vitality. Then, instead of drawing from ancestral energy, we draw from energy sources that are more easily replenished, much as we spend money from a checking account for daily needs but leave savings accounts untouched for times of emergency. Thus we constantly build up energy savings as we live a healthy, balanced life.

Herbal tonic therapies support and encourage healing. Ancient cultures used special energy-promoting herbs just as they are used today, especially in many parts of Asia. Such herbal therapies are an important part of a total program to build and maintain vital energy.

Herbal Treatments for Fatigue Illnesses

Herbs can be used to improve the many symptoms of chronic fatigue syndrome. Some herbs may even attack the possible root causes of the illness.

Relaxing Herbs

Several herbs help counteract the stress and anxiety of those suffering from fatigue illnesses by encouraging genuine relaxation and restful sleep. Herbs to relax the nervous system—calming herbs or calmatives—include skullcap, St. John's wort, and passion flower to slow the thoughts and relieve tension. Hawthorn flowers and leaves calm the restless spirit. California poppy counteracts anxiety. Valerian, hops, and linden improve sleep.

Cleansing and Protective Herbs

Cleansing the body of toxins and destructive agents is an excellent start toward good health, for it frees the body to function normally and relieves the immune system of an enormous burden.

Toward this goal, dissolve one teaspoon to one tablespoon of pectin in warm water and drink in the morning before breakfast. Follow this with two cups of cleansing tea, such as red clover, fenugreek, or burdock. These herbs help remove toxic metals and radioactive compounds from the body.

Efficient liver function is a major concern in treating CFS, for the liver is a major cleansing organ and supplies every cell with glucose. To cleanse the liver and remove fat-soluble toxins like pesticides and herbicides from the body, take bile-moving herbs such as burdock root, yellow dock root, artichoke leaf, and wormwood tea. Protect the liver from the negative effects of drugs like aspirin and antibiotics with preparations of milk thistle, turmeric, ginger, and schisandra-berry extracts.

Other body systems may require cleansing as well. The bowel responds well to cleansing with psyllium, flax seed, and bentonite clay. A number of commercial formulas available in natural food stores are also helpful. Cleansers containing red clover, mullein, and red root can help maintain a healthy lymphatic system. For more detailed information, consult *Foundations of Health*, Hobbs, 1992; or *Natural Liver Therapy*, Hobbs, 1993.

Herbs to Strengthen Digestion

Strong digestion makes the best of a good diet. To stimulate digestive "fire" and improve digestive efficiency, use bitter tonics containing gentian root, artichoke leaf, orange peel, cardamom, or ginger. To remove stagnation and aid digestion, take the herbal digestive enzymes contained in hawthorn fruits, rose hips, slightly unripe plums and apples, pineapple, papaya, and sprouted barley. These herbs can be purchased in an herb store or natural food store. Use them in powdered form sprinkled on food or add a teaspoon to warm peppermint or ginger tea. You may also find these herbs in capsule or tablet form.

Herbal Tonifiers

Tonics help the body maintain a state of dynamic equilibrium, or balance. Slow and gentle, herb tonics safely provide the body with essential compounds that promote good health. The average daily therapeutic dose of herbs is about 100 grams per day; the range is 30 to 250 grams, depending on the severity of the condition and the patient's body weight and constitution. The herbs can be steeped in water to make a tea, or the equivalent amount of powdered extract can be taken. Generally, herbal tonics should be consumed in the amount of one cup of strong tea in the morning and one in the evening around mealtime, or the equivalent in powdered extract. Continue for one to three months and perhaps a year or more, depending on the health of the individual and state of deficiency.

To Tonify the Blood. Herbs that tonify the blood improve its ability to circulate vital nutrients throughout the body. Foods rich in chlorophyll such as leafy, green lettuce and spinach are good blood tonifiers.

Superfoods such as nettles, barley grass, and spirulina also boost the blood. While various forms of these herbs are available, use a vegetable juicer or, better yet, a wheat-grass juicer to create the freshest tonifiers from nettles or other wild or garden-grown, green, leafy vegetables. You can make your own superfood juice powders by drying the juice in a food dehydrator. Take four to ten grams daily as a green drink or in size 00 capsules; two capsules equals about one gram. Lemon juice and yellow dock tincture, two droppersful, two or three times a day, act as catalysts to help increase the absorption of minerals, especially iron and magnesium. Blood tonic herbs also include *dong qui* and *he shou wu (fo-ti)*.

Tonify the Immune System. Use deep immune tonics to strengthen the bone marrow and replenish immune reserves. CFS is often linked to a nonspecific viral infection. While the exact virus is unknown, Epstein-Barr and cytomegalovirus are suspected of causing CFS.

Chronic viral infection can persist when the immune system has been weakened by stress, unhealthy diet, pollutants, and other as-yet-unidentified factors. One herbal strategy to strengthen immune function is to add immune tonics to the diet daily. Good tonifiers include reishi, shiitake, astragalus, and ligustrum. They can be purchased as bulk herbs and made into tea. Two or three cups daily of the tea (made from 35 to 100 grams of the herb) is an effective dose. The tea can also be used in soup stock, or grains, beans, or cereals can be cooked in it. Incorporating such tonic herbs into the diet strengthens the immune system and protects it.

Tonify Adrenals. Use adaptogens to strengthen adrenal glands and counteract stress. Deglycyrrhizinated licorice may be one of the most effective therapies for correcting adrenal insufficiency. This form of licorice is preferred because it contains only small amounts of the compounds that may increase blood pressure.

One researcher reported "almost complete recovery from chronic fatigue syndrome with licorice." He dissolved 2.5 grams of licorice powder in two cups of milk per day (Baschetti, 1995). Those who cannot use regular cow's milk can substitute goat's milk, soy, or almond milk.

Licorice tea can also be an effective adrenal adaptogen. Simmer three to five grams of licorice (depending on body weight) in two and one half cups of water for thirty minutes. Drink half of the resulting tea in the morning and the rest in the evening. At the same time, minimize sodium intake and supplement with about 100 milligrams per day of potassium to protect against increased blood pressure. If in doubt, consult a qualified herbalist who is familiar with the actions of licorice. Other examples of adrenal adaptogens include eleuthero or Siberian ginseng, American ginseng, rehmannia, reishi, and schisandra.

Inhibit Viral Infection. Several viruses such as Epstein-Barr and cytomegalovirus may contribute to chronic fatigue. Active viral infections are not generally the cause of chronic fatigue; rather, the viruses act as opportunistic agents that take advantage of an overloaded and stressed immune system. Viral infections stress body systems further and

NATURE'S ANTIOXIDANTS

Some antioxidants are widely available in capsules or tablets in a variety of potencies. They can be used as a part of a total nutritional program.

Vitamin E

Vitamin E, an essential fat-soluble vitamin, is one of nature's most powerful antioxidants. Nuts, seeds, and some whole grains contain good amounts of vitamin E. Protect potency by shielding vitamin E from both heat and oxygen. Take from 400 to 800 units per day as a dietary supplement. Vitamin E is nontoxic except for those who have high blood pressure or chronic rheumatic heart disease.

Vitamin C

Vitamin C is a water-soluble vitamin that cannot be synthesized or stored by the human body. It is also a powerful antioxidant. Most people get vitamin C from fresh fruits and other foods, but some researchers believe that we don't get enough to remain healthy in our stressful societies. Frequent doses of Vitamin C are necessary because the body cannot store the vitamin.

Vitamin C has antihistaminic effects and has been used in the treatment of allergies and asthma. Vitamin C deficiency is associated with depression, irritability, malaise, and fatigue. Take one to three grams per day. Powders are particularly convenient; blend one to three teaspoons into water or juice and drink.

Pycnogenol

Pycnogenol is a patented extract from grape seeds and the bark of the French maritime pine tree. A number of medical studies demonstrate that pycnogenol fights free radicals (Packer, 1997). Pycnogenol may prevent disorders associated with oxidative damage such as cancer, atherosclerosis, and aging. One of the many mechanisms of action is due to pycnogenol's protective action on vascular endothelial cells (Rong et al, 1994–95). For example, a double-blind clinical trial demonstrated pycnogenol as an effective agent in the reduction of post-operative edema (Baruch, 1984). Additional studies have demonstrated that pycnogenol stimulates the immune system, lowers cholesterol, interferes with the disease process of retinopathy, and acts against venous insufficiency, or pooling of blood in the veins (Cheshier et al, 1995; Werbach & Murray, 1994). Many physiological effects of these studies may be due to pycnogenol's strengthening effect on collagen, decrease in capillary permeability and fragility, and antioxidant properties (Werbach & Murray, 1994).

Claims for it include improvement of general brain function and eased movement across the blood-brain barrier of active molecules. It is thought to be nonallergenic, non-carcinogenic, nonmutagenic, and nonhabit-forming.

Some proponents state that pycnogenol can help up to eighty medical conditions through its antioxidant power, including the relief of joint and muscle pain associated with inflammation, reduction of blood leakage from capillaries, and lessening of muscle pains. Some researchers have suggested that most symptoms of chronic fatigue syndrome are related to free-radical stress within the body and recommend pycnogenol as an effective remedy. Potential side effects of pycnogenol include difficulty with memory and concentration and decreased spatial and motor functioning.

Anthocyanidins

These plant pigments, also called proanthocyanidins, are derived from grape seeds. Their effects are similar to pycnogenol's, and they usually cost a lot less. Look for grape-seed extracts in capsule or tablet form in your local natural food store.

force the body to burn vital energy to stave them off. Antiviral herbs can inhibit these infections, but they should be taken in combination with immune- and adrenal-strengthening herbs. Lemon-balm tea or extract, St. John's wort extract, and garlic are effective against viral infections.

Pain-Relieving Herbs (Anodynes). Some herbs help relieve the muscle pain, headaches, and back pain that some CFS patients experience. These include California poppy (tincture form), Jamaican dogwood, and Roman chamomile. For maximum effect in eliminating pain, combine herbal therapy with other natural healing techniques such as massage, stretching, and acupuncture.

Antioxidants

Free radicals are widely thought to be responsible for much of the tissue damage that occurs in many kinds of chronic disease, such as heart disease and liver toxicity. Free radicals, or highly reactive molecules, are created by the immune system and by other cells during cellular respiration in our oxygen-rich environment. They are also released by our own immune system as weapons against disease-causing organisms, but they may attack our own tissues as well. Because free radicals can disrupt cellular processes and cellular membranes or even destroy healthy cells, extra antioxidant support is helpful whenever a viral or bacterial infection occurs.

Herbs and nutrients that contain antioxidants, or free-radical scavengers, can bind free radicals and prevent cellular damage. A few examples of herbal antioxidants are rosemary tea or extract, lemon balm, hawthorn, ginkgo, and milk thistle. Several vitamins, such as E and C, possess powerful antioxidant action as well. These herbs and vitamins may relieve the symptoms that accompany fatigue illnesses.

INSOMNIA

In today's world, sleep is often considered a luxury, not a necessity; our schedules are full from morning to night. Maintaining mental and physical well-being while pursuing a career and raising a family presents great challenges, and many people sacrifice hours of sleep in order to achieve other goals. Well-known media figures brag about meeting grueling schedules in spite of minimal sleep, but is it possible that these "role models" are helping to accelerate the rise of stress-related illnesses?

A century ago, prior to the lure of radio and television, an average night's sleep was nine and one-half hours. In the 1950s and 1960s, the average dropped to eight. Today, the average American adult sleeps seven and one-half hours, and this figure is declining.

Sleep-deprived people are chronically tired, irritable, moody, and potentially depressed. All phases of their lives are effected. Those who invest in a full night's sleep, complete with dreaming, are rewarded by heightened productivity, creativity, focus, and physical and psychological well-being.

Sleep and Its Origins

Scientifically, sleep is defined as a sharp decline in the activity of the reticular activating system (RAS). Located within the brain stem, RAS regulates sleep by monitoring the sensory information coming into the brain. Rather like a border-crossing guard deciding who will be allowed to enter the country and who will be turned back, the RAS blocks unnecessary information from the brain to preserve a restful state. For example, the RAS allows us to continue sleep by blocking ordinary stimuli such as the noise of a passing car or the nip of a mosquito. Conversely, when there is an earthquake or an explosive noise, like a burst of thunder, the RAS passes the stimuli to the brain, and we awaken.

Although the exact origin of sleep is obscure, nearly all animals and even some plants undergo some form of sleep on a regular basis. The RAS and brain stem exist in all mammals and birds, leading biologists to believe that the mechanism of sleep may have evolved many millions of years ago in a common ancestor of the mammal and bird. Sleep is essential for life; without it, creatures would be unable to rest, repair, or rejuvenate.

The Stages of Sleep

Sleep is complex. There are two stages of relaxation before sleep, and when sleep begins we pass through four more stages to enter the deepest level, rapid eye movement (REM), named for its most observable characteristic. During REM sleep, our minds and bodies become refreshed and rejuvenated. We also dream during REM sleep, journeying into the unconscious world of mind and spirit.

Sleep is preceded by sleep latency, the quiet period before we fall asleep. Then come the drifting feelings, called the drowsy or pre-sleep period. The eyes are closed and the muscles are deeply relaxed.

In Stage I sleep, we lose consciousness. This transition from wakefulness to sleeping lasts only several minutes. During Stage II sleep, metabolic activity, blood pressure, and heart rate decrease. In Stages III and IV—delta sleep—body temperature drops. Blood pressure and heart rate further decrease. Restorative sleep takes over as cells start to repair and rejuvenate themselves. Stage IV sleep may be decreased or absent in the elderly, causing them to awaken more frequently during the night.

Finally we enter REM sleep. All muscles are relaxed, but blood pressure and heart rate increase. Blood flow to the brain increases, resulting in heightened brain activity. The eyes move rapidly, and dreaming occurs. Each night typically includes four or five sleep cycles of about ninety minutes each. The REM portion of the cycles lasts only twenty to thirty minutes during the first sleep cycle, but it lengthens progressively throughout the night. The longest REM state, up to fifty minutes, occurs in the early morning.

REM is the most restorative stage of sleep and influences psychological health, learning, and memory. Newborns spend almost fifty percent of their sleep time in REM; by the age of three months, the percentage of REM is thirty percent, and only twenty percent by six months (Sandyk, 1992). In rapidly growing young adults, REM sleep constitutes about twenty-five percent of a night's sleep. The cycles of sleep restore and nurture our bodies and minds after a long day of work or play.

Recognizing Insomnia

Insomnia, defined simply as the inability to sleep, affects twenty to thirty percent of American adults at some time in their lives. Reliable statistics report that twenty percent of American adults and fifty percent of American seniors have difficulty falling asleep on any given night (Reiter & Robinson, 1995). Despite the frequent occurrence of insomnia, only recently has it been viewed as a significant and potentially disabling medical condition requiring treatment.

Recognition of insomnia became official in 1993, when the United States Congress mandated a National Center on Sleep Disorders to study and report about sleeping difficulties. Today, the National Sleep Foundation identifies six major categories for the origins of insomnia: psychiatric problems, psychological problems, pre-existing medical issues, learned insomnia, poor sleep hygiene, and circadian-rhythm factors. To these I add a seventh category: inherent and constitutional factors.

Each factor plays an important part in the ability to sleep. The psychological stress of emotional events influences a majority of insomnia patients. Losing a loved one through death or divorce often results in disturbed sleep, as does conflict within important relationships or other stressful events, both good or bad. Even simple nighttime disturbances such as noisy dogs or sirens, worrying, or mentally planning the next day can create enough psychological stress to result in poor sleep. Both initial insomnia (difficulty in falling asleep) and early morning wakefulness can be associated with emotional difficulties such as anxiety, depression, or bipolar disorder.

A lifestyle that includes stimulating drugs like coffee or amphetamines can contribute to and intensify insomnia. For example, my dad had trouble sleeping at night for many years. When he switched to decaffeinated coffee after thirty years of drinking three cups daily of regular coffee, his sleep improved.

Illnesses or conditions accompanied by pain and other internal discomfort can also interfere with sleep. A cast for a broken bone, the pain of injury or sickness, or the necessity of remaining in an unaccustomed position due to surgery sometimes make sleep impossible for the patient. This is especially unfortunate, because a good night's sleep heals powerfully.

Some insomnia is learned. Perhaps it begins with necessary nightly awakenings, but then continues long after the reason for getting up is past. New babies, for instance, require night-time feedings, but their new mothers may awaken during the night long after baby sleeps blissfully until morning. Likewise, learned insomnia can result from caring for an ill family member or similar circumstances. Students who study for long hours rather than sleep also may find themselves burdened with learned insomnia.

Another cause of insomnia is poor sleep hygiene, that is, failing to manage effectively the circumstances that promote sleep. One who engages in strenuous physical activity late in the evening may find getting to sleep elusive because the process requires an initial period of relaxation.

Upsets of biological rhythm may also induce insomnia. Humans, like animals, have an internal circadian rhythm that encourages waking during daylight and sleeping during night, but modern work schedules may require the opposite. A day worker who is suddenly required to begin night-shift work is likely to experience serious sleep disturbances; even more difficult is a weekly schedule that includes widely varied hours of both day and night work.

Constitutional or genetic factors that play a role in insomnia include highly strung, sensitive nervous systems. Some people have nervous systems that are easily aroused; others may have inherent neurotransmitter or hormone imbalances. Those who experience insomnia as a result of these problems may find that positive changes in diet and lifestyle do little to resolve the sleeping problems. In such cases, learning "inner poise" requires constant practice. For instance, avoiding overexcitement, too much mental stimulation, and powerful emotional situations can be learned. The techniques of meditation, visualization, and deep breathing can be very effective when other approaches have failed.

In my practice, I have seen people achieve significant results by conscientiously learning and applying these techniques. Slow, steady gains are typical among such patients, and within six to twelve months many have shown excellent progress in overcoming insomnia.

People who suffer insomnia experience a wide range of symptoms. Although the primary symptom is the inability to sleep, individual symptoms vary. One person can sleep for several hours, wake up for an hour, then go back to sleep; another may be unable to sleep at all. Some may have daytime drowsiness while others do not. Symptoms such as fatigue, depression, lack of energy, and mental alertness also vary from patient to patient. Further, while an individual's ability to sleep well diminishes with age, the need for sleep does not.

Insomnia most commonly consists of increased sleep latency—people can't fall asleep easily—and REM latency, waking during REM sleep. Extremely stressed individuals may experience very short periods of REM sleep. In fact, those with severe insomnia may be unable to complete a single cycle of the nourishing REM in a night.

A long-term REM deficiency will impede earlier sleep stages III and IV and may eventually prevent a person from entering REM

Figure 5-1. The Deficiency Cycle

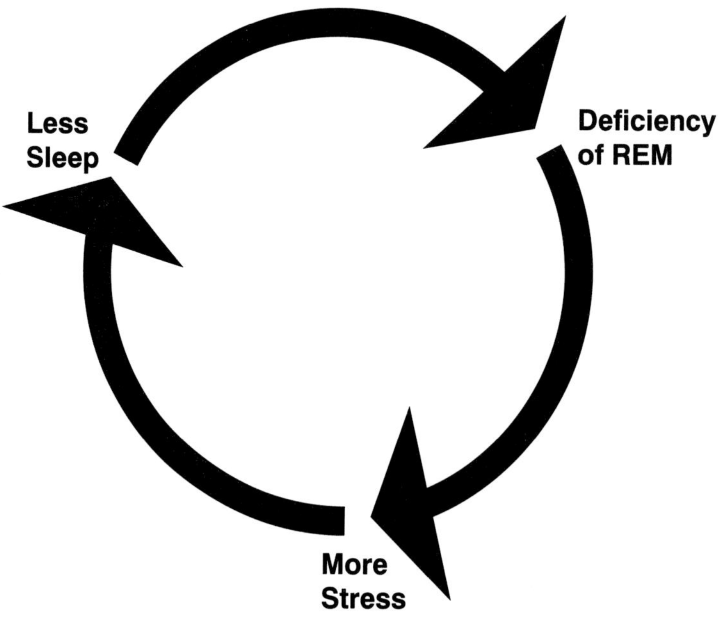

Less Sleep

Deficiency of REM

More Stress

sleep at all (Steinberg & Soyka, 1989). For almost everyone, both types of insomnia become more frequent with age.

Regardless of the reason for disrupted sleep, results are likely to include memory problems and varying degrees of physical and psychic disturbances. Inadequate sleep over a period of a few months impairs the ability to function and enjoy life. Complete sleep cycles for an adequate time every night are necessary to replenish and heal our energy stores.

The effects of REM deficiency, sleep deprivation, and fatigue are parts of a self-perpetuating cycle (see Figure 3-2). Decreased sleep reduces REM time and prevents rejuvenation; unrejuvenated, we are more susceptible to stress; feeling stressed, we are unable to sleep.

Classification of Insomnia

The National Sleep Foundation has identified three types of insomnia: transient, short-term, and chronic. These definitions are based upon the length and severity of symptoms.

Transient or situational insomnia is the least severe form, lasting only a few nights. The condition usually results from a passing emotional conflict or a momentary life stress such as a big event or vacation. A change in daily habits can cause insomnia, too. For many, eating or drinking too much alcohol interferes with sleep, as does taking a cup of coffee before bed. Trying to sleep in unfamiliar surroundings causes many to lie awake for hours.

Short-term insomnia occurs over a two- or three-week period. Typically it arises from emotional conflict, work-related stress, illness, and other periodic concerns. This is the most common form of insomnia.

Chronic insomnia is the more severe form. Fifteen percent of adults experience chronic insomnia. This condition is what most people think of when hearing about sleep disorders—the inability to fall asleep night after night. It lasts for more than a month, and some have suffered chronic insomnia for decades. The reasons for the development of chronic insomnia are unclear, but a chemical imbalance in the brain, perhaps involving serotonin, may be involved. Deep emotional conflict, inability to relax or change difficult situations (such as overwork), a constitutional imbalance aggravated by diet or other factors, or chronic illness—all are associated with chronic insomnia. Advancing age is also a factor, for chronic insomnia is observed in perhaps fifty percent of the elderly.

In Traditional Chinese Medicine (TCM), insomnia is viewed quite differently. If a person has difficulty falling or staying asleep, TCM says the Heart complex is probably involved. If people fall asleep relatively easily but then awaken at the same time(s) every night, TCM says the patterns may indicate the involvement of other organ systems, such as the Liver, Spleen, or Lungs. For example, if you can't sleep between 1 and 3 A.M., you may have a Liver imbalance, since this is the time of the Liver.

What a Doctor Will Do About Insomnia

To treat insomnia, the doctor usually takes a medical history and conducts a physical evaluation to investigate underlying problems such as a mental disturbance like depression; a physical illness like an endocrine imbalance; or a lifestyle problem like caffeine or alcohol abuse. Resolving these problems alone may take care of the insomnia. If no underlying problem is found, then the doctor will review the patient's sleep practices and recommend changes such as the following:

- Go to bed only when tired
- If you go to bed and cannot fall asleep after ten minutes, then get up and do something else until you are tired
- Use the sleep area for sleeping only
- If improved sleep hygiene fails to resolve the patient's insomnia, the doctor may recommend relaxation training. If this proves insufficient, medication may be considered.

The mainstream medical community does not consider soporific drug therapy to be the best method of treating insomnia because such therapies are addictive and have side effects. Many doctors make repeated attempts to cure sleeping disorders using dietary adjustments, improved sleep hygiene, and relaxation techniques. When drug therapy does come into play, it should be viewed as a temporary support of lifestyle and behavioral modification therapies. The patient's goal should be to use the drug(s) for as short a time as possible.

Approximately seven percent of the population use medication regularly to treat insomnia. Eighty-seven percent of these people use over-the-counter (OTC) sleep medications; the remaining thirteen percent receive prescription medication. The active ingredients in over-the-counter sleep aids are depressants that slow brain activity and cause drowsiness. The most popular OTC sleep products, including Unisom, Sominex, Nytol,

Somnicaps, and Sleep-Eze, contain antihistamines such as diphenhydramine, doxylamine, or pyrilamine maleate.

These nonprescription drugs may help with mild or occasional sleeplessness, but they are not recommended for continued use. Those who suffer from glaucoma, peptic ulcer, bronchial asthma, seizures, and prostate enlargement should avoid them completely. The most pronounced side effect, next-day drowsiness, occurs because these drugs break down slowly in the body. Patients may also experience the side effects of increased heart rate and dry mouth. These drugs are under review by a United States Food and Drug Agency advisory review panel, which seeks to eliminate many of the products as neither safe nor effective.

The most common prescription soporific drugs (non-OTC) prescribed to treat insomnia belong to the benzodiazepine family, a class of drugs that includes popular anxiety fighters like Valium, Halcion, and Xanax. In addition to preventing anxiety, most benzodiazepines are also extremely effective for inducing sleep, reducing the amount of time it takes to fall asleep, and increasing total sleep time by reducing the number of times one awakens. Benzodiazepines are ad-

dictive and thus appropriate for treating only transient and short-term insomnia. They should not be used for more than one month, and then only at the smallest effective dose to avoid side effects.

The recommended benzodiazepines for insomnia are Restoril (temazepam), Halcion (triazolam), and Dalmane (flurazepam hydrochloride). Although the benzodiazepines usually do not cause daytime drowsiness, they are addictive and the body produces a tolerance toward them. Withdrawal symptoms include increased anxiety, insomnia, and excitability. Higher doses typically lead to more serious withdrawal symptoms.

Two classes of antidepressant medications are especially effective in treating insomnia related to depression: the selective serotonin reuptake inhibitors (SSRIs), such as Prozac (fluoxetine), and tricyclic antidepressants (TCAs), such as Elavil (amitriptyline). In most cases, as these drugs slowly restore the appropriate levels of serotonin to the brain and resolve the depression, the insomnia disappears as well.

Natural Healing and Sleep Disorders

How much sleep is needed each night to maintain good

health? The answer depends on the individual's lifestyle and constitution. The National Sleep Foundation recommends approximately eight hours of sleep each night for everyone but recognizes that some may require an hour or two more while others may need only seven hours. A few may have shortened but complete sleep cycles. Most people, however, cannot afford to lose the essential restoration sleeping provides. Those who run their batteries down too fast, without recharging, will eventually suffer. It is vitally important to respect one's body and mind, nourishing them with the most effective natural therapy of all, sleep. And sleep is free!

Multifaceted, holistic treatment for insomnia may incorporate herbal medicine, vitamin and mineral supplements, lifestyle changes, improved sleep hygiene, massage therapy, behavioral therapy, meditation, diet, exercise, hypnosis, acupuncture, relaxation, guided imagery, and homeopathy. Treatment aims to resolve potential causes of insomnia rather than simply provide symptomatic relief.

Insomnia treatment begins with a detailed sleep history designed to pinpoint the most likely cause of the disorder. Patients can benefit from keeping a sleep journal for at least a month, detailing sleeping times, quality of sleep, and sources of sleep disturbance. Questions which should be asked include the following:

1. How long have you had a sleep problem?

2. Is it a problem every night or only occasionally?

3. Is the problem falling asleep or staying asleep?

4. Do you go to bed and wake up at a regular time?

5. Can you relate sleep problems to causes such as anxiety, change in work shifts, chronic diseases, or pain?

6. Is your sleeping space comfortable? Any there any disturbances such as noise or light?

7. Do you engage in any special habits or routines before going to bed?

8. How long does it take you to fall asleep?

9. Are you relaxed when you go to sleep?

10. Are you exhausted after a night of sleep?

11. Do you nap during the day? Exercise?

12. Do you drink alcoholic or caffeinated beverages and, if so, at what times of the day?

13. Do you smoke or chew tobacco?

Answers to all these questions help determine a treatment protocol. Many patients improve promptly upon eliminating habits that disrupt healthy sleep, such as eating late at night, smoking, and drinking beverages containing caffeine, while others need to adjust their sleeping environment and remove distractions that awaken them during the night. For most sleep disorders, such positive changes in sleep hygiene are potentially more effective than drugs. See Table 5-2 for a complete list of positive sleep hygiene habits.

Analyze the origins of insomnia and seek to resolve them.

Since insomnia is frequently produced by a combination of factors, examine each of the following categories, experiment, and note the results. If a particular therapeutic focus doesn't work, don't give up. Try another approach or combination of approaches and persist until you obtain some measure of success.

Could psychiatric or psychological problems, such as depression, be a factor? Such difficulties may result from traumatic or

Table 5-2. Sleep Hygiene

Maintain a regular sleep schedule. Arise at a specific hour each morning, regardless of the previous night's sleep, to help set your biological clock.

To consolidate and deepen sleep, restrict the amount of sleep to only enough to feel refreshed during the following day.

Exercising regularly helps deepen sleep, but strenuous exercise should be completed three or four hours before bedtime.

Arrange the bedroom so that it is comfortable. Insulate it against sound and light by using carpets and curtains; ear plugs and eye masks may be helpful.
Turn off the telephone.

Keep the room at a cool to moderate temperature. Excessive heat disturbs sleep.

Avoid liquids before going to sleep to minimize nighttime trips to the bathroom.
If liquids are not a problem, try drinking a small hot beverage
(dairy, rice, or soy milk) at bedtime.

Avoid alcohol, tobacco, and caffeinated beverages, especially in the evening. Although alcohol may help one fall asleep, subsequent sleep is fragmented and of poor quality.

As far as possible, work out family- or job-related problems before going to sleep.

Use the bedroom for sleeping and sexual activity only.

If you can't fall asleep, don't get angry at yourself. Get up, leave the room, and do something quiet like reading or stretching.

Hide the clock if you find yourself waking up to see the time.

Avoid napping longer than an hour; don't nap at all after 4 P.M.

To prepare the mind for sleep, try a relaxation technique such as biofeedback, meditation, yoga, progressive muscle relaxation, or massage (Rakel, 1996).

stressful life events and often lead to insomnia. For instance, one may have trouble sleeping for weeks or even months after an emotional upset such as a divorce or the death of a loved one. Counseling is recommended for insomnia of this origin; even talking to a close friend may help. Vigorous exercise usually helps relax the body and release emotions that might otherwise get "stuck inside." Make sure to complete the exercise at least three or four hours before bedtime. A regular practice of deep breathing or yoga can be very effective in releasing tension that can interfere with healthy sleep.

Are medical problems disturbing your sleep? Congestion from allergies, for instance, can be very disturbing. Pain, allergies, kidney or liver distress, and infections are only a few conditions that can provoke insomnia. If medical conditions underlie insomnia, identify and treat them. Chronic illness requires the attention of a knowledgeable health professional. A physician working with a natural health practitioner may be of help if the illness has progressed beyond a purely functional disturbance.

Has the insomnia behavior been learned? Sometimes when a stressful situation or illness disturbs one's sleep for a short period—up to several months—one may asso-

ciate the insomnia with an environmental factor, such as one's bed or bedroom. Then, even after the original situation has been resolved, the insomnia may persist due to the continued presence of the environmental factor associated with it. In such cases, it is necessary to seek clues to the association and, when found, to analyze the association to discover why it still has power. Once one becomes clear about this, the insomnia will often cease without further examination.

A friend once told me a story that illustrates this point. When he was young, between the ages of 5 and 15, he and his baby brother slept in the same bed. During the night, the brother often kicked him, and he awakened frequently. This went on for ten years or so. When my friend left home, he found himself continuing to awaken frequently during the night. It was years before he could completely relax and get a truly sound, uninterrupted night's sleep. A year of counseling helped him achieve it.

Can your sleep hygiene be improved? Several simple habits maximize the quality and quantity of sleep. First, don't try to fall asleep by counting sheep, or tossing and turning to find just the right position. It is essential to relax and allow the mind to let go of all its objectives and preoccupations. Excellent ways to distract the mind from churning include reading, conversing, listening to music, or engaging in some other enjoyable pastime. Right before bedtime, avoid tobacco, alcohol, drugs—especially caffeine or other stimulants—spicy food, intense mental work, or strenuous exercise. I have consistently found that working right up until bedtime makes it difficult for me to fall asleep and reduces the quality of my sleep when I do finally doze off. I like to stop work at least an hour before bedtime for some gentle stretching on the floor, meditation, deep breathing, or light reading.

Have your circadian rhythms been disrupted recently? Circadian rhythms are the biological rhythms that govern the body's cycles of waking and sleep, activity and rest. Most everyone has experienced some change in daily routine that upsets sleep—perhaps jet lag or a changed work schedule. Adjusting to the change in schedule is sometimes no problem, but many experience disrupted sleep in these circumstances. While some people can adjust quickly to a change in schedule, others will have a difficult time. If you are in the second group, the hormone supplement melatonin can be helpful. It is important to experiment with herbal sleep aids, calmatives, adaptogens like eleuthero, and well-timed naps in order to help settle into a new sleep rhythm.

Some people have odd sleeping schedules—7 P.M. to 2 A.M., or 3 A.M. to 2 P.M.—but this does not necessarily constitute insomnia. As long as the quality of sleep is good and one wakes up feeling refreshed, insomnia is not a problem.

Most people can temporarily circumvent their circadian rhythms without harm, but habitual disruption can lead to trouble. Like many others, if I push myself to stay awake after I am tired, I get a second wind and feel energetic and alert. Pushing myself this way from time to time is no problem, but if I should continue this habit over a period of years, I would quite likely find my energy reserves exhausted and perhaps my life shortened.

Does advancing age demand sleep adjustments to avoid insomnia? Many elderly people can neither stay awake nor fall asleep for a sustained period. Instead, they bounce between these two states all day and all night. This happens because their biological clocks have, over a whole lifetime, essentially run down, leaving their biorhythms fragmented. Light therapy is often useful for this type of insomnia. At a sleep-disorder clinic, doctors purposefully disorient the elderly patient's sense of time and then reprogram a new sleeping schedule. One may also retrain one's own rhythm, but it takes discipline.

Are your inherent and constitutional factors a possible source of insomnia? In Traditional Chinese Medicine, one of the most important elements in creating a healing program for a sleeping disorder is to ascertain the patient's constitutional type. This determines which herbs and foods will best create the inner balance so important to a healthy sleep process. For instance, a fire type—nervous-system dominant or yin-deficient type—is usually enthusiastic and excitable; this type's sleep is not improved by heavy mental work or stimulating foods before bedtime. In contrast, an earth type—digestive-system dominant—may not be troubled by such factors. See the book *Between Heaven and Earth, A Guide to Chinese Medicine* (Beinfield & Korngold, 1991) for a complete program to determine and evaluate your constitutional type.

In traditional medicine another important determination is whether the problem is related to a "deficiency" or "excess" condition. One experiencing a deficiency condition will feel weak, run down, and fatigued. A person with an excess condition will be overly robust, energetic, and full of heat. If a person is generally deficient and has sleeping problems, it is important to tonify, usually with adrenal and hormonal tonics that include these herbs:

- rehmannia, which strengthens adrenals
- eleuthero, which acts as an adaptogen, regulates adrenals, and helps relieve stress
- American ginseng, which tonifies adrenals and hormones
- Chinese wild yam, which tonifies digestion and hormones
- kudzu, which acts as a hormonal tonic
- reishi, which strengthens immunity, regulates hormones, protects the heart, and calms the mind.

Enhancing Sleep with Phytonutrients

Sleeping disorders are sometimes linked with lowered brain levels of the neurotransmitter serotonin. Before sleep, serotonin levels build up, and at a certain point the sleep response begins. Serotonin is very susceptible to the action of monoamine oxidase (MAO) enzymes, which quickly break down serotonin. Substances that inhibit the action of the enzymes, allowing serotonin to remain active for a longer period, are called monoamine oxidase inhibitors (MAO inhibitors). St. John's wort is increasingly being used to protect or sustain serotonin action by blocking MAO enzymes. A number of pharmaceutical drugs also have this action, but with more side effects.

Another way to normalize serotonin levels is by using the amino acid L-tryptophan, a raw material for the manufacture of serotonin. Some years ago this amino acid was widely available in health food stores, but it was banned by the Food and Drug Administration because a contaminated batch of genetically engineered product was believed responsible for several deaths.

Doctors can now prescribe L-tryptophan, but it is difficult to obtain. Fortunately, L-tryptophan is found in high concentrations in a number of foods (see Table 5-3).

Melatonin

Melatonin, a natural hormone, took the health-food industry by storm in 1995 when it was first marketed as a remedy for insomnia. Now an essential part of insomnia therapy, melatonin is favored particularly by travelers and swing-shift workers, since it can be used to accelerate readjustment to varying schedules.

Sometimes mistakenly associated with the skin pigment melanin, melatonin is a natural secreted by the pineal gland. Its exact function is unknown, but some believe that melatonin influences

---

Adrenal/Hormonal Tonifying Formula for People with Insomnia

3/4 ounce reishi, dried and powdered

1/3 ounce rehmannia, dried and powdered

1/3 ounce American ginseng, dried and powdered

1/3 ounce valerian, dried and powdered

1/4 ounce orange peel, dried and chopped fine

Place the herbs in one quart of water and stir. Bring water to a boil, then turn heat down to simmer. Simmer herbs for 45 minutes, then strain. Discard herbs. Drink 1 cup of the tea in the morning and 1 at night for at least three months.

Table 5-3. Natural Sources of L-tryptophan

Spirulina, a blue-green algae (Best source)
Yeast
Legumes (cooked soybeans, tofu, tempeh)
Meats
Fish and poultry
Nuts, especially almonds
Milk products: Cheese leads the dairy products. Other good dairy sources of L-tryptophan include sheep's milk, yogurt, and sheep's-milk feta.
Quinoa
Vegetables and fruits usually contain little L-tryptophan.

From *Bowes & Church's Food Values of Portions Commonly Used*, 16th ed. (Pennington, J.A.T., Ed.).

the circadian rhythm, the internal body clock that governs the biological rhythms and cycles.

Research suggests that melatonin's original purpose was to protect organisms from free-radical damage (Reiter & Robinson, 1995). It is a powerful antioxidant and twice as effective as vitamin E in protecting against free radicals, which cause extensive cellular damage. Melatonin's most noted role, the regulation of sleep, probably developed rather recently in the process of evolution.

Despite the research of Reiter and others—nearly 1,000 articles per year are published on mela-

---

Making Almond Milk at Home

Almond milk is available at health food stores, but it is not difficult to make at home. Take 1 cup of organic (if available) almonds and soak them in one quart of water overnight. The next morning, blend the water and almonds together at high speed until smooth and creamy. Try adding a little vanilla to make a delicious drink. For a good variation, add three to five dried figs presoaked in a little water and blend.

At bedtime, warm and drink a cup of almond milk. It's much higher in L-tryptophan than cow's milk and often much healthier. Use this milk on cereal and in beverages as well.

Almond milk sours after a few days, even in the refrigerator. If you are not using much of the milk daily, make a single cup: Soak one cup of almonds and store in the refrigerator; blend one-fourth cup of soaked almonds with one cup of water to make one cup of almond milk. The soaked almonds will not ferment.

Trypto Stew

1 8-ounce package tofu	2 tablespoons tahini
1 cup quinoa (can substitute millet)	1 tablespoon turmeric powder
4 tablespoons fresh or 2 tablespoons dried chives	1 tablespoon tamari
2 tablespoons nutritional yeast	

Pour one cup quinoa into two cups of boiling water. Cover and simmer gently about fifteen minutes, then let stand for ten minutes. Crumble an eight-ounce package of tofu into a steamer; sprinkle it with one tablespoon turmeric powder, and steam for five minutes.

Put the steamed tofu in a bowl and mash it with the yeast, tahini, and tamari. Then fluff the quinoa with a fork. For each individual serving, put a layer of quinoa on the plate and spoon on the tofu mixture. Sprinkle the chives on top.

tonin—no one is sure exactly how melatonin affects the body. Researchers know that the pineal gland, the organ which secretes melatonin, influences the immune and nervous systems. The gland's primary role is to translate environmental light signals into a hormonal response.

In animals, melatonin is involved in sexual maturation, seasonal mating cycles, sleep cycles (including hibernation), and temperature regulation. In humans, its role is not as clear, but it does seem to be involved in circadian rhythms including sleep cycles. It has found use as a sleep aid and to minimize the symptoms of jet lag. There is also increasing evidence that melatonin can reduce the risk of cancer, bind free radicals, participate in nerve trans-

mission, and stimulate the immune system. Previous research on melatonin has centered around farm animals, but more and more human research is being done. Soon, the role of melatonin in humans will be more fully understood.

More modestly, clinical and laboratory studies do indicate that for most individuals melatonin is a safe short-term treatment for insomnia, but long-term effects are unknown. We know that melatonin's effects are subtle compared to those of prescription sleeping pills; it provides a more natural and peaceful sleep, with ample REM. Thus melatonin may best be used for short-term insomia.

To induce sleep, melatonin is most effective taken on an empty stomach or with a small meal. The average daily dosage of melatonin is three milligrams, with a range of two and five milligrams. Sublingual lozenges seem to be most effective because the melatonin is absorbed directly into the bloodstream. The medicine should be taken between fifteen minutes and an hour before bedtime. Reading about melatonin prior to commencing its use is also recommended (see Resource Directory).

Melatonin is not without side effects. Doses greater than one milligram can cause tiredness, headaches, and depression. Continued use may lead to nightmares and lowered sex drive. Less frequently reported side effects include mild stomach upset, nausea, constipation, and itchiness (Sahelian, 1996).

Consult a health practitioner before taking melatonin if pregnant or breast feeding; if suffering a serious illness, autoimmune disease, diabetes, leukemia or lymphoma; if experiencing depression or using antidepressants or medications that suppress immune function; or if having a hormonal imbalance. Children and young adults typically do not benefit from melatonin because they have naturally higher levels of melatonin than older adults.

Herbal Treatments for Insomnia

Valerian is an excellent herbal sedative that has none of the negative side effects of synthetic sedatives such as Valium. It combines well with other sedative herbs, such as California poppy, skullcap, hops, and passion flower.

Some people achieve great results with the calming herb kava-kava. Many new types of kava-kava extracts are available in natural food stores and some drug stores. Try several brands if you are not getting the desired results, for not all kava-kava extracts are created equal. See Chapter 6 for more details on this interesting herb.

I have found that St. John's wort, used for several months at a low to moderate dose, improves sleep for some insomniacs by preserving healthy levels of serotonin in the brain. See the section on this ancient herb in Chapter 6.

My other favorite herbs for insomnia include California poppy, a calming herb, and reishi, an ancient Chinese herb that soothes the spirit and nourishes the Heart system. In Traditional Chinese Medicine, the Heart system relates to emotional and mental poise.

Finally, adrenal tonic herbs are often essential. Insomnia can be brought on by overwork, emotional and mental strain, and stress. These factors weaken the adrenal system, leading to a hormonal imbalance that interferes with proper sleep. Adrenal fatigue syndrome is often accompanied by chronic fatigue and depression. Bedtime Tea is a tried and true formula for insomnia.

Using herbs in other ways releases stress and promotes sleep. A few drops of essential oil of lavender added to a foot bath or regular bath is calming and pleasant. Sleep pillows stuffed with equal parts of dried herb of hops, lavender, and chamomile, and bath salts containing relaxing essential oils are available in some health-food stores (see Resource Directory for mail-order sources).

MUSCLE CRAMPS

A muscle spasm is an involuntary contraction of a muscle or group of muscles that causes pain and loss of function. Patients suffering from severe nervousness or anxiety attacks often report that such cramps occur on a chronic basis, disrupting work, play and sleep.

Muscle spasms are a mechanism used by the mind and body to release excess emotional energy. When the muscles are stimulated by stress but cannot use the energy, they may pull sharply and painfully. A better way to release this tension is walking, dancing, hiking, running, or other active sports activities.

Bedtime Tea

1 part valerian, dried
2 parts linden flowers, dried
2 parts kava-kava root, powdered
2 parts chamomile flowers, dried
1 part catnip, dried

Mix the herbs well. Make a tea by steeping 1 teaspoon to 1 tablespoon of the mix in 1 cup of boiled water for 20 minutes. Strain and drink 1/2 to 1 cup as desired. A little honey, licorice or stevia herb will make a sweeter tea.

What a Doctor Will Do about Muscle Cramps

Unfortunately, chronic muscle cramps often go untreated although they may indicate or foretell nervous-system exhaustion, a mineral imbalance, or nervous tension. Doctors generally do not treat muscle spasms with medication unless they are recurrent over several weeks or occur along with heat stress. When severe tissue damage and edema are apparent, perhaps after an injury, a doctor may prescribe muscle relaxants or anti-inflammatories for a short time.

Natural Healing and Muscle Spasms

Most muscle spasms respond readily to rest and physical therapy. When the spasm occurs, lightly stretch the muscle and gently massage the area to stop the contraction and accelerate healing. Rest and apply an icepack with a gentle compression bandage for several hours to reduce pain and prevent swelling. Elevate the part in which the muscle spasm occurred. After 24 hours has passed, whirlpool baths, massage, and acupuncture can effectively help heal the area. Alternating a hot compress (4 minutes) with cold compress (1 minute) for half an hour or so often yields good results.

If anxiety stimulates the cramp, relaxing the mind will help stop it. Hot baths or compresses are very effective in relieving anxiety. Aromatherapy, meditation, biofeedback, and behavioral therapy can all help expedite relaxation. One of the most effective herbal remedies is kava-kava, a popular herb from the Pacific. It is relaxing and leaves the mind clear and without drowsiness.

ADDICTIONS

Addictions and dependencies cross all borders, genders, races, and cultures. The addict's object of desire may be a substance, such as coffee or cocaine, or it may be a practice, such as compulsive gambling. Physical craving produces addiction; psychological craving produces dependency. Tobacco and some other substances stimulate both physical and psychological cravings, producing both addiction and dependency.

The mark of addiction/dependency is intense craving for a particular substance/activity that does not give the person significant pleasure or gain. In fact, the addict may understand clearly that the substance or behavior is destructive but be unable to stop it. An alcoholic, for example, becomes preoccupied with getting alcohol and cannot function at certain times without it; aggression, insomnia, or severe anxiety ensues if the alcohol is somehow unobtainable. After drinking, the alcoholic may feel shame and sorrow, as well as the misery of hangover, but the knowledge of these disadvantages does not interfere with the cycle of behavior.

Most addicts claim to use the substance or behavior only to produce relief from anxiety, achieve a temporary pleasant mood, and feel self-confident. Some seek increased sensitivity to sights and sounds, altered activity levels, or easing unpleasant or painful symptoms that occur without their "fix". Given the prevalence of stress in our society today, these goals seem reasonable; however, addiction grows to rule a person's life.

Some say that everyone is addicted to something—sex, food, tobacco, drugs, drama, strong emotions, relationships. Maybe the saint is addicted, in a sense, to God. However, devotion to fulfilling positive, life-affirming human needs such as love, friendship, or worship differs substantially from addiction to drugs that harm mind and body and to habits that harm human relationships. Even smoking and drinking, under the proper circumstances, can be healthy, or at least not unhealthy. For example,

drinking a glass of wine daily may have a preventive role in heart disease, and century-old Russians report drinking a glass of vodka and smoking two cigarettes every day. These old folks may or may not be addicted, but they clearly enjoy their habits as a celebration of life. Nonetheless, it is best to avoid any regular consumption of potentially addictive drugs to preclude compulsive use. As any addictive person knows, it is much easier to never start an addictive behavior than to try to quit after becoming addicted.

The Anatomy of Addictions

Addictions go hand in hand with stress. Fatigue and overwork aggravate addictive tendencies, and our society accepts the use of certain addictive drugs for relieving stress and stimulating energy.

Addictive behavior in families, observed in one generation after another, raises important questions about addiction. Genetic predisposition may play a role in addiction, and family and community life contribute as well, although this interplay is poorly understood.

If this research is confirmed, individuals susceptible to addiction could perhaps be identified shortly after birth. With early education and the development of healthy habits and attitudes, the nightmare of addiction and its companions crime and social destruction can possibly be avoided. Reducing addiction promotes the financial and spiritual health of nations as well as the health of individuals and communities.

Rebellious young people are the focus of most efforts against addiction. Tobacco use by the young is one example. Unfortunately, however, the use of even illegal drugs cuts across generations and socioeconomics; some young folks say they learned about illegal drugs by watching their parents; in the 1980s, cocaine was trendy among ambitious young professionals. Addiction among the elderly now consists primarily of addictions to smoking, alcohol, and prescription drugs. As the Baby Boomers reach the age of 50 or 60, will the first generation to glorify the widespread use of addictive legal and illegal drugs change their ways? Probably not. The next century's health practitioners will face a strange new landscape of geriatric addictions.

Signs and Symptoms

Although addicts abuse numerous legal and illegal substances today, this book focuses on the most common addictions: tobacco, prescription drugs, and alcohol.

Tobacco Addiction

Smoking and chewing tobacco are dangerous, addictive habits. Each day about 1,000 American smokers die from their addiction; daily, the tobacco industry recruits 1,000 replacements from among children and the Third World (Boyd et al, 1995). Although the number of adult American smokers is fewer, the incidence of smoking among teenagers and young adults is on the rise.

Smoking has been strongly implicated in lung and heart disease, cancer, and low birth weight. In the United States alone, smoking costs $23 billion and more than 500,000 lives per year. Cigarette smoke contains about 4,000 chemicals, including not only addictive nicotine and tar but trace amounts of dangerous carcinogens such as DDT, arsenic, and formaldehyde.

Second-hand smoke, also known as passive smoke, is a problem for many as well. Passive smoke is implicated in the aggravation of diseases such as asthma, bronchitis, rhinitis, chronic coughing, and other respiratory illness. It also exacerbates allergy-related illnesses, heart disease, arteriosclerosis, cancer, and childhood developmental problems. (Cohen, 1995; Stone, 1994). Epidemiologic studies have suggested that passive smoke is responsible for tens of thousands of deaths annually in the United States, mostly from heart disease (Cohen et al, 1994).

Lung cancer is the most common cause of all cancer deaths and the most common cancer in men; it is increasing among women. Oral cancers related to tobacco chewing and snuff contribute up to two percent of cancer rates in the United States. Within the developing Third World, chewing-tobacco-related cancers are increasing, and in India, oral cancers from betel quid (containing areca nut, tobacco, slaked lime, and sometimes other ingredients) cause forty percent of all cancer deaths (Saranath et al, 1993).

Considering these alarming facts, why do people continue to use tobacco, rejecting the pleas of family and friends while they persist in damaging their health? Why? Because nicotine is one of the most highly addictive stimulants known.

Commonly experienced tobacco-withdrawal symptoms include irritability, anxiety, craving, headache, sleep problems, tremors, and lethargy. Withdrawal symptoms usually last four to six weeks, but cravings can go on for years. Some people find it helpful to use nicotine gum or nicotine skin patches when trying to quit smoking. Gradual withdrawal from nicotine

reduces the dependency and severity of symptoms for many; others report success by quitting abruptly. Behavioral therapy and psychotherapy may help reduce the discomfort of nicotine withdrawal.

Prescription Drugs

Patient complaints of nervousness, poor sleep, or anxiety often prompt physicians to prescribe addictive central-nervous-system depressants such as Xanax, Ativan, and Valium. Without careful monitoring, these patients can easily become addicted. The elderly are particularly vulnerable because their livers often are not capable of breaking down the offending drugs and eliminating them quickly from the body. Some physicians issue prescriptions for months-long supplies of these dangerous drugs or reorder them month after month without insisting that patients visit the office for regular evaluations.

Patients with growing addictions to the drugs often devise ways of circumventing the medical community's safeguards. Some hop from one doctor to another, gathering prescriptions to increase their supplies; use of different pharmacies prevents records from being flagged for the overprescription of dangerous drugs. Researchers report that many "senile" elderly are actually befuddled by prescription-drug addictions—confusion is not a part of the aging process itself (Carroll, 1995). Some patients can succeed in hiding their drug addictions for long periods without detection. Only when the addiction creates problems, such as impaired ability to work or relationships that falter and perhaps fail, do others take notice.

When a person decides to kick these drugs, a gradual reduction of the dose over an extended period—perhaps months—is essential. Abrupt withdrawal from prescription drugs can stimulate troublesome symptoms such as anxiety, weakness, profuse sweating, insomnia, seizures, drowsiness, memory impairment, confusion, tremor, and agitation.

Alcoholism

Alcoholism results from both psychological dependence on and physiological addiction to alcohol, a degenerative process that begins at whatever age the drinking begins. The cause of alcoholism is not fully understood, but medical evidence suggests that contributing factors include a genetic predisposition, family habits and social pressures, and personality factors rooted in brain chemistry. Men are more likely to become alcoholic than women.

Alcoholism affects almost everyone in developed countries, directly or indirectly. Drinking costs the United States alone $100 billion in lost productivity. Between ten and thirty percent of all patients seen by physicians consume enough alcohol to aggravate their presenting condition or cause ill health (Rakel, 1996). Innocent victims of drunken drivers and the permanently damaged children of mothers who drank during pregnancy suffer directly from the alcohol abuse of others. The actions of alcoholics cost taxpayers millions for special education for children of alcoholics, additional law enforcement directed toward drunken driving and alcohol-related domestic violence, alcohol detoxification centers, and indigent hospitalization. Even those who exclude or carefully monitor alcohol intake are subject to the harm of those who don't.

Alcoholism often results in the disruption of interpersonal, family, and work relationships. Early signs of alcoholism include needing alcohol at the beginning of the day or during times of stress, insomnia, nightmares, habitual hangovers, absence from work, preoccupation with obtaining alcohol, hiding drinking from family and friends, and irritability when others suggest drinking is excessive.

Withdrawal from Alcohol

Even the occasional drinker may experience a hangover, a minor withdrawal syndrome during which the body readjusts to a nonalcoholic state. Hangovers occur four to twelve hours after the peak blood-alcohol concentration is reached. Symptoms may include headache, dizziness, nausea, vomiting, increased heart rate, fatigue, and thirst. During a hangover, most individuals suffer from reduced ability to perform complex skills such as driving (Maisto, 1991).

Although numerous remedies have been proposed for hangovers, no proof supports their effectiveness. It is not uncommon for individuals to drink more alcohol to remove symptoms, yet this solution only postpones the inevitable. Supposed hangover cures include:

- Taking medications such as Tylenol, aspirin, or tranquilizers
- Taking megadoses of vitamins so the body will have strength to ward off the hangover
- Inhaling pure oxygen to hasten the body's oxidation of alcohol
- Exercising
- Eating a huge breakfast
- Drinking a lot of coffee

Regardless of what one does, the liver processes alcohol at a certain rate. Taking drugs such as antihistamines with alcohol produces a synergistic effect, making the intoxication last longer.

Long-term excessive abusers of alcohol have a particularly difficult time quitting drinking. Symptoms of physical dependence can be severe and, if not treated professionally, may result

Table 5-4. Symptoms of Alcohol Withdrawal Syndrome

Phase 1. A few hours after drinking stops, the alcoholic begins to experience agitation, tremors, sweating, and weakness. Headache, cramps, high heart rate, rapid reflexes, visual and auditory hallucinations are also common. The alcoholic seeks alcohol or other drugs to ease the discomfort.

Phase 2. Within twenty-four hours of drinking cessation, grand mal seizures begin. The severity ranges from one seizure to continuous, severe seizures with little interruption.

Phase 3. Delirium tremens (DTs) begin about thirty hours after drinking ceases and last nearly continuously for three or four days and as many as seven days. The alcoholic is severely agitated, confused, and disoriented. Terrifying hallucinations, such as attacks from animals or bugs crawling on the skin, are common and the alcoholic may become violent. The heart rate is abnormally rapid, and the body temperature is elevated. Deaths occur from high fever, cardiovascular collapse, or trauma injury (Jacobs & Fehr, 1987).

in death. During withdrawal, monitored care can prevent a life-threatening reaction. According to statistics from the United States Department of Health and Human Services, approximately twenty percent of alcohol-related deaths are caused by alcohol withdrawal syndrome (USDHHS, 1987). The symptoms of this syndrome occur in three phases, summarized in Table 5-4.

Over time, alcoholism damages many parts of the body. Neurological deterioration is reflected in blackouts and memory loss, numb and tingling extremities, reduced sexual potency and interest, confusion, seizures, and finally coma and death.

Delirium tremens, or DTs, is a dramatic and dangerous complication of alcoholism which can occur during a period of alcohol withdrawal. Its onset is usually sudden and involves restlessness, irritability, confusion, and tremors that may progress to convulsions. DTs can involve hallucinations, disorientation, and overactivity of the autonomic nervous system. It may persist for three to seven days and can cause death. The internal organs are also affected by alcoholism: chronic liver disease is a widely recognized consequence, but no less intimately associated with alcoholism are stomach ulcers and inflammation, pancreatic distress, and congestive heart failure. Family members of an alcoholic may develop psychological problems resulting from verbal or physical abuse.

What A Doctor Will Do About Addiction

Successful treatment programs for smoking, prescription-drug, and alcohol addiction provide medical support along with psychological, social, and behavioral counseling. Any one or two factors, without the third, is far less effective for the patient than the three-part approach.

Alcohol

Today, primary-care doctors may take a long-term, active role in treating alcoholism. They may prescribe Antabuse or naltrexone to help the alcoholic avoid the drug, and refer the patient to counseling services or Alcoholics Anonymous. Psychologists and psychiatrists also treat alcoholism. Due primarily to insurance regulations, some doctors refer alcoholic patients to addiction-treatment centers, typically chemical-dependency units at hospitals, where the patients receive specialized care.

Patients seek treatment for numerous reasons. Many businesses today offer employee-assistance programs that provide referrals for alcoholism. Some patients begin treatment as a result of court orders following convictions for domestic violence, drunken driving, or similar situations. Some are persuaded by family members to get help, and others do so of their volition.

Medical treatment for alcoholism should include a complete medical history. Physical examination should include a neurological exam and blood tests for liver function. Tests for sexually transmitted diseases, particularly HIV, should be conducted. Because advanced alcoholics prefer alcohol to food and may experience a decreased ability to absorb nutrients, they often suffer malnutrition. Consequently, the doctor may prescribe a diet high in protein, vegetables, and complex carbohydrates, and perhaps recommend additional vitamin and dietary supplements.

During detox, the patient may be treated with benzodiazepines to ease withdrawal symptoms, which begin six or eight hours after the last drink. The drugs also limit convulsions. Because alcoholics can easily substitute a new addiction for the old, however, no drugs should be prescribed after the detoxification period.

Recovery programs offer inpatient treatments for up to thirty days with varied periods of outpatient support. Counseling, classes, and group therapy, including Alcoholics Anonymous meetings, form the core of the treatment. Outpatient supervision continues for a varied amount of time, and may include half-way houses or recovery homes where treatment continues. Complete abstinence from alcohol is required.

Those who struggle to abstain from drinking may be helped by disulfiram (Antabuse), a drug that interrupts the liver's alcohol metabolism, resulting in severe nausea, vomiting, abdominal pain, and other symptoms; it has helped many patients stay sober. Naltrexone, currently used for opoid overdose, may also decrease one's craving for alcohol. As a last resort, patients may be prescribed SSRIs such as Prozac, Zoloft, or Paxil.

Drug Addiction Addictions to prescription drugs often involve the benzodiazepines and barbiturates, both of which can cause severe physical discomfort during withdrawal. Those who mix these drugs with others, such as alcohol, complicate their withdrawal further. Thus, to free a patient from this addiction, a doctor is likely to require hospitalization during the detoxification phase of withdrawal.

To evaluate the patient's level of dependence on the drug, the doctor must determine the patient's tolerance and then decrease the dose by about ten percent per day. During this time, phenobarbital may be used as both a substitute intoxicant and an anticonvulsant.

Within twelve to twenty hours after the dosage is reduced, the patient experiences weakness, trembling and restlessness. These symptoms intensify during the next day, and from the second to fifth day, convulsions may begin. Even those who extend withdrawal for up to two weeks are at risk for seizures after the second week; the stabilization of the nervous system requires up to thirty days. Follow-up treatment includes counseling, social support, and close medical monitoring.

Gradual withdrawal is essential to kicking the prescription-drug habit. A number of drugs abused in this way, when abruptly discontinued, can cause life-threatening symptoms that are very similar to the delirium tremens (DTs) of alcoholism.

Quitting Smoking

The risk of death related to heart disease, cancer, stroke, and chronic respiratory disease drops dramatically when the patient quits smoking. Those who quit before the age of 35, after 17 years of smoking, will add two to three years to their life expectancy. A doctor who is helping a patient stop smoking will likely develop a strategy that includes behavioral modification and drug treatment to help alleviate withdrawal symptoms. The doctor may prescribe an agent that contains nicotine to satisfy the body's craving for stimulation; two of the most popular and successful products are Nicotine polacrilex gum and the nicotine skin patch. Both are easy to use, although many prefer the gum because the chewing action helps satisfy the oral craving that occurs with tobacco withdrawal (Tierney et al, 1996).

The doctor may also direct the patient to the American Lung Association (1-800-586-4872) for information and support while quitting smoking. The Lung Association supplies free literature on effective quitting techniques and continually offers classes on quitting smoking in conjunction with local medical clinics or hospitals. These classes may be found in almost every community in North America with a population greater than 15,000.

Preventing Addictions

These three addictive substances—tobacco, alcohol, and prescription drugs—are widely ac-

prescription drugs—are widely accepted in our society today, so preventing addiction is very difficult. Experience shows that education about the negative effects of addiction has limited value. More successful is long-term change in social acceptance of the substance. For instance, since the 1950s tobacco smoking has become less and less acceptable, and regulations to isolate smokers or to ban smoking entirely are common. Alcoholism and drunken driving have been the subjects of public awareness campaigns, leading to new legislation and social sanctions against drinking and driving. These strategies support addiction-free living:

- Avoid socializing with those who use and abuse drugs
- Work toward developing healthy interests and leisure activities
- Seek counseling for mental health problems, such as depression or chronic anxiety, before they lead to drug problems
- Following surgery, injury or illness, use prescription pain relievers/tranquilizers for as short a time as possible.

Natural Healing and Addictions

I am eminently qualified to talk about addictions, because I have struggled with and let go of many, especially sugar addiction. Overcoming these addictions has taken great effort, but it was well worth it. I feel stronger and more confident about all aspects of my life because of this struggle.

Well-known steps to recovery include admitting you have a problem, being open and honest with family and friends, asking for help, and avoiding people and situations that tempt you to resume the habit. To this general process I add "sitting with the addiction"—that is, deliberately examining the addiction and its role in your life. Recovering from the addiction may involve psychological and spiritual methods such as that offered by AA or group therapy, and dietary approaches that include cleansing, herbs that support recovery, and natural bodywork methods. Some find a spiritual path that requires abstinence, such as Hinduism or Church of the Latter-Day Saints. Combinations that suit the individual can also be very effective.

Sitting with an Addiction

An important first step in resolving an addiction is to sit with it, to be with it as in meditation. Addictions often develop slowly over a period of years and become such a part of our behavior that we are not aware of them or we deny them. For instance, when I was smoking many years ago, I eventually noticed that sometimes I would light a cigarette and smoke it, then put it out, unaware of what I had done.

I began to watch closely my ritual of smoking, and there were many things I did not like about my habit. I began to use this close observation as a meditation: My desire for a cigarette rose, and I watched any judgments that would come. I became deliberately aware of my feelings about others who criticized my smoking or supported it because they smoked also.

I fully experienced my own emotions and body sensations when I was out of cigarettes and wanted more. Sometimes I sat in meditation and simply followed my emotions about smoking back to the beginning of the need. I believed that the sucking response was tied to my lack of breast-feeding when I was an infant (breast-feeding wasn't fashionable then). I particularly noticed that my smoking ritual was a barrier to hide behind when I came into contact with others. I also observed how nicotine affected my biochemistry, changed my blood pressure, made me feel slightly dizzy and speeded up, and suppressed my hunger when I wanted to rush around rather than take time to eat.

Sitting with an addiction in this manner, with faith and good intentions and asking for the grace to see it clearly for what it is, led me to the practical steps that healed my addiction naturally and without tremendous effort. My effort was focused on working through resistance to attaining clarity about the addiction. Before clarity can be reached, one must face one's darkest, deepest, and most painful fears and weaknesses. This is the mystical journey to the God-self that requires courage and concentration. Everyone has the ability to make this journey, though not all choose to make the effort.

As a practical exercise for attaining insight and clarity, try sitting in a quiet place for fifteen minutes. Concentrate on the process involved in your addiction. For instance, if you are a drinker, think about the drink. Envision going to the store and buying the bottle. Honestly examine your feelings: Are you fearful or embarrassed? Do you feel guilty or angry, or maybe excited or apathetic? Then imagine the first drink from the bottle. Are you anxious to have it? How does it taste—good or foul? Do you gulp it eagerly, or choke it down almost against your will? Imagine the first sensations of the alcohol entering your blood. Watch closely as you start to lose yourself to the sensations of getting high. Watch as long and as closely as you are able. Now, how do you feel the morning after, both physically and emotionally? Do you feel guilty? Do you feel prepared to meet the day?

Also pay attention to your perceptions about the brand or label you prefer. Advertising for both liquor and cigarettes is pervasive and powerful. Do you feel any subconscious allure to be like the cowboy in the cigarette ads who is so strong and self-assured, or like the smartly dressed, powerful woman who is in control of her life?

Watch carefully, without judgment. When we judge ourselves or our behavior, we are using the ego to try to control the ego and encouraging self-deception, which leads backward, not forward. The only way to make the watching process truly productive is through exquisite attention and dedication, without thinking about right or wrong. In this state of choiceless awareness, we are closer to our God-self. In other words, by accessing our higher intuition, we are able to open ourselves to universal knowledge about our healing process.

When you watch yourself, do it fully. Be the smoker or the drinker absolutely. Don't play games by saying, "I am not really a smoker" or "I will quit soon". Be the smoker all the way: "I am the smoker. I smoke. I smoke often. I light the cigarette, I inhale, I feel the smoke go into my lungs, and I feel the chemicals pervade my body." Embrace every aspect of your addiction unconditionally.

Now that you've taken the crucial first step toward healing your addiction, choose the method or combination of methods of healing that most appeals to you. Remember, however, that thinking about an improved diet, or fantasizing about quitting drinking or smoking, or deciding to work out or taking a long walk tomorrow is not the same as healing. Health is created moment by moment in what we do right now. Only the choices we make at this instant can create health—and heal addiction.

Diet and Herbal Remedies

The role of nutrition in alcoholism has been the focus of extensive research. For instance, it appears that vitamin B insufficiencies in the diet can enhance the craving for alcohol, and that supplementation with thiamine, pyridoxine, and vitamin B_{12}, folate, nicotinic acid, and pantethine can prevent or at least help manage the disease (Cleary, 1990; Smith, 1978). Daily oral supplements of 500 to 1,000 milligrams of niacin over a three- to four-week period reduced drug and alcohol craving in patient volunteers (Cleary, 1990). In another study, 507 alcoholics were given three grams or more of nicotinic acid daily for five years. From thirty to sixty percent of the volunteers reported reduced alcohol-related symptoms (Smith, 1978).

Chronic alcohol use can interfere with nutrition. Alcohol blocks the conversion of linoleic acid to gamma-linolenic acid (GLA), which plays a role in the development of prostaglandins, hormone-like substances that regulate blood pressure and inflammation, among other effects. Some researchers have stated that the toxic effects of alcohol can be counteracted with the consumption of GLA-rich products such as evening primrose oil, borage-seed oil, and black currant-seed oil (Horrobin, 1980; Jiang, W. C. et al, 1995).

The recommended diet for recovering addicts is supportive, nurturing, and varied. A warm, nutritious diet that contains some fish and organic chicken, vegetables, grains, legumes, and a moderate amount of high-quality dairy products, along with some cleansing foods, is ideal for most people. Following is a recommended balance of food; the percentages are only approximate and should be varied according to climate, age, type of work, and time of year:

- Cooked food: Eighty percent in the winter; sixty to seventy percent in the summer
- Raw fruits and vegetables: Twenty percent in the winter; thirty to forty percent in summer
- Protein foods: Thirty percent total, consisting of about thirty-five percent beans; twenty percent meats, mostly fish, organic chicken and turkey, and a little red meat; twenty percent tofu and tempeh; fifteen percent dairy, if no allergies are present; and ten percent seeds and nuts.
- Carbohydrates: Thirty percent total, consisting of approximately fifty percent whole grains; twenty percent refined flour products such as baked goods, bread, or pasta; thirty percent vegetables such as yams, potatoes, squash; ten percent fresh fruit in season; and ten percent refined foods such as ice cream, cookies, and candy (if desired). Beware however: alcoholics often substitute sugary foods for alcohol after breaking their addiction.

Antioxidant supplements can help protect the body against free-radical damage to the lungs, digestive tract, and other organs from tobacco smoke, alcohol, and drug use. These include vitamin E (400 to 800 units per day), vitamin C (one to four grams per day), zinc, and selenium. Herbal antioxidants include ginkgo, milk thistle, and hawthorn extracts. Grape-seed extract, about 200 milligrams, two to three times daily, is also effective.

Cleansing

In clearing addictions, various forms of cleansing, if done properly, can be a great help. It is beneficial to assist the body in ridding itself of any toxic residues of addictive substances, including drugs of all kinds. Because the liver is the main organ of elimination and detoxification, their continual use can place a great strain on that organ. Powerful antioxidant herbs

that protect the liver include milk thistle (follow instructions on the product), turmeric (cook with it or use a commercial tablet or capsule product), schisandra (in capsule or tablet form), and ginger (cook with it or use a tablet or capsule product). Liver-cleansing herbs include Oregon grape root, fenugreek, burdock, dandelion, centaury herb, gentian root, and artichoke root.

Other systems of the body can also be cleansed of toxic substances with herbs. These help the systems function properly and work against lingering effects of the addiction. Red clover, burdock, and dandelion cleanse the blood. Red root, cleavers, echinacea, and mullein cleanse the lymphatic system.

The Liver Flush

Mix any fresh-squeezed citrus juices (orange and/or grapefruit and lemon) together to make one cup of liquid. Add one or two cloves of fresh-squeezed garlic and a small amount of fresh ginger juice. Mix in one tablespoon of olive oil and blend (or shake well in a glass container).

Follow with one to two cups of a purifying tea blend, such as fennel, fenugreek, licorice, flax, or burdock.

Use the liver flush for ten days during addiction withdrawal, up to three rounds per day, with a rest of three to five days between.

Pectin Therapy

Mix one tsp. of citrus or apple pectin in a glass of water; let it sit for at least one hour; then drink the liquid. The pectin forms a highly charged gel that removes heavy metals, some toxins, and radioactive compounds out of the body.

A diet consisting mostly of cleansing foods for short periods (up to a week at a time) helps remove toxic drug residues from the body. Fruits and vegetables and their juices tend to be the most cleansing of foods.

Other Herbal Remedies

A number of herbs are helpful to recovering addicts. Some should be chosen according to the addict's symptoms, and others are good for general support of the body.

Adrenal tonic herbs (adaptogens) counteract stress and support the efforts of the recovering addict to stay away from the abused substance. They include eleuthero, American ginseng, ashwaganda, and schisandra.

Calmatives such as California poppy, an excellent antianxiety herb, also help relieve stress. Other herbs that are good for this include valerian, passion flower, hops, catnip, chamomile, lemon balm, and linden flower.

Some recovering addicts experience depression during recovery. To help these individuals, St. John's wort, rosemary or lavender extract, and essential oils of lavender, chamomile, clary sage, and neroli may bring relief.

Liver protectors such as milk thistle are also excellent in supporting and healing the liver during recovery from addiction. These are particularly important for those recovering from alcohol or prescription-drug addictions.

Digestive tonics

Bitters can help support the vital energy of the body, allowing more resources for breaking addictions. These herbs include red ginger, gentian, artichoke leaf, orange peel (many commercial formulas available). Warming digestive herbs, such as ginger, cardamom, cinnamon, American calamus, may also be helpful. See the Resource Directory for books that can help with addictions.

High Blood Pressure

According to the National Health and Nutrition Examination Survey (NHANES III, 1988-1991), an estimated fifty million people, or twenty-five percent of adults in the United States, have high blood pressure (hypertension). Blood pressure tends to increase with age and is most common in the elderly. Twice as many African-Americans suffer from hypertension as do people of European ancestry. According to medical population studies, life expectancy is significantly shortened in individuals with increased blood pressure. For example, the life expectancy of a 35-year-old man with mild hypertension may be shortened by as many as twenty years (Rakel, 1996).

The primary causes of high blood pressure are lifestyle choices: obesity, excessive alcohol and caffeine consumption, smoking, and a diet high in sodium and saturated fat. Such a diet may lead to arteriosclerosis, a hardening or thickening of the arteries which reduces their elasticity. Heredity also plays a role, as do environmental factors (Berkow, 1982). Certain prescription drugs, such as oral contraceptives, steroids, nasal decongestants, estrogens, and anti-inflammatories, can raise blood pressure.

A person with hypertension usually experiences no symptoms

Almond Oil

We use this oil in my clinic to enhance circulation, nourish tissues, and help relieve pain. It is a favorite of many of my patients.

To one ounce of almond oil, add one or more to suit: ten to thirty drops of essential oils of cinnamon, calamus, chamomile, orange, or valerian (if you like the smell). Half an ounce of St. John's wort oil can act as a relaxing and nerve-healing addition.

If desired, the oil can be warmed before use.

until specific organs are damaged. At that time, cardiovascular complications such as coronary heart disease, congestive heart failure, and stroke may occur. Additional complications include ventricular failure, retinal hemorrhages, cerebrovascular insufficiency, and kidney failure (Berkow, 1982). These hypertension-related diseases also may produce symptoms such as dizziness, blurred vision, headaches, fatigue, and nervousness.

The Anatomy of Hypertension

The heart cycle has two alternating phases, systole and diastole. Systole occurs when the heart contracts and the ventricles, the major pumping chambers of the heart, are emptied. The diastole occurs when the heart muscle rests and the ventricles fill. These phases of the heart cycle are transmitted to the major arteries and are detected when measuring blood pressure. The healthy range of blood pressure is wide and depends upon the age, gender, and lifestyle of the patient. A normal systolic pressure is less than 130 millimeters of mercury (mmHg) and a normal diastolic pressure, less than 85. This blood-pressure reading is notated as systolic over diastolic, or 130/85. In mild hypertension, systolic is 140-159, diastolic is 90-99. In severe

hypertension, systolic is 160 or greater, diastolic 120 or greater.

Most major drugstore chains offer free use of blood-pressure machines; unfortunately, sometimes these machines are not accurate. Although home blood-pressure machines and ambulatory monitors provide the most accurate measurements, one study showed that more than sixty percent of blood-pressure readings from a popular ambulatory machine were inaccurate and inconsistent (Whitcomb et al, 1995). If you're using a drugstore machine, always choose the same one so your measurements are consistent. Everyone should have a periodic blood-pressure measurement.

What a Doctor Will Do about Hypertension

A medical doctor diagnoses hypertension with accurate and consistent blood-pressure measurements. Before an official diagnosis is given and medication prescribed, blood pressure is monitored daily for several weeks. The goal of medical treatment for hypertension is to minimize damage to the body.

Lifestyle changes and nondrug therapies comprise initial treatment of mild, early hypertension (systolic below 180, diastolic below 110). Table 5-5 reviews the recommended lifestyle modifications. Because drug therapy does not significantly improve *mild* hypertension and can have dangerous side effects, it is not typically used as a first recourse. After six months, if the preliminary treatment proves to be inadequate, drug therapy will be recommended by your physician.

Numerous effective antihypertensive drugs are available. Individualized therapy is required, since many drugs are contraindicated for specific diseases and health conditions. The medical doctor must consider parameters such as risk factors, demographics, and family-health history when formulating a therapy. A patient should beware if a physician attempts to prescribe a "cookbook" treatment without thorough research.

There are many effective drugs to treat hypertension. They include diuretics, drugs that affect the sympathetic nervous system, vasodilators, and those that directly affect hormones involved in regulating blood pressure. Because these drugs act on different mechanisms, they can be combined with each other to treat more severe hypertension.

Diuretics act on the kidneys to increase the excretion of sodium and water through the urine. This decreases the volume of blood, thereby decreasing blood pressure. These drugs are normally used for mild cases of hyperten-

TABLE 5-5. Lifestyle Modification for High Blood Pressure

Reduce body weight to normal range.
Stop using all tobacco products.
Reduce or stop using entirely alcohol and caffeine.
Under guidance of a healthcare professional, start an aerobic exercise program and work up to 30 minutes, 3 times a week.
Avoid anaerobic exercise such as weightlifting, which can increase blood pressure.
Avoid drugs that may increase blood pressure, such as oral contraceptives, steroids, decongestants, and nonsteroidal anti-inflammatory drugs (Tylenol, Aspirin, Advil).
Learn biofeedback and relaxation techniques.
Supplement with potassium, calcium, and magnesium.
Restrict dietary sodium and simple sugars.
Increase intake of crude fiber, trace minerals, and amino acids.
Include plenty of garlic and cold-water fish, such as tuna and salmon, in your diet.
(Rakel, 1995)

sion and include thiazide and amiloride. Side effects include depletion of other minerals through the kidneys and increased serum lipids.

Drugs that affect the sympathetic nervous system include the beta-blockers. These drugs act by blocking the transmission of certain nerve impulses that use epinephrine or norephinephrine as neurotransmitters. The result is to decrease blood pressure by slowing the heart rate. Unfortunately, these drugs act throughout the body, inhibiting neurons in the respiratory tract, eye, and other cells. Patients with asthma and diabetes should not take these drugs. Among these drugs are propranolol and metaprolol. When discontinuing these drugs, patients should taper off gradually. Abrupt withdrawal can cause nervousness, increased heart rate, and increased blood pressure.

The vasodilators, such as hydralazine and verapamil, relax the smooth muscle cells of the small arteries, allowing them to open. They can cause headache, nausea, anorexia, fluttering or throbbing of the heart, and sweating.

Finally, there are drugs that act directly on the body's hormones. These include the ACE inhibitors that inhibit angio-converting enzyme, which cause the blood vessels to constrict. By inhibiting production of the enzyme, the ACE inhibitors lower blood pressure by stimulating vessel relaxation. In some patients, these drugs can cause a severe drop in blood pressure and kidney failure.

Natural Healing and High Blood Pressure

Drug therapy should be followed only when the patient is unwilling to make changes in diet, exercise, and amount of relaxation conducive to an actual cure for hypertension, or when making these changes does not lower blood pressure. Medical doctors often prescribe blood-pressure medication for the duration of the patient's life, and although these drugs may lengthen life, they can significantly reduce its quality. Unfortunately, some patients will risk the serious side effects of medications rather than make lifestyle changes and take up healthy practices.

To treat hypertension naturally, consult a health-care provider about implementing an aerobic exercise program. Exercise can be dangerous for hypertensives, as it can increase blood pressure; if it is safe, however, it is very effective in lowering blood pressure and perhaps eliminating the need for antihypertensive drugs. Begin an easy to moderate exercise program and increase it over a period of several months to a more strenuous routine. Consult a physician or other qualified health-care practitioner for a safe program tailored to your needs.

Secondly, adopt a strict dietary regimen. Recommended dietary changes include restricting salt intake, including the salt hidden in many processed foods; ingesting less saturated fat and animal protein (especially red meats); and eating more fresh fruits and vegetables. It may also be beneficial to restrict alcohol intake, avoid caffeine, and supplement with magnesium, potassium, and omega-3 fatty acids.

Lifestyle changes can also reduce stress. Biofeedback can have dramatic, beneficial results. For mild to moderate cases of hypertension, dietary changes and a good relaxation program that includes walking, deep breathing, meditation, and herbal therapy may be sufficient. In severe cases, combining drug therapy with a natural healing program may be necessary.

Herbal Programs

Herbal therapy safe for treating high blood pressure without professional supervision includes three to four doses per day of hawthorn (one to two tablets per dose of standardized extract; four droppersful per dose of liquid extract; three to four cups of tea per day of flowers and leaves) and three to four garlic tablets or capsules per day, plus plenty of garlic in cooking. Positive hypotensive effects have been shown with preparations made from fresh garlic, and hawthorn has an undisputed reputation for improving cardiac function (Weiss, 1983; Koch & Lawson, 1996).

Relaxing herbs, especially passion flower, California poppy, and hops, can help reduce tension. In Europe, mistletoe and shepherd's purse are commonly recommended for reducing hypertension, but both should be used with caution and preferably under the supervision of a trained herbalist.

CHAPTER 6:

THE HERBAL

ALTHOUGH THOUSANDS of years of experience throughout the world indicate the usefulness of herbs for healing, much remains unknown about the active constituents—the chemicals that cause the medicinal action—of many plants. Chemists in Europe and Asia, where most of the analytical work on medicinal plants is conducted, have come full circle in understanding the role of active constituents in the overall effectiveness of healing herbs. For instance, it was once agreed that the action of St. John's wort was probably due to one or two important compounds, or perhaps a group of compounds.

Yet it now appears that the most potent and friendly extracts from St. John's wort and other plants contain the entire plant. These whole-plant extracts include small amounts of secondary compounds such as alkaloids, ter-penes, phytoesterols, essential oil components, and other components that have significant biological activity.

Plant extracts often lack primary constituents such as starches, cellulose, and sugars because they are abundant in the modern diet, and thus considered nonessential to the plant's precise medicinal effect. This may also turn out to be a false assumption. Perhaps the most profound medicinal activity can be found in the fresh, whole, live plants that are harvested and made into a tea, or simply eaten on the spot. It is my experience that well-made liquid and powdered extracts have significant biological activity as well.

The constituent section for each herb contains a summary of analytical work reported for that plant in the literature. The information on the chemical constituents of the following plants was gathered from these sources: List, P. H. and L. Hörhammer. 1973. *Hagars Handbuch der Pharmazeutischen Praxis* (7 vols.). New York: Springer-Verlag; Leung, A. Y. and S. Foster. 1996. *Encyclopedia of common ingredients* (2nd. Ed.). New York: John Wiley; Bisset, N. G. and M. Wichtl (Eds.). 1994. *Herbal drugs*. Stuttgart: Medpharm; Newall, C. A., et al, 1996. *Herbal medicines: A guide for health-care professionals*. London: Pharmaceutical Press.

CALIFORNIA POPPY
(Eschscholtzia californica)

Parts Used The whole, fresh plant in flower, including the root.

Range California poppy is native west of the Coastal Ranges of California and Washington. Almost weedy in habit, it is now successfully cultivated elsewhere in North America and Europe.

California poppy

Related Species Ten related species are listed, but only *E. californica* has been tested; other species should be avoided.

Etymology of Nomenclature The botanical name of California poppy, *Eschscholtzia*, honors Eschscholtz, a Russian surgeon and naturalist who is credited with discovering the plant.

History This beautiful, golden-flowered herb was first described by botanists who came to California in 1820 as part of a Russian expedition. These explorers sent specimens of the California poppy to Europe, where it quickly became a popular garden plant. Today it is the California state flower and is legally protected, since once-vast fields of *Eschscholtzia* have been replaced by condominiums, shopping centers, and freeways.

The first people to write about the medicinal properties of the California poppy were early Spanish explorers who traveled up the Camino Real along California's coast. They considered the whole, flowering plant to be a sedative. The Spaniards undoubtedly learned of its uses from Native Americans who lived in California and southern Oregon. The Costanoan people laid the flowers under children's beds to help induce sleep, while various tribes used the leaves and roots to help ease toothache (Bocek, 1984). The Cahuilla of Southern California used the whole plant as a sedative for babies (Bean & Saubel, 1972).

Constituents Eschscholtzine, californidine, protopine, aporphines, sanguinarine, chelerythrine, and allocryptopine (Kleber et al, 1995).

Pharmacology Clinical and laboratory work on California poppy has demonstrated the plant's sedative and antianxiety properties; it has been shown to improve both sleep latency and quality (Bruneton, 1995).

The alkaloids in California poppy have a gentle sedative and sleep-inducing properties. Some of these alkaloids have been studied individually and found to relax uterine muscles (Weiss, 1988; Kleber, 1995).

Modern Use California poppy is anxiolytic, analgesic, antispasmodic, and sedative. It is one of the best herbs for relaxing muscle spasms, twitches, or tics. California poppy can currently be found in a few herbal remedies sold in the United States for easing mild anxiety and promoting sleep and relaxation. Because of its mild sedative and analgesic properties, California poppy preparations can be given safely to children.

Dose Tea, 1 cup, 2 to 3 times daily; tincture, 30 to 40 drops, 2 to 3 times daily. Note: Since the tea is mild, a tincture is recommended for stronger doses.

Side Effects and Contraindications California poppy may increase the effects of MAO inhibitors. Otherwise, the herb is safe to consume when used appropriately.

Notes Because California poppy is protected by law, it is advisable to grow it at home for fresh or dried-plant preparations, and this is easy to do. Sprinkle a packet of seeds, available from any nursery, into a well-prepared, sunny bed and watch the little plants grow! Harvest the whole plant when in flower and make a tea or tincture.

To preserve the herbs, clean the roots and dry the plants in a well-ventilated area out of direct sunlight. Then store the dried herb in airtight amber jars, or in heavy paper. Prepare the poppy plants for use by chopping or crumbling them finely and making a tea or tincture.

CATNIP

(Nepeta cataria)

Parts Used Leaves.

Range Catnip was naturalized from Europe and is now found growing by roadsides and in waste places throughout the United States.

Catnip

Etymology of Nomenclature
The common name catnip (or its relative, cat mint) derives from the fact that cats are attracted to the herb because it intoxicates them. The botanical name, *Nepeta*, refers to Nepet, the Tuscan town where the plants were first discovered (Paxton, 1840).

History Catnip has a soothing, quieting effect on the nervous system and has traditionally been used for nervousness, hysteria, and nervous headaches (Hutchens, 1969; De Bairacli-Levy, 1974).

Gerard, Parkinson, and the later English herbalists used catnip not for its sedative properties, but as a female herb. They also used it for babies who were very fussy and colicky with flatulence.

Originally, catnip was taken as a tea, juice, tincture, or poultice; it was also smoked or chewed. Some Eclectic doctors used catnip as a foot bath to relieve nervous irritation (Scudder, 1830). Like Gerard, Cazin (1886) prescribed it for hysteria, and it has been said to be beneficial for various acute nervous disorders, causing no withdrawal effects upon discontinuation (Hutchens, 1992). The tops and leaves of catnip were official in the *U.S. Pharmacopoeia* from 1840–1870 and in the *National Formulary* from 1916 to 1945.

Constituents Nepetalactone; volatile oils such as citronellol, geraniol, and citral; tannins; and a bitter element.

Pharmacology Weak, non-dose-dependent, sleep-promoting effects were demonstrated in a study involving young chicks given both cold-water and acetone-pretreated, hot-water extracts of catnip (Sherry et al, 1948). The constituent nepetalactone has been shown to account for catnip's mildly sedative and antispasmodic characteristics (Leung & Foster, 1996).

Modern Use Catnip is a calmative and mild antispasmodic. It is good for coughs and relaxing sore muscles and is recommended for children as a tea or a bath (specifically, for restless children who cannot fall asleep). Herbalist Rosemary Gladstar, author of *Healing Herbs for Women*, describes catnip as "the herb of choice for many childhood problems." She writes, "Years ago when my son was just a baby, I had read in my handy herbal 'bible' *Back to Eden*, about the marvelous benefits of using catnip for soothing fussy babies. Catnip not only saved my child from much suffering, but also saved his mother from many a sleepless night. Those early experiences with catnip convinced me to try it on many other ailments of childhood. Whenever my son had a fever, restless evening, or was fussy, I would brew up a cup of catnip tea for him, and in most cases it worked wonders. I even sewed catnip in his sleep pillow, and it did seem to soothe and calm him to sleep, this fragrantly scented herb pillow of catnip, hops, roses, chamomile, and lavender."

Dose Tea, 1 cup 2 to 3 times daily; tincture, 30 to 40 drops, 2 to 3 times daily.

Side Effects and Contraindications Avoid catnip during pregnancy.

CHAMOMILE
(Anthemis nobilis)
and *(Matricaria recutita)*

Parts Used Flowers.

Range Chamomile originated in western and southern Europe. Several species of chamomile have naturalized in southern England, Europe, North Africa, North America, and Asia. Elsewhere, it is cultivated with great success.

Etymology of Nomenclature *Anthemis* derives from the Greek *anthemidos*, meaning flower, and the Latin *nobilis*, meaning well-known. *Matricaria* is from the Latin *matrix* for womb, an allusion to its medicinal properties, and *recutita* is from the Latin for skinned.

History Chamomile was well-known to the ancient Greeks, who likened its scent to apples and hence named it "earth apple" *(kamai melon)*. The Spanish call it *manzanilla*, or little apple. It was also revered by the Egyptians, who dedicated it to their gods. In Europe chamomile was used as an aromatic stewing herb throughout the Middle Ages because of its fragrance.

Chamomile

Surprisingly, perhaps, neither the Greeks nor Gerard (1633) used the chamomiles as a sedative. One of the earliest references to chamomile's use in this capacity is in 1799, when Woodville mentions Roman chamomile for hysteria. King (1866) used the oil for the same purpose. Likewise Cazin (1886) used German chamomile for nervousness, especially hysteria, while Fernie (1897) recommended Roman chamomile to decrease nervous excitability reflected from an affected organ, for nervous colic of the bowels, and in the young for restlessness and discomfort during teething. Fernie also extolled that a potted plant of chamomile was helpful in the garden: "Singularly enough, if another plant is drooping, and apparently dying, in nine cases out of ten it will recover if you place a herb of [German] Chamomile near it" (1897).

Scudder (1898), the Eclectic physician, wrote that chamomile could be prescribed with certainty for any nervous or restless condition in children, or to calm adults who were touchy and impatient. To nourish the nervous system, Scudder prescribed ten drops to one teaspoon of chamomile tincture in half a glass of water (Scudder, 1883), though Felter, another Eclectic physician, found that very small doses of chamomile were most effective for nervous complaints (Scudder, 1900).

Anthemis nobilis was official in the *U.S. Pharmacopoeia* from 1820 to 1900, and *Matricaria chamomilla* from 1840 to 1916. The latter was also official in the *National Formulary* from 1926 to 1942.

Constituents German: A volatile oil, 0.24–1.9% [primarily α-bisabolol, and chamazulene]; sesquiterpene lactones (matricin, matricarin, desacetylmatricarin); flavonoids (flavones and flavonols such as apigenin, luteolin, quercitrin); coumarins (umbelliferone, herniarin), mucilage. Roman: A complex volatile oil, 0.6–2.4% (angeloyl, methacryl, nobilin); flavonoids (apigenin, luteolin, quercitrin, apiin); polyacetylenes, phenolic constituents (trans-caffeic, ferulic acids, scopoletin); triterpenes, mucilage, coumarins.

Pharmacology *In vitro*, chamomile has shown an antispasmodic effect similar to that of papaverine (Wren, 1988). The tea has been reported to have a hypnotic effect (Reynolds, 1993). Chamazulene and α-bisabolol, constituents found in chamomile oil, have shown anti-inflammatory and antispasmodic activity (Foster & Leung, 1996).

Modern Use In general, German chamomile is preferred when a mild calmative that helps the digestion is desired. Roman chamomile is preferred for its pain-relieving and sedative qualities. Both are very safe and particularly well-suited for children (Hoffmann, 1983).

Mindy Green, co-author of *Aromatherapy, A Complete Guide to the Healing Art*, writes that the "anti-inflammatory action of chamomile is mild enough for the treatment of many childhood ailments that require sedation, such as fever, teething, and tantrums, yet strong enough to treat adult problems such as insomnia, rheumatic pain, and depression."

Five or six drops of chamomile oil can be put in bath water to soothe overwrought nerves (Maybe, 1988), diluted to two percent to make an excellent massage oil, used as an inhalant, or applied as a compress (Green, 1994). In Mexico, chamomile is known as manzanilla and is commonly served as iced tea in restaurants. It is also used in countless households for stomach complaints, colic in babies, and nervousness (Martinez, 1992). Chamomile is widely used in Russia as a sedative and nervine and in Pakistan as a calmative for children (Hutchens, 1992).

Dose Tea, 1 cup 2 to 3 times daily; tincture, 30 drops 3 times daily.

Note For severe muscle spasms or pain, take one-half teaspoon of tincture of Roman chamomile *(Anthemis nobilis)* combined with one-half teaspoon of tincture of valerian *(Valeriana officinalis)*, three to four times daily in a little water or lemon balm tea.

Side Effects and Contraindications Very strong chamomile tea can cause vomiting. Keep chamomile tea away from the eye area; it can produce irritation.

Notes Don't underestimate chamomile. It is considered a mild herb, but if you make a strong tincture or tea and take enough of it, it can produce miracles. Pineapple weed, *Matracaria matracaroides*, works in much the same way as chamomile.

HAWTHORN
(Crataegus oxyacanthus)

Parts Used Flowers, leaves.

Range *Crataegus* is a genus of the Rosaceae (rose family). Approximately two hundred species are native to temperate zones. They are primarily concentrated in East Asia, Europe, and eastern North America.

Etymology of Nomenclature The name *Crataegus* comes from the Greek *kratos* (strength), referring to the strength and hardness of the plant's wood. *Oxyacantha* is a Greek name that has been applied by ancient writers to barberry, sweetbriar, hawthorn, and other plant groups.

History The history of hawthorn's medicinal use is relatively brief. It was mentioned for various ailments by Al-Samarquandi (ca. A.D. 1210) and by Parkinson and Gerard in the early seventeenth century; its current use for heart conditions dates back to that time, according to Leclerc (Madaus, 1976). The first conspicuous American reference to the use of hawthorn to treat heart disease was in an article published by J.C. Jennings of Chicago in 1896 (Lloyd, 1917). In homeopathy, hawthorn is used as a sedative for irritable patients with cardiac symptoms.

Constituents A number of antioxidant procyanidins (also called pycnogenols), 1.3%; numerous flavonoids which vary from species to species and the time relative to flowering when they are harvested, 1–2% (hyperoside, vitexin, rutin, spiraesoside); amines, catechols, phenolcarboxylic acids (chlorogenic acid), triterpene acids, sterols, purines.

Modern Use Although hawthorn is predominantly used for its normalizing action on the heart and circulation, one of its major clinical uses is as a mild sedative (in combination with lavender or lemon balm) where mild heart disease is accompanied by nervousness (Hobbs & Foster, 1990). In Italy, hawthorn preparations are used more for mild anxiety and other nervous disturbances than for heart ailments (Loggia et al, 1983). Hawthorn has also been indicated for insomnia related to nervous conditions (Paris & Moyse, 1981).

Pharmacology Potter's *New Cyclopaedia of Botanical Drugs and Preparations* (1988) lists hawthorn as hypotensive and mentions that *Crataegus* species have been described as sedatives, but without scientific evidence to support the assertion. Hawthorn's cardiotonic and hypotensive activity has been widely reported (Leung & Foster, 1996).

Dose Tea, 1 cup 2 to 3 times daily; tincture, 2 to 3 droppersful, 2 to 3 times daily.

Side Effects and Contraindications Consult your health-care professional before taking hawthorn if using digitalis. Hawthorn can increase the effect of digitalis, so a smaller dose of digitalis may be required.

HOPS
(Humulus lupulus)

Parts Used Strobiles, the female flowers notable for their casing of small scales.

Range Hops is native to North America and Europe. It now is found as far north as New

Hops

Brunswick, in the Midwest, and in New Mexico.

Etymology of Nomenclature The word *humulus* is thought to derive from the Latin *humudus* (wet) or *humus* (fresh, damp earth), as the plant prefers a moist soil (Pratt, ca. 1800). According to Pliny (Grieve, 1931), the name *lupulus* derived from the plant known as "willow wolf" *(Lupus salictarius)*, so-called because it destroys willows by twining around and choking them.

History Hops has been cultivated for brewing since Roman times and has been used medicinally for at least that long. Gerard (1633), the English herbalist, praised the health-promoting qualities of beer in his *History of Plants*. In nineteenth-century European herbalism, hops was used for its narcotic action; it lacks the side effects, such as constipation and weakened stomach tone, that often accompany narcotic drugs. It was also said to be an anaphrodisiac, having a sedative effect on the genital organs (Cazin, 1886). Scudder (1891) recommended hops for anxiety and worry, for nervous conditions in general, and to induce sleep. For mild insomnia it was used in pillows (Wood et al, 1926). Homeopaths have also traditionally used hops for conditions of the nervous system.

In the early 1900s, Eclectic physicians used hops as a gentle tonic, hypnotic, and sedative. It was used specifically for insomnia due to worry, nerve weakness, or alcohol abuse (Bell, 1925; Ellingwood, 1983). Hops fomentations, or hot, moist preparations, were applied to acute inflammations.

Humulus lupulus was official in the *U.S. Pharmacopoeia* from 1820 to 1916 and in the *National Formulary* from 1926 to 1942.

Constituents Bitter substances, including acylphloroglucides, 15–30% (humulone and lupulone); essential oil, 0.3–1% (myrcene, linalool, farnesene, caryophyllene, etc.); tannins, 2–4%; flavonoids (kaempferol, quercetin) and closely related chalcones.

Pharmacology Modern research shows that extracts from hops relax smooth muscles, particularly in the digestive tract (Caujolle et al, 1969). The lupulin from fresh hops has been known to cause contact dermatitis, as well as uneasiness, headache, conjunctivitis, and sleepiness in field workers. In Germany, this syndrome is called "hop pickers' disease." In animal studies, hops has shown sedative effects on rats (Wohlfart et al, 1983). There are many unanswered questions regarding the optimum use of hops—whether its effects are better from fresh or dried preparations, whether the drug increases or decreases in potency during storage, and whether the extracts have any identifiable active constituents or work by some unexplained synergism.

Modern Use Hops has bitter, tonic effects on the digestive tract, and thus is useful for irritable bowel syndrome, nervous stomach, and to counteract the effects of excessive indulgence in food, drugs, or drink. It is also used as a mild sedative to promote sleep and counteract restlessness and anxiety (Weiss, 1988; Fintelmann et al, 1989). Hops is generally mixed with other herbs, among them valerian and sometimes St. John's wort (Klein, 1995). Steidle (1931) suggests that hops could also be used as a daytime sedative, perhaps in combination with passion flower and lemon balm. Fresh hops preparations are good for atonic dyspepsia, whereas dried preparations combined with valerian are indicated for hysteria, restlessness, and sleep disturbances. Herbalist Cascade Anderson (1994) emphasizes the importance of using dried hops preparations when a sedative action is desired, as she has found that fresh hops (tea or tincture) can be quite stimulating.

Hops contains phytoestrogens and has a mild estrogenic effect in both men and women (Hesse et al, 1981). For this reason, I sometimes recommend hops as a calmative for nervousness and anxiety in women who have had hysterectomies, or are menopausal or postmenopausal.

Dose Tea, 1 cup 2 to 3 times daily; tincture, 30 to 40 drops, 2 to 3 times daily.

Side Effects and Contraindications Some writers advise against using hops if depression is present. Otherwise, none noted.

Notes Hops is one of the most effective herbs that I have found for settling a restless heart. When your heart is jumpy or if irregular heartbeats occur, or if you are concerned about your heart for no apparent reason, hops tea or a teaspoon of tincture added to a little warm water is a fast and effective remedy. Of course, if your symptoms persist, visit your physician for a thorough evaluation and diagnosis.

A good quality hops is rich in essential oil, and should contain at least 0.35 percent. In addition, it should be very aromatic (Blumenthal et al, 1996).

JAMAICAN DOGWOOD
(Piscidia erythrina)

Parts Used Bark.

Range This tree grows in the West Indies, South America, Mexico, Florida, and Texas.

Jamaican dogwood

Etymology of Nomenclature
Piscidia derives from the Latin *piscis* (fish) and *caedo* (to kill), alluding to the stupefying effect the plant has on fish.

History Jamaican dogwood entered widespread medical use in the late nineteenth century, after early research revealed an active constituent, piscidin, that has narcotic properties similar to morphia (Ott, 1880). Physicians began using it in fluid extract form for nervous bilious attacks, hysteria, and nervous headaches (Auxence, 1953) and sometimes as an opium substitute for promoting sleep, relaxing spasms, and allaying pain (Shoemaker, 1891). It was also used as an analgesic, antispasmodic, and to allay nervous anxiety (Felter & Lloyd, 1898). Griffith (1847) recommended the use of Jamaican dogwood in extract form, made from one ounce of bark powder to twelve ounces of alcohol. Potter (Wren, 1988) classified Jamaican dogwood as an analgesic, sedative, and antispasmodic with a particular usefulness in insomnia. In homeopathy, *Piscidia* was used as a nerve sedative for insomnia caused by excitement or worry.

Constituents Saponin glycosides, (piscidin, which may be a mixture of two); hydroxybenzoic acid derivatives [piscidic acid (r-hydroxybenzyltartaric acid), fukiic acid, malic acid, succinic acid, tartaric acid); isoflavonoids (icththynone, jamaicin, etc.); rotenoids (rotenone, sumatrol, milletone, etc.);

alkaloid (from the stem), resin, volatile oil, sterols (β-sitosterol); tannin.

Pharmacology The active constituent is most likely piscidin, which produces intoxication with subsequent sleep. The whole plant's effect is similar to that of codeine and hashish, being at first irritating and stimulating, then relaxing, and ultimately causing quiet sleep without any unpleasant side effect. *Piscidia* paralyzes nerves in the central nervous system, respiration being increased at first but then suddenly diminished. Due to this soporific action, it has been used as a sleep-inducing drug in cases where morphine and other remedies failed to calm the patient (Madaus, 1976).

Modern Use Today, Jamaican dogwood is used as a sedative and anodyne, primarily for insomnia caused by pain or nervous tension. It is sometimes combined with hops and valerian for this purpose (Hoffmann, 1983). "Herbal Ed" Smith (1994) says that Jamaican dogwood "is an effective nonopiate anodyne, but its action can be strongly pronounced, so it must be used with caution and discretion." He reports that it is particularly effective for neuralgia such as sciatica, toothache, earache, and migraine headaches.

Dose Tincture, 20 drops to 2 droppersful 2 to 3 times daily.

Side Effects and Contraindications The maximum dose has not yet been determined, but caution is advised in the prescription of larger doses or long-term use. It is important to consult an herbalist experienced in its use.

KAVA-KAVA
(Piper methysticum)

Parts Used Root.

Range Kava-kava is probably indigenous to the South Sea Islands, originating somewhere west of Fiji. Because it has been cultivated for so many centuries, from New Guinea to Polynesia to Micronesia, it is difficult to determine the exact original range.

Kava-kava

Etymology of Nomenclature *Piper methysticum* means "intoxicating pepper" in Latin. In various parts of the Pacific islands, *Piper methysticum* has been called kava-kava, awa, waka, lawena, or yaqona.

History Up to twenty-one distinct varieties of kava, each with slightly different medicinal effects, have been identified. In Hawaii, kava-kava has been used to soothe and relax the nerves and to induce sleep (Titcomb, 1948). In other Pacific Island cultures, it has been used to relieve fatigue, promote deep sleep, and strengthen children recovering from illnesses. Kava-kava has been described as stimulating to the nervous system in small doses but depressing in larger amounts. It has been used as a local anesthetic (Foster, 1897). Kava-kava has also been used to alter one's consciousness, preparing the way for interaction with the spirit world (Fackelmann, 1992). One historical way of preparing kava-kava for medicinal use, called the Tongan method, consisted of chewing the root to mix it with saliva and then storing the final, well-moistened concoction. Missionaries who came to the Pacific Islands forbade the use of kava, partly because of their revulsion with this practice.

Constituents The root contains varying amounts (3–20%) of resinous material with numerous cavalactones; α-pyrones include kavain, yangonin, and methysticin. The levels of these compounds vary from variety to variety and are thought to play a significant role in their relaxing and euphoriant qualities. The roots also contain large amounts of starch (43%) and sugars (3%), proteins, minerals, and other constituents.

Pharmacology Animal and human testing over the last century or so has given variable results. Some of the identified constituents have shown stimulating activity, some sedative activity, and some no activity. Early testing was flawed due to problems with uncertain identification and adulterations of the samples studied. Recent research has shown effects such as cerebral depression, steadying of heartbeat (Lewis & Elvin-Lewis, 1977), and reduction of anxiety (Singh, 1981). One double-blind study showed reduced feelings of nervousness and anxiety in patients taking 100 milligrams of the extract three times daily for one month (Kinzler et al, 1991). For a review of animal tests, see Keller & Klohs (1963).

Modern Use Kava-kava is used as a general relaxant and calma-

tive. Kava-kava prepared from the fresh roots and rhizomes is said to have a stronger effect than that prepared from the dried material. Some authors emphasize that kava-kava prepared by the Tongan method (chewing and mixing with saliva) is stronger than that made by crushing the rhizomes and macerating them in cool water. Also, kava-kava prepared by boiling is said to have a stronger, quicker effect than that prepared by maceration in cool water.

I have noticed only mild relaxing effects from two cups of hot kava-kava tea prepared from the commercially available, cut-and-sifted rhizome. A good quality extract produces a pronounced feeling of euphoria, a numbing of the tongue, and a feeling of heaviness in the limbs.

Dose Tea, 1 cup, 2 to 3 times daily; tincture, 3 to 4 droppersful, 2 to 3 times daily.

Side Effects and Contraindications Avoid large doses, as oversedation can occur. Begin with doses of one-half teaspoon of the liquid tincture, and do not exceed one teaspoon, three to four times per day.

Use caution when driving or operating dangerous equipment. Do not take with alcohol or barbiturates. Do not take during pregnancy or lactation. Do not exceed recommended dose.

LADY'S SLIPPER
(Cypripedium pubescens)

Parts Used Rhizome.

Range Lady's slipper, also known as American valerian, is native to North American and Europe. It is found in dry to moist woodlands and bogs.

Etymology of Nomenclature *Cypripedium* derives from the Greek *cypris*, another name for Venus, and *podion*, meaning slipper or shoe.

History Lady's slipper resembles valerian in its therapeutic action, having been used traditionally for spasmodic conditions, nervousness, and insomnia (Shoemaker, 1891). Lady's slipper roots were used by Native Americans as a sedative and antispasmodic, and they are said to have been used successfully for hysteria (Griffith, 1847). Rafinesque (1828) believed that all the *Cypripedium* species have equal medical merit and considered lady's slipper to be the best American substitute for European valerian.

Lady's slipper was used in homeopathy for nervousness and insomnia in young children. Felter, the Eclectic physician, described lady's slipper as a safe and simple remedy for nervous children and proclaimed it as one of the best remedies for insomnia (Scudder, 1906). Lady's slipper was official in the *U.S. Pharmacopoeia* from 1866 to 1905 and in the *National Formulary* from 1916 to 1926.

Constituents The rhizome of lady's slipper has not been thoroughly analyzed. It is possible that an essential oil, resinous fraction, unknown glycosides, and a group of phenanthraquinones, one of which is named cypripedin, all contribute to the plant's medicinal activity.

Dose Tincture, 2 droppersful, 3 to 4 times daily; tea, one-half to one cup, 2 to 3 times daily.

Lady's slipper

Side Effects and Contraindications None known.

Notes In 1990, the American Herbal Products Association recommended that lady's slipper not be traded because of its endangered status in many states. Therefore, valerian and other relaxing herbs are recommended in its place.

LAVENDER
(Lavandula angustifolia)

Parts Used Flowers.

Range Lavender is native to the Mediterranean regions of Europe and is cultivated extensively for its aromatic flowers in Europe and North America.

Lavender

Etymology of Nomenclature The name *lavender* derives from the Latin *lavo* (to wash), referring to the use made of its distilled water to scent baths and water for washing clothes.

History Lavender was used traditionally much as it is used today—as a sedative, relaxant, and antispasmodic. Although it was not mentioned by ancient Greek authors, it does appear in *The Medical Formulary* of Al-Samaquandi of the Arabian school. One of the earliest references to lavender in European medicine is by Hildegard of Bingen, a twelfth-century abbess, who said it refreshes and frees the spirit and fosters "pure knowledge and a clear understanding" (Flückiger, 1879). In the nineteenth century, lavender oil was recommended for hysteria, nervous headache, and other nervous afflictions (Bentley & Trimen, 1880; Shoemaker, 1891). In Fernie's *Herbal Simples* (1897), it is said that ". . . the lions and tigers in our Zoological gardens, are powerfully affected by the smell of Lavender-water and become docile under its influence." Lavender-flower tea was also used as a remedy for headache due to fatigue or weakness, and the essential oil was taken internally to counteract faintness, nervous palpitations, spasms, and colic. The Eclectics, too, extolled lavender for its "kindly" influence on the nervous system (Scudder, 1870). Spirit of lavender (lavender oil in an alcohol base) was official in *The National Formulary* in 1950, and lavender flowers were official in the *U.S. Pharmacopoeia* from 1820 to 1880. Lavender oil was official from 1820 to 1942.

Constituents An essential oil (0.5–3%) containing over 100 compounds, including linalool, linaloyl acetate, 1,8-cineole, camphor, and sesquiterpenes such as caryophylene oxide, cadinene is prominent. Constituents vary considerably depending on the chemical race or species of the lavender. The plants also contain coumarins (coumarin, umbelliferone), flavonoids (like luteolin), triterpene phytosterols (ursolic acid), and tannins (5–10%).

Pharmacology In a laboratory study with mice, hyperactivity induced by caffeine was reduced and nearly eliminated by inhalation of lavender oil. This aromatherapy study serves to sanction the popular use of lavender-herb pillows to facilitate falling asleep and reducing stress (Buchbauer et al, 1993). Another study done by a nurse in an English hospital suggests that massaging the feet of intensive-care patients with lavender oil reduces wakefulness (Hewitt, 1992).

Modern Use Lavender flowers have carminative, spasmolytic, tonic, sedative, and antidepressant properties. Lavender (infusion or oil) is used for spasms, colic, neuralgia, and nausea, internally as well as externally (Leung, 1980). It may also be effective for headaches and for inducing sleep. Lavender is a gentle strengthening tonic for the nervous system and benefits those suffering from nervous exhaustion (Hoffmann, 1983). A few drops of lavender oil added to a bath before bedtime is recommended for those with sleep disorders.

Herbalist and aromatherapist Kathi Keville, co-author of *Aromatherapy, A Complete Guide to the Healing Art*, says about lavender, "Of all the many oils available to the aromatherapist, lavender is one of my favorites for relaxation. It is easily available, relatively inexpensive, useful for many disorders and, best of all, one of the best-loved fragrances. I find that I use it in my aromatherapy practice more than any other oil. Applied externally as a compress, poultice, or diluted essential oil (such as massage oil), lavender relaxes muscles. When inhaled, the scent alone is quite relaxing. Both methods of application help to decrease insomnia, nervousness, physical or emotional exhaustion, and anxiety. The diluted oil rubbed on the temples also calms headaches." She also recommends making a compress to apply to the forehead and/or back of the neck; adding two to four drops of the essential oil to bath water for a whole-body or foot bath; and using the scent as an atmospheric agent to ease emotional conflicts and promote decision-making, including in work environments.

Dose Tea, 1 cup, 2 to 3 times daily; essential oil may be inhaled; diluted essential oil massaged into the skin (use 10 drops essential oil per ounce of vegetable oil), or added to baths (3 to 10 drops).

Side Effects and Contraindications Do not ingest essential oil; more than two drops may cause toxic reaction. Otherwise, safe to consume when used appropriately.

LEMON BALM
(Melissa officinalis)

Parts Used Leaves.

Range Lemon balm is native to southern Europe and is naturalized in Middle Asia, North America, and Europe.

Etymology of Nomenclature The name *Melissa* (bee) derives from the fact that lemon balm is

Lemon balm

a sweet-smelling plant that attracts bees.

History Paracelsus (1493–1541) is said to have claimed that lemon balm could completely revivify a person, and the plant was once esteemed beneficial for all maladies stemming from nervous disorders (Grieve, 1931). Lemon balm's essential oil was traditionally considered of great medicinal value as a "corroborant of the nervous system" (Lewis & Akin, 1791), and Fernie (1897) suggested making a cold-water infusion (so as not to lose volatile oils by evaporation) of the plant for "hysterical headache" and as a nervine stimulant. Cazin (1886) described *Melissa's* use in Europe for nervous afflictions such as hysteria, palpitations, spasms, and melancholy. In the early twentieth century, a popular English formula, called Carmelite water, combined lemon balm with lemon peel, nutmeg, and angelica root to treat nervous headaches (Grieve, 1931). *Melissa* was official in the *U.S. Pharmacopoeia* from 1840 to 1890.

Constituents Small amounts of a sedative essential oil (0.02–0.3%), with more than seventy individual compounds (monoterpenes, mostly citronellal, citral, geranial, neral; and sesquiterpenes, mostly β-caryophyllene and germacrene). The exact content of the essential oil varies with climate and race of the plants. The polyphenols, or tannins (up to 4%) are also biologically active (antiviral) and this fraction is used in creams and other preparations externally for treating herpes lesions. Also present are flavonoids and triterpenes.

Pharmacology As early as 1889, French researchers proved that lemon-balm oil can cause narcotic effects such as drowsiness, chronic sleepiness, and sleep. Seel found a sedative and sleep-promoting action with a twenty-drop dose, which slowed breathing and heart rate and diminished blood pressure (Koch-Heitzmann & Schultze, 1988). In 1956, research conducted in Yugoslavia on the central nervous system of fish demonstrated the sedative effects of *Melissa* oil, which worked by reflex action to stimulate the olfactory lobes. The strongest effects were attributed to the presence of terpene alcohols in the oil. These results were confirmed by reports in the patent document of Laboratories Meram (Koch-Heitzmann & Schultze, 1988). In other animal studies, *Melissa* oil has shown sedative and spasmolytic activity (Wagner & Sprinkmeyer, 1973). Interestingly, equal sedative action was found with dosages from 3.16 up to 100 milligrams per kilogram of body weight. The effect was minimal, however, with a dosage of one milligram per kilogram of body weight (Koch-Heitzmann & Schultze, 1988). Terpenes from spirit of *Melissa* have shown spasmolytic effects comparable to those of papaverine, a strong, alkaloidal, smooth-muscle relaxant. The sedative action of both lemon balm and lavender oils was confirmed in pharmacological studies and clinical examinations performed by Schilf (Wagner & Sprinkmeyer, 1973).

Modern Use Herbalists today use lemon balm as a gentle sedative for nervous stomach and to relieve tension. In German trade, its use is officially listed for "nervous disorder of sleep" (Bisset, 1994). The essential oil of lemon balm is effective for melancholy and depression. In Europe, the oil is considered to have strong sedative properties and is sometimes taken in the amount of two to four drops, combined with other relaxing herbs.

Dose Tea, 1 cup 2 to 3 times daily; tincture, 2 to 3 droppersful, 3 to 4 times daily.

Side Effects and Contraindications None noted with tincture or tea; consult a qualified herbalist before using the essential oil.

LINDEN
(Tilia europea)

Parts Used Flower.

Range Grows throughout Europe and many parts of North America.

Etymology of Nomenclature Linden is also known as lime tree

Linden

or tilia, the later deriving, perhaps, from *ptilon* (feather), in reference to the feathery appearance of the leaves. However, Paxton (1840) says the etymology of *Tilia* is completely unknown.

History Linden has been used since the nineteenth century for its sedative, antispasmodic, and anodyne properties (Fernie, 1897). Cazin (1886) used a hot infusion of the flowers for nervous affections, hysteria, vomiting caused by nervousness, and general sedation of the nervous system. He advocated its daily use because it has a sweet, pleasant aroma and is non-irritating, unlike regular tea. Many herbalists have used an infusion of linden flowers in a bath for nervousness and hysteria (Fernie, 1897; Grieve, 1931), or in a hand or foot bath for insomnia, especially in babies and children (Mességué, 1973). Leclerc (1937) considered linden blossoms to be antispasmodic and especially useful after psychological or physical stress. In folk medicine, this herb continues to be used as an antispasmodic and sedative (Bisset, 1994).

Constituents Flavonoids, about 1% (rutin, hyperoside, quercitrin, and more), mucilage (about 10%), leucoanthocyanadins, caffeic, r-coumaric, chlorogenic acids), and a very small amount of essential oil, about 0.2%.

Pharmacology Little research has been done on the pharmacological aspects of linden flowers (Bruneton, 1995).

Modern Use Linden is a generally safe and relaxing nervine and is good for tension headaches, nervous tension, and mild hypertension. It is mild with a definite relaxing, sedative effect.

Dose Tea, 1 cup, 2 to 3 times daily; tincture, 1 teaspoon, 3 to 4 times daily.

Side Effects and Contraindications None noted. Safe to consume when used appropriately.

PASSION FLOWER
(Passiflora incarnata)

Parts Used Leaves.

Range Passion flower originated in South America and the East Indies. Of about 300 species, most are native to the United States. In Europe, passion flower is a popular garden plant; in America it thrives in dry soils from Virginia to Florida and westward to Missouri and Arkansas.

Passion flower

Etymology of Nomenclature
The name *Passiflora* (passion flower) derives ultimately from *fior della passione*, the popular Italian name applied to the flower due to a fancied resemblance of its parts to a cross. This association with Christian symbolism may have begun in 1610, when a Mexican friar brought a drawing of a passion flower to Jacomo Bosio, who was then preparing a work about the Cross of Calvary (Moldenke & Moldenke, 1986).

History Passion flower was probably introduced into medicine around 1840 by a doctor from Mississippi, its uses being mainly for restlessness and insomnia (Wood et al, 1926). In the mid-1800s and early 1900s, the Eclectics used the entire plant in moderate doses as an antispasmodic and mild narcotic. It was specifically indicated by them for restlessness and wakefulness due to nervous exhaustion or overwork. It was also used for insomnia in the very young and the very old; for excess mental activity in any age group; for warding off attacks of epilepsy; and for heart palpitations resulting from excitement or shock (King, 1898). Karl found the plant to be quite effective for treating nervous restlessness during menopause (Spaich, 1978). Homeopaths used passion flower for its quieting effect on the nervous system, for insomnia resulting from exhaustion, and for mental overwork. The dosage was thirty to sixty drops of mother tincture, taken several times a day. This tincture is an alcohol-and-water solution made with one part herb to ten parts solution.

Constituents The biological activity appears to be a result of a synergy between small amounts of harman alkaloids, 0.1–0.9% (harmine, harmaline), the levels of which depend on the stage of development of the flowers and leaves when the plant is harvested, up to 2.5% flavonoids (apigenin, luteolin, quercetin, kaempferol, rutin, etc.) and the γ-pyrone maltol. The plant also contains phytosterols (stigmasterol, sitosterol), and small amounts of cyanogenic glycosides.

Pharmacology *Passiflora* extracts can depress the central nervous system and are used for their sedative and soothing properties (Windholz, 1976). Early studies on passion flower demonstrated its sedative action and effectiveness for hysteria, fatigue, and insomnia in alcoholics (Madaus, 1976). Recent animal studies have shown that passion-flower extracts, given both orally and intraperitoneally, significantly prolong sleeping time (Speroni & Minghetti, 1988). One company in Japan makes a chewing gum for inhibiting anxiety that contains passion flower and valerian powder in addition to L-tryptophan (Yamaji et al, 1986).

Modern Use Passion flower is an important herb for anxiety, insomnia caused by mental worry, nightmares, and hysteria. In England it is an ingredient in forty popular sedative preparations. Passion flower has been recommended as a sedative in neurasthenia, anxiety states, and nervous disorders, particularly in children (Bisset, 1994). It is indicated for nervous restlessness (Blumenthal et al, 1996) and especially in cases of disturbed sleep or heart palpitations (ESCOP, 1992). Passion flower is used for arrhythmia and minor sleep problems in both children and adults (Bruneton,

1995). It is an excellent sedative with no side effects even when used in large doses (Spaick, 1978). The tincture is also beneficial for premenstrual syndrome and for menopausal women with nervous restlessness.

Dose Tea, 1 cup, 3 times daily; tincture, 30 to 60 drops, 3 to 4 times daily.

Side Effects and Contraindications None noted. Safe to consume when used appropriately.

SKULLCAP
(Scutellaria lateriflora)

Parts Used Leaves, flowers.

Range Skullcap is found in temperate regions in various parts of the world but is particularly abundant in America.

Skullcap

Etymology of Nomenclature Skullcap derives its name from the Latin *scutella*, meaning "a little cap," which the calyx resembles.

History Rafinesque (1830) and Gunn (1872) both reported skullcap's use as a nervine. King (1866) prescribed skullcap as a warm infusion for all nervous affections, including restlessness, wakefulness, nervous headache, mental excitement in pregnant women, and nervous excitability. Millspaugh (1887) confirmed its use as a nervine in his work *American Medicinal Plants*, and Fernie (1897) mentioned its use as a decoction combined with extract for epilepsy and "depressed and disordered states of the nervous system." A dried extract (pill form) was used for insomnia due to excess mental activity. In the *Homeopathic Materia Medica* of 1927, skullcap was listed as a nerve sedative for use especially with "nervous fear" and irritation in teething children. Skullcap was official in the *U.S. Pharmacopoeia* from 1860 to 1900 and in the *National Formulary* from 1916 to 1942.

Constituents Active sedative or antispasmodic compounds are little understood. The activity may be partly due to flavonoids (apigenin, luteolin, scutellarein, etc.), a volatile oil with monoterpenes (limonene, terpineol) and sesquiterpenes (caryophyllene, humulene), and iridoids (catapol). The plant also contains a resin and tannin.

Pharmacology While skullcap enjoys popularity as a folk remedy, virtually no scientific research has been done on this herb.

Modern Use Skullcap is well-respected for its sedative, nervine, and antispasmodic properties. It is used for nervousness manifesting in the muscles (spasms, tics, tremors, convulsions), insomnia, nervous exhaustion, and for premenstrual syndrome. In Traditional Chinese Medicine, it is considered to have a tonic effect on the nerves.

Medical herbalist and doctor Tierona Low Dog says that skullcap will sedate gently if one is feeling anxious. She considers this herb a true tonic, because it brings one back to the center, to balance, and it has a lot of food for the nerves. Her experience shows it to have a quieting and enriching effect throughout the day, and precludes her having to give people anything else to help them sleep at night.

Dose Tea, one-half cup, 3 to 4 times daily; tincture, 30 drops, 3 times daily.

Side Effects and Contraindications If purchasing commercial preparations of this herb, avoid any that contain germander *(Teucrium* spp.). Some reports indicate that this combination of herbs can cause hepatitis. Use only as recommended; large doses may cause excitability, disorientation, and stupor.

ST. JOHN'S WORT
(Hypericum perforatum)

Parts Used Flowers and leaves.

Range St. John's wort is native to Europe, West Asia, North Africa, Madeira, and the Azores. It is naturalized in many parts of the world, notably North America and Australia (Hickey & King, 1981; Wichtl, 1986).

History St. John's wort has been used for centuries in folk medi-

St. John's wort

cine for nervous disorders, particularly injured nerves and sciatica. King (1876) mentions its use for hysteria and nervous imbalances with depression. In homeopathy, St. John's wort was used for excessive pain (Boericke, 1927). St. John's wort is currently official in the pharmacopoeias of Czechoslovakia, Poland, Romania, and Russia (Hobbs, 1988).

Constituents A group of dianthraquinones, which are red pigments found in the flower (0.05–0.3%), especially hypericin, pseudohypericin. Modern phytopharmaceutical extracts of St. John's wort are often standardized to 0.3% hypericin (probably containing other related compounds). Research shows that the whole-plant extract containing the naturally occurring compounds is more effective than extracts containing a highly purified fraction of these compounds. Flavonoids (hyperoside), a phloroglucinol derivative (hyperforin), which is related to compounds found in hops as well as a volatile oil (0.05–0.3% with α-pinene and other monoterpenes) may also play a role in the activity of the herb.

Pharmacology Because of St. John's wort's history of use for psychiatric conditions, it has been tested for MAO-inhibiting activity (Suzuki et al, 1984). A standardized (hypericin) extract was found to extend the narcotic sleeping time of mice, depending on dose (Okpanyi & Weishcer, 1987). One research team found an improvement in symptoms of anxiety, dysphoric mood, loss of interest, hypersomnia, depression, insomnia, and feelings of worthlessness (Muldner & Zoller, 1984). In a placebo-controlled, double-blind study consisting of patients with mild to moderately severe depression, 66.6 percent reported favorable results, and hypericum did not cause any impairment of attention, concentration, or reaction (Schmidt & Sommer, 1993). A significant reduction in depression was also reported in another double-blind study with 105 patients given 300 milligrams three times daily, with no adverse effects (Sommer & Harrer, 1994).

Modern Use Modern herbalists use St. John's wort for many of the same conditions for which it has been recommended throughout the ages. It is taken internally to treat mild depression, fear and/or nervous disturbances, and to help heal gastric ulcers.

In one review article about St. John's wort, the author writes, "Recent studies have shown that it is clinically effective for the treatment of the symptoms of depression. It has proved superior to a placebo, equally effective as standard medication, and has a clear advantage over the latter in terms of side effects. It follows that, on the basis of our present knowledge, St. John's wort can be recommended for use as an antidepressant" (Ernst, 1995).

Overall, more than 23 randomized clinical trials with St. John's wort for depression in 1,757 human volunteers have been performed in Europe. Recently, an overview and critical analysis of these studies was published in the *British Medical Journal* (Linde et al, 1996). The researchers found that 15 of the trials were placebo-controlled, and 8 of the studies compared St. John's wort with other psychoactive drug treatments. They concluded that the St. John's wort extracts were significantly superior to the placebo and just as effective as pharmaceutical antidepressants.

In comparisons of the side effects of pharmaceutical antidepressants with St. John's wort, only two patients taking St. John's wort withdrew from a study because of side effects, compared with seven who took pharmaceuticals. Overall, side effects were reported by 52.8 percent of the patients on pharmaceuticals, and only 19.8 percent of those taking St. John's wort. The dose given in these studies varied widely, from less than one milligram of the standardized extract, up to one gram.

St. John's wort extract and calmative herbs such as California poppy extract, valerian, passion flower, and kava-kava can help ease the symptoms of anxiety, nervousness, and depression. They should not be abruptly substituted for pharmaceutical drugs used to treat these conditions, however. If you seek to treat these ailments with herbs, work closely with a physician and herbalist trained in the use of these substances. Don't abruptly stop taking these pharmaceutical drugs, because serious withdrawal symptoms can occur.

St. John's wort oil is one of the most useful remedies for any type of muscle pain, neuritis, neuralgia, or muscle or nerve weakness. Its main active component, hypericin, is a strong anti-inflammatory and can penetrate through the skin if applied locally as an oil or liniment. The oil is warming and soothing, whereas the tincture, which is more stimulating and cooling, can be used as a liniment. St. John's wort is a tonic nervine and is recommended for people who have nerve damage. It can be used either externally (as an oil) or internally (as a tea or in extract form) for trauma, accident, cut nerves, or any type of nerve damage. It has even been used for epilepsy. St. John's wort oil is thus extremely useful for body workers and chiropractors, because it helps strengthen and regenerate nerves and removes pain.

To make St. John's wort oil, cut the flowering tops off fresh flowers and grind them. Put them in high-quality olive oil and let them soak in the sun for two weeks. Then strain out the flowers and store the bright red oil in amber bottles, away from heat and light.

Dose Tea, 1 cup, 3 times daily; tincture, 2 droppersful, 2 to 3 times daily; extract, 40-milligram tablets, at a dose of 1 or 2 tablets, 3 times daily. For severe depression, larger doses—up to 1 teaspoon, 3 times per day of tincture—may be necessary.

The recommended dose of St. John's wort extract in Germany is 2 to 4 grams of a standardized extract (to 0.3% hypericin). Since the whole dried herb can contain up to 0.3% hypericins, it is possible that the carefully dried flowering tops can be dried, powdered, and put into capsules. The dose is 2 to 4 "00" capsules taken every morning and evening between meals. Hypericin is soluble in slightly alkaline watery solutions, so when making a tea, it is best to add a teaspoon of baking soda to a quart of water.

The best commercial tinctures should be cherry red to dark red. Do not purchase products that are clear or light pink; the richer the color of the tincture, the more likely it is to contain a good amount of hypericins and flavonoids, which may account for much of the activity of the herb.

Side Effects and Contraindications Those with fair skin may find that they sunburn more easily when taking St. John's wort and should protect themselves accordingly. People who are taking MAO inhibitor antidepressants such as Nardil, Parnate, and Marplan should consult a professional health-care provider before ingesting St. John's wort.

Notes For a complete review of the botany, history of use, chemistry, pharmacology, clinical applications, side effects and contraindications, commercial preparations, and quality control of St. John's wort, see the monograph on the herb in the Fall 1988/Winter 1989 issue of *HerbalGram*.

VALERIAN
(Valeriana officinalis)

Parts Used Rhizome.

Range *Valeriana* species are indigenous to most parts of Europe and parts of northern Asia, ranging from Spain to Iceland, to the North Cape and Crimea, to the coast of Manchuria in northern Asia (Flückiger & Hanbury, 1879; Tutin et al, 1964). The plant is cultivated in many parts of the world. It spreads rapidly by means of runners and can become invasive.

Etymology of Nomenclature
The name *Valeriana* is thought to derive from the Latin *valere* (to be in health) or *valeo* (to be strong), referring either to the plant's powerful healing properties or to its strong odor. Some claim it was named after Valerius Cordus, a Roman emperor, who may have used it in medicine.

History Down through the ages, valerian has been and continues to be one of the most popular and widely used medicinal herbs. In Traditional Chinese Medicine, it is used for headaches and mental depression. In the West, since the seventeenth century, valerian has been used as a primary treatment for nervous conditions such as epilepsy, hysteria, anxiety, and insomnia. Valerian was so widely used for nervous afflictions in women during the nineteenth century that it has been called the "Valium of the nineteenth century." Nonetheless, and contrary to popular belief, there is no chemical similarity between the two substances (Hobbs, 1989).

While most people find the smell of old valerian roots disgusting—it has been likened to the odor of well-seasoned socks—the fresh roots and the essential oil have a surprisingly sweet, musky odor that is quite pleasant. These were used in some ancient cultures as a perfume and sexual attractant similar to musk. Modern research has shown that some of valerian's sedative activity may be due to its odor, and at least one currently available valerian product (tablets) combines the essential oil with the herb in order to enhance the herb's activity. Valerian was listed as official in most drug books in both England and the United States until only forty years ago. In 1967, it was still official in the pharmacopoeias of Austria, Belgium, Brazil, Chile, Czechoslovakia, France, Germany, Hungary, Yugoslavia, the Netherlands, Poland, Portugal, Romania, Russia, Spain, and Switzerland (Hobbs, 1989).

Constituents the most active fractions of valerian appear to be the essential oil (0.3%–0.7%, containing the monoterpene bornyl acetate, and the sesquiterpenes β-caryophyllene, valeranone, valerenal, etc.) and 0.5–2% valepotriates including valtrate, isovaltrate, etc., which are bicyclic iridoid monoterpenes. These latter constituents are heat sensitive and are more active in fresh-plant extracts or carefully dried rhizomes (below 100°C). The smelly valerenic and acetoxyvalerenic acids provide the "dirty socks" smell characteristic of dried valerian roots. It is not known what role these components play in the overall sedative effect of valerian. A minute amount of alkaloids is also present (0.01–0.05%).

Pharmacology In well-controlled studies, valerian has been shown to depress the central nervous system (Krieglstein & Grusla, 1988) and improve sleep in humans, as measured by a variety of subjective and objective parameters (Leathwood et al, 1982; Chauffard et al, 1981; Leathwood & Chauffard, 1985). It was once thought that valepotriates (bicyclic iridoid esters) were the plant's major active components. Generally, valepotriates have shown spasmolytic, sedative, and anticonvulsant activity (Thies, 1970; Finner et al, 1984; Marekov, et al, 1983). However, more recent research has shown that water extracts of valerian, which contain no valepotriates and little essential oil, still have sedative effects and can improve sleep in humans (Koch, 1982); and that neither valepotriates nor valerian's major essential oil components affect the central nervous system (Krieglstein & Grusla, 1988).

Thus, for the moment, it appears that valerian's sedative effect is caused by a combination of depression of some centers of the central nervous system and direct relaxation of smooth muscle (Houghton, 1988). The most likely active compounds are essential oil components, the valepotriates, and as yet unidentified water-soluble components. Bruneton (1995) reports that in Germany the valepotriates are used generally for mood enhancement and for depression and anxiety in the elderly.

Modern Use Valerian's major application is as a sedative, especially as a potential substitute for stronger synthetic sedatives such as Valium and Xanax, which, unlike valerian, can cause severe dependence *(Physicians' Desk Reference*, 1989); a "drugged" feeling; losses in locomotor coordination (Von Eickstedt, 1969); and a potentially dangerous synergism with alcohol. In Germany, many doctors already prescribe valerian preparations for mild to moderate cases of depression while doctors in this country still resort to Valium (Weiss, 1988) and Xanax (Weil, 1983).

In the United States, herbalists use valerian extensively for its sedative and antispasmodic action against emotional stress, muscle pain, tension headaches, insomnia, nervousness, and restlessness (Moore, 1979; Anderson, 1989; author's experience). One clinical herbalist especially recommends it to break dependency on pharmaceutical antidepressants (Anderson, 1989). Valerian is recommended for people who have a hard time falling asleep because it shortens sleep latency. It also reduces nighttime waking.

Other uses for valerian include nervous heart conditions, children's anorexia caused by overexcitement (taken one-half hour before meals), "inner unrest," trembling, and stomach complaints (Koch, 1982). A German valerian-hops preparation has been recommended as a good daytime sedative because it does not reduce reaction time, while another German preparation called Recvalysatum Burger can be helpful in cases of hysteria, neurasthenia, excitement, anxiety, and psychosomatic illness induced by stress (Bühring, 1976).

Dose Tea, 1 cup as needed; tincture, 2 to 5 droppersful, 2 to 3 times daily.

Side Effects and Contraindications Some who have weakened adrenal systems due to severe, sustained stress may find that valerian acts as a stimulant; if this idiosyncratic effect occurs, discontinue the herb. Excessive use of valerian may lead to headache, insomnia, and excitability.

Notes For a complete review of valerian's botany, history of use, chemistry, pharmacology, clinical applications, commercial preparations, quality, and cultivation, see *Valerian, The Relaxing and Sleep Herb*, (Hobbs, 1993).

VIOLET
(Viola odorata)

Parts Used Flowers, leaves.

Range Violet flowers are widely distributed throughout Europe, northern Asia, northern Africa, and North America.

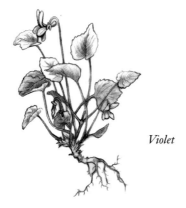

Violet

Etymology of Nomenclature Violet is derived from the Latin *viola*, which refers to the blue-red color.

History The ancient Greeks used violets for insomnia. Likewise, in a recipe for sleeplessness from Askham's *Herbal*, he states that those who ". . . may not slepe for sickness seeth this herb in water and at even let him soke well hys feete in the water to the ancles, wha he goeth to bed, bind of this herbe to his temples" (Grieve, 1931). Gerard (1633) also believed that syrup of violets could induce sleep; it was once used as the syrup base for children's cough medicines and various remedies for nervous irritability

Constituents Possible active constitutes include triterpenes, saponin, glycosides, flavonoids, or phenolic glycosides. Minute amounts of alkaloids and considerable quantities of mucilage is also present. Very little research has been performed on these constituents.

Modern Use Today, violet is used much as it has always been, for hysteria, insomnia, and other nervous problems (Lust, 1974).

Dose Tea, 1 cup, 2 to 3 times daily.

Side Effects and Contraindications None noted.

WILD LETTUCE
(Lactuca virosa)

Parts Used Leaves.

Range The origin of wild lettuce is unknown. It was introduced to the United States from Europe, where it grows in England, southern Europe, and as far east as western Siberia. In the United States, it can be found on roadsides, dumps, and other areas where the soil has been disturbed.

Wild lettuce

Etymology of Nomenclature

The botanical name *Lactuca* refers to the milky juice *(lacto)* that the plant contains.

History Wild lettuce has long been used as an opium-like sedative. According to ancient Greek legend, after the death of Adonis, Venus used a bed of lettuce leaves to calm her mind and assuage her grief. The Greeks are said to have extracted lettuce juice, dried it in the sun to reduce it to powder, and then mixed it with opium (Cazin, 1886). Gerard (1633) recommended wild lettuce for sleeplessness and pain. After that time, wild lettuce seems to have fallen out of favor until the late 1700s, when a Dr. Coxe reintroduced it to the medical profession. It then regained popularity both in England and the rest of Europe and became official in the pharmacopoeias.

Rafinesque (1830) cited wild lettuce as a strong pain reliever and sedative for nervous complaints and sleeping difficulties. Dr. Griffith (1847) claimed that wild lettuce could relieve pain, create relaxation, and slow the pulse while increasing its tone. Christison (1848) identified wild lettuce as a calming, pain-relieving, and hypnotic agent. King (1866) described wild lettuce as a substitute for opium, but without its side effects. He prescribed the dried juice in five- to twenty-grain doses.

According to Trousseau and Pidoux (1880), four to eight grams of wild lettuce are needed to obtain a stupefying effect in humans, as compared to two and one-half to five centigrams of opium. Cazin (1886) found that wild lettuce, unlike opium, did not cause constipation but could cause nausea when taken in large doses. He used it successfully for nervousness, starting with twenty centigrams and working up to sixty. Fernie (1897) prescribed three to eight grains taken at bedtime for insomnia due to overstimulation of the brain. It was used as syrup in children's cough medicines and various remedies for nervous irritability (Shoemaker, 1891).

Grieve (1931) later mentioned that the French used water distilled from lettuce as a mild sedative in two- to four-ounce doses.

Boericke (1927) used wild lettuce homeopathically for restlessness and insomnia. Wild lettuce leaves were official in the *U. S. Pharmacopoeia* from 1820 to 1840.

Constituents The sedative and antispasmodic effects of wild lettuce are often attributed to sesquiterpene lactones (lactucin, lactupicrin, β-amyrin, germanicol, taraxasterol, and others) found in the milky sap. Known as lactucarium, the dried latex was considered active as a sedative in official medicine. Contributing to the activity might be the flavones (apigenin, luteolin), flavonols such as quercetin, and other similar molecules. Coumarins (aesulin, cichoriin), simple plant acids (citric, malic, oxalic), the phenolic acid cichoric acid, a resin, sugars, and proteins are also present.

Pharmacology Wild lettuce has long been considered a hypnotic (Schenck & Graf, 1936). *Lactuca* extracts are believed to depress the activity of skeletal muscle, smooth muscle, the heart, and nervous tissues.

Modern Use *Lactuca* is mildly soporific, and while different preparations contain varying degrees of strength, it is nontoxic and safe for children and the elderly. Brian Weissbuch, certified acupuncturist and herbalist, uses a fluid extract of wild lettuce in a variety of formulas for the treatment of acute and chronic pain and insomnia. He states, "In my clinical practice, I have found wild lettuce extract very beneficial for patients experiencing moderate to severe musculoskeletal pain and insomnia due to pain and/or anguish. *Lactuca*'s calming effects and great safety provide a fine children's sedative useful for trips to the dentist and relief of various painful and emotional crises. Wild lettuce combines well with other calming and analgesic herbs, including valerian, corydalis, and Jamaican dogwood. In fact, I find that wild lettuce is most effective in combination [with other herbs], rather than individually."

Dose Tincture, 2 to 3 droppersful, 3 to 4 times daily.

Side Effects and Contraindications Do not use if glaucoma or prostate enlargement is present. Otherwise, safe when used appropriately.

WILD OATS
(Avena fatua)

Parts Used Spikelets.

Range Wild oats grow in fields and waste places from Newfoundland to British Columbia, from Pennsylvania to New Mexico, and in Mexico (Fernald, 1970).

Wild oats

Etymology of Nomenclature
The name *Avena* is said to originate from the Celtic *aten*, or *etan>*, meaning "to eat." This eventually became the English word *oat*.

History The oat was mentioned by many ancient Greek authors mainly for its nutritive value (Griffith, 1847). American doctors in the late nineteenth century made a strong tincture of wild oats with spirit of wine and used the preparation as a nervine restorer, especially for nervous debility brought on by overwork in lawyers, public speakers, writers, and so on. It was recommended for insomnia due to nervous exhaustion (Fernie, 1897) and for nervous debility during convalescence (Felter & Lloyd, 1898). Grieve (1931) listed it as a nervine and antispasmodic. Homeopathically, wild oats were used for their nutritive action on the nervous system (Boericke, 1927). In folk use, oat straw baths have been credited with sedative properties (Bisset, 1994). *Avena sativa* was official in the *National Formulary* from 1926 to 1946.

Constituents The active constituents are not well-known. Flavones, triterpenoid saponins, and small amounts of an alkaloid, avenine, in the outer hull may are possibilities. The plant may contain phytoestrogens, as feeding large amounts to livestock has led to increased fertility. Carotenoids and chlorophyll derivatives are also present.

Pharmacology Wild oats has not yet been well-defined pharmacologically, although it does have an alkaloid called avenine. The active constituent that is presumably responsible for its calming effects has not yet been found. Nonetheless, there are no proven side effects in humans (Tschesche et al, 1969).

Modern Use Wild oats is used today for nurturing the nervous system that is under stress, for counteracting exhaustion caused by depression, and for general nervous system weakness. The mild sedative effects of oats are said to be useful for withdrawal from addictions (Weiss, 1980). Von Hartungen (1952) contends that *Avena* is specifically indicated in cases of mental overwork and reports that it imparts psychological calm and prolongs sleeping time.

For treating insomnia, *Avena* may also be reliable when the disorder results from psychological exhaustion. Menge and Goebel (1954) report the cases of three women who suffered insomnia due to the psychological traumas of war. After taking *Avena* for only one week, their sleep returned to normal—which is a much quicker recovery than one would expect when dealing with long-term insomnia. Further, in a sanitarium with an herbal treatment program, Loben (1935) succeeded in completely replacing the usual sleeping and relaxing remedies with tincture of *Avena*.

Dose Tea, 1 cup, 3 times daily; tincture, 3 to 6 droppersful, 3 to 4 times daily.

Side Effects and Contraindications None noted. Safe to consume when used appropriately.

Notes To make your own tincture, harvest the spikelets in the stage where a milky starch can be squeezed out. Make an alcohol tincture with the fresh herb.

WOOD BETONY
(Stachys betonica)

Parts Used Dried leaves.

Range Wood betony is a common woodland plant in England.

Wood betony

Etymology of Nomenclature The word *Stachys* means "spike," in Latin, referring to the plant's inflorescence; *vettonica* was the name of an ancient Iberian culture.

History The ancient Greeks held wood betony in high esteem as a healing plant. A physician to the Emperor Augustus (63 B.C.-A.D. 14) wrote a treatise on wood betony, proclaiming it as a cure for no less than forty-seven diseases. The plant was also valued highly in the Middle Ages. Culpeper (1840) wrote, "This is a precious herb well worth keeping in your house." At one time, wood betony was the primary herb used for physical maladies of the head, and it is still recognized as a valuable tonic and nervine, although in present times it is most often used in formulas with other nervines (Grieve, 1931). An old Italian proverb was "Sell your coat and buy betony," while a modern Italian saying is "He has as many virtues as betony."

Constituents Tannins, saponins, and alkaloids.

Pharmacology Wood betony contains the alkaloids, stachydrine and betonicine, as well as abetaine, choline, tannins, and other components.

Modern Use Wood betony is often touted for strengthening the central nervous system and is especially indicated for nervousness and headaches due to anxiety and tension (Hoffmann, 1983). It is also recommended for neurasthenia (Lust, 1974).

Dose Tea, 1 cup, 2 to 3 times daily; tincture, 30 to 40 drops, 2 or 3 times daily.

Side Effects and Contraindications Safe to consume when used appropriately.

CHINESE HERBS FOR RELAXATION AND SLEEP

By Lesley Tierra, L.Ac.

Lesley Tierra, herbalist, acupuncturist, and author of The Herbs of Life, *explains the role of sedatives from the standpoint of Chinese medicine, along with how to use some popular Chinese patent remedies for relaxation and insomnia.*

In Traditional Chinese Medicine (TCM), restlessness, tension, stress, and insomnia can stem from several different causes. Overthinking, working, or eating; excessive concentration, studying, or deliberation; mental agitation, "burning the candle at both ends," depression, and fatigue— all contribute to the inability to relax or sleep properly. Which factors are present and where the body's imbalances lie ultimately determine which organ system or systems are involved and need to be addressed to create relaxation or adequate sleep. Following are the general categories for relaxation and sleep disharmonies according to the times of dis-

Table 6-1. Overview of Major Relaxing Herbs

Common Name	Latin name	Primary Uses
California poppy	Eschscholtzia californica	Calmative
Catnip	Nepeta cataria	Mild calmative
Chamomile	Anthemis nobilis	Calmative
Hawthorn	Crataegus laevigata	Mild sedative, mild heart sedative
Hops	Humulus lupulus	Mild sedative, sleep problems
Jamaican dogwood	Piscidia erythrina	Sedative, insomnia
Kava-kava	Piper methysticum	Nerve tonic, euphoric
Lady's slipper	Cyprepedium calceolus	Nervousness, insomnia
Lavender	Lavandula officinalis	Mild sedative, nerve tonic
Lemon balm	Melissa officinalis	Calmative, antispasmodic
Linden flowers	Tilia europa	Nervous irritability
Passion flower	Passiflora incarnata	Mild sedative, nervine
St. John's wort	Hypericum perforatum	Nerve restorative
Skullcap	Scutellaria lateriflora	Antispasmodic, sleeplessness
Valerian	Valeriana officinalis	Anxiolytic, sleep aid, nerve tonic
Vervain	Verbena hastata	Nerve tonic, strengthener
Violet, sweet	Viola odorata	Sedative, insomnia
Wild oats	Avena satua	Sedative, nervous exhaustion, addiction withdrawal
Wild lettuce	Lactuca virosa	Mild sedative, nerve irritation
Wood Betony	Stachys officinalis	Nervousness, nerve tonifier

Herb	Dose	Availability	Energy
California poppy	45 drops liquid extract, 3 times a day	Herb store; liquid extract	Bitter, acrid, slightly cool
Catnip	Warm tea, as needed.	Herb store; garden	Spicy, cool
Chamomile	1–2 cups tea, warm, 3 times a day; as a convenient alternative to tea, give children liquid extract in the amount of 5 drops to 3 droppersful, depending on age.	Herb store; garden	Pungent, cool, sweet
Hawthorn	2 to 3 tablets per day	Herb store; standardized extract	Cool, sweet
Hops	1 to 4 droppersful, liquid extract, 3 times per day	Herb store; liquid extract, herb	Acrid, warm, bitter
Jamaican dogwood	Toxic; use with caution	Herb store; liquid extract	Cold, bitter, pungent
Kava-kava	1 to 3 droppersful liquid extract, 3 times per day	Herb store; liquid extract	Acrid, spicy, slightly hot
Lady's Slipper	1 to 3 droppersful liquid extract, 3 times per day	Endangered plant	Bitter, pungent, sweet, neutral
Lavender	20 to 40 drops, liquid extract, 3 times per day	Common garden plant, herb store	Spicy, cool, pungent
Lemon balm	Warm tea as needed	Garden, wild plant	Spicy, cool
Linden Flowers	Tea as needed; can add to baths	Herb store	Pungent, sweet, astringent, cool
Passion Flower	2 to 3 droppers, liquid extract, 3 times per day	Herb store; cultivated vine	Bitter, sweet, cool
St. John's wort	1 to 2 droppersful or 2 to 3 tablets per day	Herb store; standardized extract or liquid	Bitter, acrid, cool
Skullcap	45 drops per day liquid extract	Herb store; herb, liquid extract	Bitter, spicy, cool
Valerian	1 to 2 droppersful liquid extract, 3 times per day	Herb store; liquid extract	Spicy, warm, sweet
Vervain	1 to 2 droppersful liquid 3 times per day	Herb store; herb, liquid extract	Cool, bitter
Violet, sweet	1–2 droppersful liquid extract, 3 times per day	Herb store; herb, liquid extract	Bitter, cool, slightly sweet
Wild Oats	Tea, 1 cup 3 times daily; tincture, 3 to 6 droppersful, 3 to 4 times daily.	Herb store; herb, liquid extract	Slightly warm, sweet
Wild lettuce	2 tablespoons fresh herb per 1 cup water	Wild plant, herb store, dried herb	Bitter, cool
Wood betony	Tea or liquid extract, twice a day	Herb store; herb, liquid extract	Sweet, bitter astringent

Table 6-2. Pharmacology of Important Nervines

Herb	Pharmacology—Major Actions	Main Uses
Valerian *Valeriana officinalis*	Central nervous system sedative, soporific (induces sleep), improves quality of sleep	Tension, anxiety, sleeplessness, insomnia, inner unrest, trembling, nervous stomach, hysteria, neurasthenia (with other tonic herbs)
Hops *Humulus lupulus*	Antispasmodic, sleep-inducing and calming, mildly anxiety-relieving	Helps with sleeplessness due to tension or anxiety, to relieve headaches, tension, mild anxiety
Passion Flower *Passiflora incarnata*	Central nervous system depressant, hypotensive (lowers blood pressure), pain-relieving, sedative	Can help relax the imagination in people who are worried or anxious; in my experience, helpful for people who have elevated blood pressure, especially when due to mental tension and worry
Catnip *Nepeta cataria*	Anti-spasmodic, sedative, diaphoretic	Helps increase elimination through sweating, especially during colds and flu, where it can also help reduce fever; also a mild sleep-inducing herb, safe for children; mild digestive tea and antispasmodic for colic, intestinal cramps
Skullcap *Scutellaria lateriflora*	Antispasmodic, sedative, anticonvulsant	As a tincture or powdered extract, often used to reduce nervous tension, relieve hysteria, and mitigate epileptic or other spasms; also as a mild bitter tonic; little scientific verification.
California Poppy *Eschscholtzia californica*	Some of the alkaloids have been individually studied and found to have relaxing effects on the muscles of the uterus, antispasmodic (muscle relaxing), anxiolytic (anxiety-relieving), and pain-relieving.	The tincture or powdered extract can calm, help relieve pain, and produce sleep, helping one to relax; also useful for relieving mild anxiety and spasms in coughs or intestinal cramps; it is considered safe for children.
Lady's Slipper Orchid *Cypripedium bulbosum,* *C.* spp.	Helps to relieve mild anxiety headaches, and nerve pain; relaxes one during emotional stress	Sedative, nervine, mild hypnotic
Note: Lady's slippers are listed as rare and endangered in some states.		
Lavender *Lavandula officinalis*	Sedative	Relieves nervousness and muscle spasms
Kava-kava *Piper methysticum*	Antispasmodic, sedative	Counteracts insomnia, mild depression
Wild oats *Avena fatua*	Nervine	Used for nerve weakness, exhaustion and addictions
St. John's wort *Hypericum perforatum*	Sedative, antidepressant	Used for nervous disorders, anxiety symptoms, and depression

Table 6-3: Herbal Treatments for Nervous Disorders

Symptom or condition	Herbal Treatment
Anxiety	Valerian, hops, California poppy
Depression	Lavender, St. John's wort
Emotional exhaustion	Lavender, wild oats
High blood pressure	Hawthorn, passion flower
Hysteria	Skullcap, valerian, violet
Insomnia	Valerian, hops, passion flower, wild oats
Insomnia in children	Catnip, California poppy
Muscle tension	Skullcap, valerian, kava
Muscle pain	Valerian
Nerve pain	St. John's wort
Nervousness	Valerian, skullcap, California poppy
Pain	Valerian, Jamaican dogwood
Painful digestion	Valerian, skullcap, chamomile
Restlessness	Valerian, passion flower, hops
Tension	Valerian, hops, linden, lemon balm, kava
Ulcers	Licorice, chamomile, St. John's wort

Note: If symptoms persist after several weeks of an herbal program coupled with other natural healing methods, we recommend consulting a qualified health care practitioner.

harmony and the common Chinese herbal patent medicines used to treat them. Table 6-4 details the times of sleep disturbance and the body systems and emotions involved.

Sleep Difficulties All Night

Because the Heart is the residence of the Mind, when the Heart is full of blood, the Mind will be peaceful and happy. If it isn't, then the Mind is deprived of its residence, and mental restlessness, anxiety, and insomnia occur. Difficulties can take three forms:

- difficulty in falling asleep; but once asleep, the sleep is good
- difficulty falling asleep, and once asleep, the sleep is poor, with several periods of wakefulness per night
- there is no problem falling asleep, but restlessness and frequent and disturbing dreams occur.

To receive the best results, choose your formula by matching as many symptoms as possible with those that the formula helps.

Find the right dosage for you. The standard dosage is eight pills, three times per day. For those with chronic stress or insomnia, however, a higher dosage may be beneficial, such as sixteen pills, three times per day. Some require twenty-four pills, three times per day.

Be sure to take the herbs during the day and not just before bed, as their effects are cumulative. Often a formula may not be fully effective until it has been taken regularly on a daily basis for one or two weeks. For a sleeping disorder, it is best to take a dosage one hour or so before bed. Keep the pills, along with water, by your bed. If you awaken during the night, take the pills if you can't easily go back to sleep. It may be necessary to take two or even three different formulas together for the best results if your insomnia pattern changes or alternates between one time of night with another. The following Chinese patent herbal formulas help these general sleep problems:

An Mien Pian, "Peaceful Sleep Pills," for insomnia, anxiety, agitation, overthinking, excess dreaming, and poor memory.

Action Nourishes blood, calms the Mind, clears Heat, regulates digestion, strengthens the Spleen and smooths Liver energy.

Dosage Eight pills, 3 times per day (a total of 24 pills), after or between meals.

Ding Xin Wan, "Settle the Will Pill" or "Stabilize the Heart Pill" for palpitations, insomnia, poor memory, dizziness, hot flashes, dry mouth, and restlessness. These symptoms often occur in those who suffer a severe emotional shock, are badly frightened, or are anxious, resulting in a difficulty coping with change.

Action: Strengthens the energy of the Heart, tranquilizes the Heart, calms the Mind, clears Heat, nourishes the Blood of the Heart, Liver, and Spleen.

Dosage Eight pills, three times per day, after or between meals.

Tian Wang Bu Xin Dan, "Emperor of Heaven's Special Pill to Tonify the Heart" for insomnia with poor memory, very restless sleep, short attention span, palpitations, restlessness, uneasiness, restless legs during sleep, irritability, nerve weakness.

Action Nourishes the Blood of

TABLE 6-4. Times of Awakening Associated with Symptoms

Time of Awakening	Organ	Psychological Symptom
1 A.M.–3 A.M.	Liver	Irritability, anger
3 A.M.–5 A.M.	Lung	Grief, sorrow
5 A.M.–7 A.M.	Large intestine	Grief, sorrow
7 A.M.–9 A.M.	Stomach	Worry, too much thinking
9 A.M.–11 A.M.	Spleen	Worry, too much thinking
11 A.M.–1 P.M.	Heart	Joy, mania, overexcitement, hard-heartedness
1 P.M.–3 P.M.	Small intestine	Joy, mania, overexcitement, hard-heartedness
3 P.M.–5 P.M.	Urinary bladder	Fear
5 P.M.–7 P.M.	Kidney	Fear
7 P.M.–9 P.M.	Pericardium	None
9 P.M.–11 P.M.	Triple-burner; connections among the lungs, stomach, and bowels	None
11 P.M.–midnight	Gallbladder	Indecisiveness, strong-willed, prideful

the Heart, cools and moistens the Heart, clears Heat, strengthens energy of the Heart, Kidneys, and Spleen, calms the Mind and stops agitation. This is also a very good remedy for those who study a lot and/or do a lot of thinking, as it protects the Heart from becoming depleted as a result of these mental activities.

Dosage Eight pills, three times per day, after or between meals.

Sleeping Difficulties from 11 A.M. to 3 A.M.

The Wood Element, encompassing the Liver and Gallbladder, flourishes at this time of night. Thus, anyone repeatedly awakening during these hours, those who go to sleep easily before 11 p.m. but not after, or people who display many of the symptoms listed below could benefit by rebalancing the Liver. The pattern causing this is often Liver-energy stagnation or energy that is not flowing properly or in the correct direction. This is a very common pattern in Western societies due to our fast, complex, and stressful lifestyles. Use the following formula.

Xiao Yao Wan "Bupleurum Sedative" for symptoms of insomnia, nightmares, palpitations, headache, vertigo, dry mouth and/or throat, fatigue, poor appetite, moodiness, depression, frustrations, irritability, premenstrual syndrome, menopause, chronic hepatitis.

Action Nourishes the blood of the Liver and Spleen and harmonizes them, calms the Mind, clears Heat, smooths the Liver and moves stuck energy. In TCM, the Liver is the "Mother" of the Heart and so nourishes it. When the Liver, or Mother, is in disharmony, the Heart, or Child, doesn't always receive the nourishment it needs, and then the Mind becomes agitated, often resulting in insomnia. This formula "sedates" the energy without causing sleepiness during the day. Rather, it relaxes people and helps them handle stress better.

Dosage: *Eight pills, three times per day, before or between meals.*

Sleeping Difficulties from 3 A.M. to 5 A.M.

The Metal Element, or Lungs and Colon, flourishes at this time of day. Any long-term Lung weakness such as asthma, bronchitis, or grief often causes a person to wake during this time period. One of the best ways to strengthen the Lungs is to treat the Spleen, as the Spleen is "Mother" to the Lungs and nourishes them.

The Spleen is also the "Child" of the Heart, which means if the Mind is agitated or overworked or the Heart imbalanced, the Spleen suffers. Disharmony between the Spleen and Heart can also cause insomnia, restlessness, and mental agitation. Furthermore, when the Spleen is weak, the blood becomes deficient and cannot nourish the Heart. This, in turn, deprives the Mind of its residence and the Spleen of its Intelligence, and the person loses the ability to concentrate or sleep well and becomes forgetful. Thus, treating the Spleen can calm the Mind and nourish the Lungs. The following herbal patent formulas do this. They are good for those who overstudy or overconcentrate and who have anxiety or worry over a long period of time.

Kwei Pi Tang for symptoms of

dream-disturbed sleep, forgetfulness, anxiety and phobia, insomnia, fatigue, nightmares, restlessness, dizziness, overthinking, palpitations, excessive deliberation or obsessive behavior, reduced appetite, wan complexion, hypoglycemia.

Action: Strengthens energy and blood, nourishes the Heart and Spleen, and harmonizes them. This is also a good formula for those with digestive problems.

Dosage Eight pills, 3 times per day before, between, or after meals. Before meals, helps digestion more; and after meals, helps sleep and emotions more.

Shen Ching Shuai Jao Wan, "Nerve Weakness Pills," for symptoms of fatigue, insomnia, nightmares, night sweats, poor memory, poor concentration, dizziness, tinnitus, restlessness, agitation, panic attacks, and other mental problems.

Action Strengthens energy and blood, improves mental health, tranquilizes and calms the Mind, strengthens Heart and Liver Blood and the Kidneys and Spleen, improves energy and stops sweats, clears heat from the Heart.

Dosage Eight pills, 3 times per day, after or between meals.

REFERENCES

Anderson, C. 1989. Personal communication.

Anderson, C. 1994. Personal communication.

Auxence, E.G. 1953. A pharmacognostic study of *Piscidia erythrina*. *Economic Botany.* July-September. 272.

Baba, T. et al. 1979. Suppression of cell-mediated immune reactions by monosaccharides. *Journal of Immunology.* Mar. 122: 838-41.

Bak, A. and D. Grobbee. 1990. Coffee, caffeine and homeostasis: A review. *Netherlands Journal of Medicine.* 37: 242-6.

Bar-Meir, E. et al. 1995. Multiple autoantibodies in patients with silicone breast implants. *Journal of Autoimmunity.* 8: 267-77.

Barnett, A. 1997. FDA gears up to put tobacco regulations into effect. *Lancet* February 15, 349(9050):483.

Baruch, J. 1984. Effect of Endotelon in postoperative edema. Results of a double-blind study versus placebo in 32 female patients. *Annales de Chirurgie Plastique et Esthetique.* 29(4):393-95.

Baschetti, Riccardo. 1995. Chronic fatigue syndrome and licorice. *New Zealand Medical Journal.* April 26. 157.

Bates, D. W. et al. 1993. Prevalence of fatigue and chronic fatigue syndrome in primary care cractices. Archives of Internal Medicine. 153: 2759.

Bates, D. W. et al. 1995. Clinical laboratory test findings in patients with chronic fatigue syndrome. *Archives of Internal Medicine.* 155: 97-103.

Bean, L. and K. Saubel. 1972. *Temalpakh: Cahuilla Indian knowledge and usage of plants.* Banning, CA: Malki Museum Press.

Beinfield, H. and E. Krongold. 1991. *Between heaven and earth: A guide to Chinese medicine.* New York: Ballantine Books.

Bell, V. L. 1925. *A glossary of indicated remedies and disease names and definitions.* Cincinnati: Lloyd Brothers Pharmacists.

Bentley, R. and H. Trimen. 1880. *Medicinal plants.* London: J. and A. Churchill.

Berkow, R. (Ed.) et al. 1992. *The Merck man-*

ual of diagnosis and therapy (16th ed.).Rahway, NJ: Merck, Sharp, and Dohme Research Laboratories.

Berkow, R., (Ed.). 1982. *The Merck manual* (14th ed.). Rahway, N.J.: Merck Research Laboratories.

Bisset, N.G. (Ed.). 1994. *Herbal drugs and phytopharmaceuticals.* Stuttgart: Medpharm.

Bliwise, D.L. 1996. Historical change in the report of daytime fatigue. *Sleep.* 19: 462-4.

Blonde-Hill, E. and S. Sharfran. 1993. Treatment of the chronic fatigue syndrome: A review and practical guide. *Drugs.* 46: 639-52. October.

Blondeau, J. et al. 1993. Stress-induced reactivation of latent herpes simplex virus infection in rat lumbar dorsal root ganglia. *Journal of Psychosomatic Research.* December, 37(8): 843-49.

Blumberg, D. et al. 1995. The physician and unconventional medicine. *Alternative Therapies.* 1: 31. July.

Blumenthal, M. et al. 1996. *Commission E Herbal Monographs.* Austin: American Botanical Council. (work in progress)

Bocek, B. R. 1984. Ethnobotany of Costanoan Indians, California; based on collection by J. P. Harrington. *Economic Botany.* 38:2. 240-55.

Boericke, W. 1927. *Materia medica with repertory* (9th ed.). Philadelphia: Boericke and Runyon.

Bohner, K. 1994. Siesta time (benefits of napping). *Forbes.* 153, 3. Jan 31. 119.

Bombardier, C. H. and D. Buchwald. 1995. Outcome and prognosis of patients with chronic fatigue vs. chronic fatigue syndrome. *Archives of Internal Medicine.* Oct. 23. 155: 2105-10.

Bonham, G. S. and R. W. Wilson. 1981. Children's health in families with cigarette smokers. *American Journal of Public Health.* March, 71(3):290-93.

Boulenger, J. et al. 1984. Increased sensitivity to caffeine in patients with panic disorders. *Archives of General Psychiatry.* 14: 1067-71.

Boyd, J. et al. 1995. The tobacco/health-insurance connection. *Lancet.* July 8, 346(8967):64.

Braverman, E. R. 1987. *The healing nutrients within. New Canaan, CT: Keats Publishing.*

Breznitz, S. 1988. The seven kinds of denial. In Peter B. Defares, Ed., *Stress and anxiety, vol. II: The series in clinical and community psychology.* Washington, D.C.: Harper Row.

Brody, T. M. 1994. *Human pharmacology—molecular to clinical.* St. Louis: Mosby-Year Book, Inc.

Bruneton, J. 1995. *Pharmacognosy, phytochemistry medicinal plants.* Paris: Lavoisier Publishing.

Buchbauer, G. et al. 1993. Fragrance compounds and essential oils with sedative effects upon inhalation. *Journal of Pharmaceutical Sciences* June. 82: 660-4.

Buchwald, D. and Garrity, D. 1994. Comparison of patients with chronic fatigue syndrome, fibromylagia, and multiple chemical sensitivities. *Archives of Internal Medicine* Sept. 26. 154: 2049-53.

Buchwald, D. et al. 1992. A chronic illness characterized by fatigue, neurologic and immunologic disorders, and active human herpes virus type 6 infection. *Annals of Internal Medicine.* Jan. 116: 103-13.

Bühring, M. 1976. The effects of valerian-hops preparation on the reaction time of clinic patients. *Der Kassenarzi.* 16.

Burt, V. L. et al. 1995. Trends in the prevalence, awareness, treatment, and control of hypertension in the adult U. S. Population. *Hypertension* July, 26(1):60-69.

Caan, B. et al. 1989. Caffeinated beverages and low birthweight: A case-control study. *American Journal of Public Health.* Sept. 79: 1299-1300.

Carey, B and Lee, K. 1996. The slumber solution: Researchers have discovered a surprising secret to waking up refreshed-and maybe even staying younger. *Health.* 10: 4. 70-6. July-August.

Carroll, Linda. 1995. Drug use in elderly debated. *Medical Tribune.* January 19. 1, 6.

Carskadon, M. A. (Ed.). 1993. *Encyclopedia of sleep and dreaming.* New York: Macmillan Publishing.

Caujolle, F. et al. 1969. Spasmolytic action of hop *(Humulus lupulus). Agressologie.* 10: 405-10.

Cazin, F. J. 1886. *Traité practique et raisonné des plantes médicinales indigenes et acclimatés.* Paris: Asselin and Houzeau.

Chase, M. 1996. How too much of a good thing stresses us out. *Wall Street Journal.* Jan. 9, 1995.

Chauffard, F. et al. 1982. Detection of mild sedative effects: Valerian and sleep in man. *Experientia* 37: 622.

Cheshier, J. et al. 1995. Immunomodulation by pycnogenol in retrovirus-infected or ethanol-fed mice. *Life Sciences.* 58(5):PL87-PL96.

Christison, R. 1848. *A dispensatory.* Philadelphia: Lea and Blanchard.

Clark, M.R. et al. 1995. Chronic fatigue: risk factors for symptom persistence in a 2 1/2-year follow-up study. *American Journal of Medicine.* Feb. 98: 187-95.

Cleary, J. P. 1990. Niacinamide and addictions. Letter. *Journal of Nutritional Medicine.* 1: 83-4.

Cohen, L. 1995. Indoor air quality a major public-health issue, workshop told. *Canadian Medical Association Journal.* July 1, 153(1):92-3.

Consumer Reports. 1987. Review of caffeine. *Consumer Reports.* Sept.

Consumer Reports. 1993. High anxiety. *Consumer Reports.* Jan. Medicine. Winter. 24-6.

Consumer Reports. 1995. *Complete drug reference.* Yonkers, NY: Consumer Reports Books.

Conway, C. 1991. Truth and consequences of coffee. *Stanford Medicine.* Winter, 24-26.

Cordova, A. and M. Alvarez-Mon. 1995. Behavior of zinc in physical exercise: A special reference to immunity and fatigue. *Neuroscience and Behavioral Reviews.* 19: 439-44.

Criqui, M. H. and B. L. Ringel. 1994. Does diet or alcohol explain the French paradox? *Lancet.* Dec. 24-31, 344(8939-40):1719-23.

Culpepper, N. 1840. *The British herbal and family physician to which is added a dispensatory for the use of private families.* Halifax: Nicholson.

D'Avanzo, B. et al. 1992. Coffee consumption and bladder cancer risk. *European Journal of Cancer.* 28A: 1480-4.

Dadd, Debra Lynn et al. 1992. *Nontoxic,natural, and earthwise: How to protect yourself and your family from harmful products and live in harmony with the earth* (rev. Ed.). Los Angeles: J. P. Tarcher.

Dawber, T. et al. 1974. Coffee and cardiovascular disease. Observations from the Framingham study. *New England Journal of Medicine.* 291: 871.

De Bairacli-Levy, J. 1974. *The illustrated herbal handbook.* London: Faber and Faber, Ltd.

Delaney, Lisa et al. 1993. Gentle remedies. *Prevention.* 45(7):66.

Dubbels, R. et al. 1994. Melatonin determination with a newly developed ELISA system: Inter-individual differences in the response of the human pineal gland to magnetic fields. *Advances in Pineal Research.* vol 7, pp. 27-33.

Duesberg, P. 1996. *Inventing the AIDS virus.* Washington, D.C.: Regnery Publishing.

Dunstan, R. et al. 1995. A preliminary investigation of chlorinated hydrocarbons and chronic fatigue syndrome. *The Medical Journal of Australia.* Sept. 18. 163: 294-7.

Elin, R. 1994. Magnesium: The fifth but forgotten electrolyte. *American Journal of Clinical Pathology.* 102: 616-22.

Ellingwood, F. 1983. (1898). *American materia medica, therapeutics and pharmacognosy.* Portland: Eclectic Medical Publications.

Elliott, G. R. and C. Eisendorfer. 1982. *Stress and human health.* New York: Springer Publishing Co.

Ernst, E. 1995. St.-John's-wort as antidepressive therapy. *Fortschritte der Medizin.* 113: 354-5.

ESCOP. 1992. Proposal for a European monograph on the medicinal use of *Passifloarae Herba Passiflora.* European Scientific Cooperative for Phytotherapy.

Etherington-Smith, Meredith. 1992. *The persistence of memory: A biography of Dali.* New York: Random House.

Fackelmann, K. A. 1992. Pacific cocktail. *Science News.* 141: 424-5.

Faltermayer, E. 1994. Will the cost-cutting in health care kill you? *Fortune Magazine* Oct. 31.

Farnsworth, N. R. 1985. Medicinal plants in therapy. *Bulletin of the World Health Organization.* 63: 965-1170.

Fawin, F. Cocaine and other stimulants: Actions, abuse, and treatment. *New England Journal of Medicine.* 318:1127.

Feldman, E.G. and D. Davidson. 1986. *Handbook of nonprescription drugs* (8th ed.). Washington, D.C.: American Pharmaceutical Association.

Felter, H. W. and J. U. Lloyd. 1898. *King's American dispensatory.* Cincinnati: The Ohio Valley Co.

Ferguson, T. 1990. How we take care of ourselves. *Self-Care Journal.* May/June.

Fernald, M. L. 1970. *Gray's Manual of Botany.* New York: D. Van Nostrand Co. 1970.

Fernie, W. T. 1897. *Herbal simples.* Bristol: John Wright and Co.

Finner, E. et al. 1984. ber die wirkstoffe des baldrians. *Planta Medica.* 50: 4-6.

Fintelmann, V. 1992. Klinisch-ärztliche bedeutung des hopfens. *Zeitschrift für Phytotherapie.* 13: 165-8.

Fintelmann, V. et al. 1989. *Phytotherapie manual.* Stuttgart: Hippokrates Verlag.

Flückiger, F. A. and D. Hanbury. 1879. *Pharmacographia: A history of the principal drugs of vegetable origin.* London: Macmillan and Co.

Foster, F. P. (Ed.). 1897. *Reference book of practical therapeutics.* New York: D. Appleton and Co.

Foster, S. and A. Leung. 1996. *Encyclopedia of common natural ingredients used in food, drugs, and cosmetics.* New York: John Wiley and Sons .

Friedman, L. et al. 1979. Testicular atrophy and impaired spermatogenesis in rats fed high levels of the methylxanthines caffeine, theobromine, or theophylline. *Journal of Environmental Pathology and Toxicology.* Jan.-Feb. 2: 687-706.

ftp.cdc.gov/ncidod/diseases/fatigue/fatigue.html (pg 3).

Fukuda, K. et al. 1994. The chronic fatigue syndrome: A comprehensive approach to its definition and study. International CFS study group. *Annals of Internal Medicine.* Dec. 121: 953-9.

Gawin, F. 1988. Cocaine and other stimulants: Actions, abuse and treatment. *New England Journal of Medicine.* 318: 1127.

Gawin, F. 1989. Cocaine abuse and addiction. *Journal of Family Practice.* 29: 193-7.

Gerard, J. 1975 (1633). *The herbal of general history of plants.* New York: Dover Publications.

Gilbert, R. 1976. Caffeine as a drug of abuse. In Gibbins et al. (Ed.), *Research advances in alcohol and drug problems.* New York: John Wiley and Sons.

Gilbert, R. 1984. Caffeine consumption. In G.A. Spiller, (Ed.), *The methylxanthine beverages and foods: Chemistry, consumption, and health effects.* New York: Liss.

Gladstar, R. 1993. *Herbal healing for women: Simple home remedies for women of all ages.* New York: Simon and Schuster.

Glantz, L. 1997. Controlling tobacco advertising: The FDA regulations and the First Amendment. *American Journal of Public Health.* 87(3):446.

Glavin, G. B. 1993. Vulnerability to stress ulcerogenesis in rats differing in anxiety: A dopaminergic correlate. *Journal de Physiologic.* 87(4), 239-43.

Gould, M. 1995. Power napping. *Nation's Business.* 83, 2. Feb.

Green, M. 1994. Personal communications.

Grieve, M. 1978. (1931). *A modern herbal.* New York: Penguin Books, Ltd.

Griffith, R. E. 1847. *Medical botany.* Philadelphia: Lea and Blanchard.

Gunn, J. C. 1872. *Gunn's new family physician.* Cincinnati: Wilstach, Baldwin and Co.

Hesse, R. et al. 1981. Demonstration of phytoestrogens in feed plants and hops by means of receptor test. *Zentralblatt fur Veterinarmedizin* 28(6):422-54.

Hewitt, D. 1992. Massage with lavender oil lowered tension. *Nursing Times.* 88: 25.

Hickey, M. and C. King. 1981. *100 families of flowering plants.* Cambridge: Cambridge University Press.

Hobbs, C. 1988-1989. St. John's-wort: A literature review. *Herbalgram.* Austin: American Botanical Council.

Hobbs, C. 1989. Valerian, a literature review. *Herbalgram.* 21.

Hobbs, C. 1993. *Valerian, the relaxing and sleep herb.* Santa Cruz, CA: Botanica Press.

Hobbs, C. and S. Foster. 1990. Hawthorn, a literature review. *Herbalgram* 22: 19-33.

Hoffmann, D. 1983. *The holistic herbal.* Findhorn, Scotland: Findhorn Press.

Holtmann, G. and N. Talley. 1993. Functional dyspepsia: Current treatment recommendatrions. *Drugs.* June, 45(6):918-30.

Horrobin, D. F. 1980. A biochemical basis for alcoholism and alcohol-induced damage including the fetal alcohol syndrome and cirrhosis: Interference with essential fatty acid and prostaglandin metabolism. *Medical Hypotheses.* 6: 929-42.

Houghton, P. 1988. The biological activity of valerian and related plants. *Journal of Ethnopharmacology.* 22: 121-42.

Hutchens, A. 1992. *A handbook of Native American herbs.* Boston: Shambhala Publications.

Hutchens, A. R. 1969. *Indian herbology of North America.* India: Homeo House Press.

Jacobs, Michael R. and Kevin Fehr. 1987. *Drugs and drug abuse: A reference text* (2nd ed., revised). Toronto: Alcoholism and Drug Addiction Reserach Foundation, 1987.

Jamel, H. et al. 1996. Taste preference for sweetness in urban and rural populations in Iraq. *Journal of Dental Research.* November, 75(11):1879:84.

James, J. E. 1991. *Caffeine and health.* San Diego, CA: Academic Press: Hartcourt Brace Jovanovich.

Jiang, W. D. et al. 1995. Inhibition of hepatocyte growth factor-induced motility and in vitro invasion of human colon cancer cells by gamma-linolenic acid. *British Journal of Cancer.* April, 71(4):744-52.

Kannel, W. and R. Ellison. 1996. Alcohol and coronary heart disease: The evidence for a protective effect. *Clinica Chimica Acta. March 15, 246(1-2):59-76.*

Kaufmann, M. et al. 1985-86. Psychosomatic aspects of myocardial infarction and implications for treatment. *International Journal of Psychiatry in Medicine.* 15(4):371-380.

Keller, F. and M. W. Klohs. 1963. A review of the chemistry and pharmacology of the constituents of *Piper methysticum.* *Lloydia* 26: 1-15.

Keller, Mark (Ed.). 1979. *Research priorities on alcohol: Proceedings of a symposium.* New Brunswick, NJ: Center for Alcohol studies, Rutgers University.

Keltner, N. and D. Folks. 1993. *Psychotropic drugs*. St. Louis: Mosby-Yearbook, Inc.

Keville, K. and M. Green. 1995. *Aromatherapy: A complete guide to the healing art*. Freedom, CA: The Crossing Press.

King, J. 1866. *The American family physician*. Indianapolis: A.D. Streight.

King, J. 1898. *King's American dispensatory*. Cincinnati: Ohio Valley Co.

Kinzler, E. et al. 1991. Effect of a special kava extract in patients with anxiety, tension, and excitation states of non-psychotic genesis. *Arzneimittel-Forschung*. June. 41. 584-8.

Klag, M.J. et al. 1994. Coffee intake and coronary heart disease. *Annals of Epidemiology*. 4: 425-33.

Kleber, E. et al. 1995. Modulation of key reactions of the catecholamine metabolism by extracts from Eschscholtzia californica and Corydalis cava. *Arzneimittel-Forschung* 452:127-31.

Klein, A. 1995. *The medicine burns*. London: High-Risk Books.

Koch, H. 1982. *Valeriana officinalis* (Baldrian). Bonn: Bundesfachnerbnad der Arzneimittel-Hersteler e. V. (BHI).

Koch, H. and L. Lawson. 1996. *Garlic: The science and therapeutic applications of Allium sativum L. and related species*. Baltimore: Williams and Wilkins.

Koch-Heitzmann, W. and W. Schultze. 1988. 2000 jahre *Melissa officinalis*. Von der bienenpflanze zum virustatikum. *Zeitschrift für Phytotherapie*. 9: 77-85.

Krieglstein, J. and D. Grusla. 1988. Central depressant constituent in *Valeriana*. *Deutsche Apotheker Zeiting*. 128: 2041-6.

Leathwood, P. D. et al. 1982. Aqueous extract of valerian root *(Valeriana officinalis L.)* improves sleep quality in man. *Pharmacology, Biochemistry, and Behavior*. 17: 65-71.

Leathwood, P.D. and F. Chaufford. 1985. Aqueous extract of valerian root (Valeriana officinalis L.) reduces sleep latency to fall asleep in man. *Planta Medica*. 51: 144-8.

Leclerc, H. 1927. Précis de phytothérapie. 187. In Madaus, G. 1976. *Lehrbuch der bioligischen heilmittel*. New York: Georg Olms Verlag.

Leclerc, H. 1937. La presse mdicale. *Dtsch.*

Dtschr. 28: 578. In Madaus, G. 1976. *Lehrbuch der biologischen Heilmittel*. Hildesheim: Georg Olms Verlag.

Leung, A. Y. 1980. *Encyclopedia of common natural ingredients*. New York: John Wiley and Sons.

Leung, A. Y. and S. Foster. 1996. *Encyclopedia of common natural ingredients*. New York: John Wiley and Sons.

Lewis, W. and J. Akin. 1791. *An experimental history of the materia medica*. London: J. Johnson.

Lewis, W. H. and M. Elvin-Lewis. 1977. *Medical botany*. New York: John Wiley and Sons.

Linde, K. et al. 1996. St. John's wort for depression: An overview and meta-analysis of randomised clinical trials. *British Medical Journal*. 313:253-8.

Linn, S. et al. 1982. No association between coffee consumption and adverse outcomes of pregnancy. *New England Journal of Medicine*. 306: 141.

Lloyd, J. U. 1917. *A treatise on Crataegus*. Cincinnati: Lloyd Brothers Pharmacists, Inc.

Loggia, R. D. et al. 1983. Depressive effect of *C. Laevigata* L. on central nervous system in mice. *Scientia. Pharmaceutica*. 51: 319-24.

Low Dog, T. 1996. Personal communication.

Lust, J. 1974. *The herb book*. New York: Benedict Lust Publications.

Madaus, G. 1976. *Lehrbuh der biologischen heilmittel*. Hildesheim: Georg Olm Verlag.

Maisto, S. A. et al. 1991. *Drug use and misuse*. Ft. Worth, TX: Holt, Rinehart and Winston.

Marcus, A. C. et al. 1989. Prevalence of cigarette smoking in the United States: Estimates from the 1985 current population survey. *Journal of the National Cancer Institute*. March 15, 81(16):409-14.

Marekov, N. L. et al. 1983. Chemistry of pharmaceutically important cyclopentane monoterpenes from some *Valeriana* plants. Chemistry and Biotechnology of Biologically Active Natural Products, 2nd international conference, Budapest.

Martinez, M. 1992. *Los plantes medicinales de Mexico*. Mexico City: Ediciones Botas.

Masoro, E. J. 1993. Dietary restriction and

aging. *Journal of the American Geriatrics Society.* September, 41(9), 994-99.

Maybe, R. 1988. *The new age herbalist.* New York: Macmillan.

McCarter, R. J. 1995. Role of caloric restriction in the prolongation of life. *Clinics in Geriatric Medicine.* November, 11(4), 553-65.

Menge, F. and G. Goebel. 1954. Die heilkunst. 66: 265. In Spaich, W. 1978. *Moderne phytotherapie.* Heidelberg: Karl F. Haug Verlag.

Mesch, U. et al. 1996. Lead poisoning masquerading as chronic fatigue syndrome. *Lancet.* April 27. 347: 1193.

Mésségue, M. 1973. *Of men and plants.* New York: Macmillan.

Millspaugh, C. F. 1887. *American medicinal plants.* New York: Boericke and Tafel.

Moldenke, H. N. and A. L. Moldenke. 1986 (1952). *Plants of the Bible.* New York: Dover.

Moore, M. 1979. *Medicinal plants of the mountain west.* Santa Fe: Museum of New Mexico Press.

Morris, M. B. and L. Weinstein. 1983. Caffeine and the fetus: Is trouble brewing? *American Journal of Obstetric Gynecology.* 146: 231.

Muldner, Von H. and M. Zoller. 1984. Antidepressive wirkung eines auf den wirkstoffkomplex hypericin standardisierten hypericum-extraktes. *Arzneim-Forsch.* 34: 918.

Murray, J. (EdD.). 1933. *The Oxford English dictionary.* Oxford: Clarendon Press.

Murray, J. 1986. An overview of cocaine use and abuse. *Psychological Reports.* 59: 243-64.

Musto, D. F. 1973. *The American disease: Origins of narcotic control.* New Haven: Yale University Press.

Narod, S. A., S. De Sanjose, C. Victora. 1991. Coffee during pregnancy: A reproductive hazard? *American Journal of Obstetrics and Gynecology,* Apr. 164(4):1109-14.

Okpanyi, S. N. and M. L. Weishcer. 1987. Tierexperimentelle Untersuchungen zur psychotropen wirksamkeit eines Hypericum-extraktes (Animal experiments on the psychotropic action of a Hypericum extract). *Arzneimittel-Forschung.* 37: 10-13.

Osol, A.and G. E. Farrar. 1955. *The dispensatory of the United States of America* (25th Ed.). Philadelphia: J.B. Lippincott Company.

Ott, I. 1880. A new narcotic—*Piscidia erythrina*—Jamaican Dogwood—Its physiological and toxicological action. *Lancet.* 3: 533.

Pace-Asciak, C. et al. 1995. The red wine phenolics trans-resveratrol and quercetin block human platelet aggregation and eicosanoid synthesis: Implications for protection against coronary heart disease. *Clinica chimica Acta,* March 15, 246(1-2):59-76.

Packer, L. 1997. Natural source antioxidants: Free-radical scavenging activity. 213th National meeting of the American Chemical Society, San Francisco, CA, USA, April 13-17, 1997. *Abstracts of papers American Chemical Society.* 213(1-3):AGFD33.

Panksepp, J. 1982. Toward a general psychobiological theory of emotions. *The Behavioral and Brain Sciences.* 5: 407-67.

Paris, R. R. and H. Moyse. 1981. *Matire mdicale.* Paris: Masson.

Paxton, J. 1840. *A pocket botanical dictionary.* London: Bradbury and Evans.

Penn, A. et al. 1994. Inhalation of steady-state sidestream smoke from one cigarette promotes arteriosclerotic plaque development. *Circulation.* Sept., 90(3), 1363-67.

Pennington, J. A. T. (Ed.). 1994. *Bowes and Church's food values of portions commonly used* (16th ed.). Philadelphia: J. B. Lippincott Company.

Pratt, A. ca. 1800. *The flowering plants, grasses, sedges, and ferns of Great Britain.* London: Frederick Warne and Co.

Prince, T. et al. 1995. Chronic fatigue in a 43-year-old woman. *Annals of Allergy.* June. 74: 474-8.

Puccio, E. M. et al. 1990. Clustering of atherogenic behaviors in coffee drinkers. *American Journal of Public Health.* Nov. 80: 1310-13.

Puglisi-Allegra, S. and A. Oliverio (Eds.). 1990. *Psychobiology of stress.* Boston: Kluwer Academic Pubs.

Raczkowski, U. et al. 1991. Cocaine acts in the CNS to inhibit sympathetic neural activity. *Journal of Pharmacology and Experimental Therapeutics.* 258: 511.

Rafinesque, A. M. 1828. *Medical flora.* Philadelphia: Atkinson and Alexander.

Rafinesque, A. M. 1830. *Medical flora, v. 2.* Philadelphia: Atkinson and Alexander.

Rakel, R. E. (Ed.). 1996. *Conn's current therapy.* Philadelphia: W. B. Saunders Co.

Ratner, D. and Z. Carey. 1995. Medical effects of indoor air pollution. *Hospital Medicine.* May. 41-6.

Reiter, F. and J. Robinson. 1995. *Your body's natural wonder drug, melatonin.* New York: Bantam Books.

Renner, A. 1937. The activity of valerians. *Deutsche Medizinische Wochenschrift.* 63: 916-9.

Resch, B. A. and J. G. Papp. 1983. Effects of caffeine on the fetal heart. *American Journal of Obstetric Gynecology.* 146: 231.

Reynolds, J. (Ed.). 1993. *Martindale. The extra pharmacopoeia.* London: Pharmaceutical Press.

Robinson, J. 1989. Up close and personal. *American Demographics.* 11: 11. Nov. 10-11.

Rolls, B. J. 1995. Carbohydrates, fats, and satiety. *American Journal of Clinical Nutrition.* Apr. 61: 960-67s.

Rong, Y. et al. 1994-95. Pycnogenol protects vascular endothelial cells from t-butyl hdroperoxide-induced oxidant injury. *Biotechnology Therapeutics.* 5(3-4):117-26.

Rowe, P. et al. 1995. Is neurally mediated hypotension an unrecognized cause of chronic fatigue? *Lancet.* March 11. 345: 623-4.

Sahelian, R. 1996. *Melatonin: Nature's sleeping pill.* Marina Del Rey, CA: Be Happier Press.

Sandyk, R. 1992. Melatonin and maturation of REM sleep. *International Journal of Neuroscience.* 63: 105-14.

Saranath, D. et al. 1993. Molecular lesions in human oral cancer: The Indianscene. *European Journal of Cancer. Part B, Oral Oncology.* April, 29B(2):107-12.

Schenck, G., and H. Graf. 1936. Archiv der Pharmazie. 274: 537.

Schmidt, U. and H. Sommer. 1993. St. John's-wort extract in the ambulatory therapy of depression. *Fortschritte der Medizin.* 10;111: 339-42.

Schneeman, B. 1994. Carbohydrates: Significance for energy balance and gastrointestinal function. *Journal of Nutrition.* Sept. 124: 1747-53s.

Schwantes, D. 1975. *The unsweetened truth about sugar and sugar substitutes.* Walla Walla, WA: Doubletree Press.

Scudder, J. (Ed.). 1883. *The Eclectic Medical Journal.* V. XLIII. Cincinnati: The Scudder Brothers.

Scudder, J. (Ed.). 1900. *The Eclectic Medical Journal.* V. LX . Cincinnati: The Scudder Brothers.

Scudder, J. 1870. *The Eclectic Medical Journal.* V. XXX. Cincinnati: The Scudder Brothers.

Scudder, J. 1898. *The Eclectic Medical Journal.* V. XVIII. Cincinnati: The Scudder Brothers.

Scudder, J. 1898. *The Eclectic Medical Journal.* V. XVIII. Cincinnati: The Scudder Brothers.

Seyle, H. 1978. [1955]. *The Stress of Life.* New York: McGraw-Hill.

Sherry, C. J. et al. 1948. Catnip: An evaluation of the cold-water and acetone-pretreated hot water extracts. *Quarterly Journal of Crude Drug Research.* 1: 31-5.

Shoemaker, J. V. 1891. *A practical treatise on materia medica and therapeutics.* Philadelphia: F.A. Davis.

Shoemaker, J. V. 1893. *A practical treatise on materia medica and therapeutics.* Philadelphia: F.A. Davis.

Shopland, D. R. and C. Brown. 1985. Changes in cigarette smoking prevalence in the U. S.: 1955-1983. *Annals of Behavioral Medicine.* 7, 5-8.

Silverman, K. et al. 1992. Withdrawal syndrome after the double-blind cessation of caffeine consumption. *New England Journal of Medicine.* Oct. 327: 1109-14.

Simeons, A. T. W. 1960. *Man's presumptuous brain: An evolutionary interpretation of psychosomatic disease.* New York: Dutton.

Singh, Y. N. 1981. A review of the historical, sociological and scientific aspects of kava and its uses in the South Pacific. *Fiji Medical Journal.* April/May.

Sipple, H. and K. McNutt. 1974. *Sugars in nutrition; The Nutrition Foundation monograph series.* New York: Academica Press.

Smith, A. G. 1988. Caffeine reduction as an

adjunct to anxiety management. *British Journal of Clinical Psychology.* 298: 568-9.

Smith, Ed. 1994. Personal communication.

Smith, R. F. 1974. A five-year trial of massive nicotinic acid therapy of alcoholics in Michigan. *Journal of Orthomolecular Psychiatry.* 3 :327-31.

Smith, R. F. 1978. Status report concerning the use of megadose nicotinic acid in alcoholics. *Journal of Orthomolecular Psychiatry.* 7: 1.

Smith, R. F. 1985. A history of coffee. In M.N. Clifford and K.C. Wiollsons (Eds.). *Coffee: Botany, biochemistry, and production of beans and beverage.* London: Croom-Helm.

Smith, U. 1994. Carbohydrates, fat, and insulin action. *American Journal of Clinical Nutrition.* Mar. 59: 686-89s.

Sommer, H. and G. Harrer. 1994. Placebo-controlled double-blind study examining the effectiveness of an hypericum preparation in 105 mildly depressed patients. *Journal of Geriatric Psychiatry and Neurology.* Suppl 1: S 9-11.

Spaich, W. 1978. *Moderne phytotherapie.* Heidelberg: Karl F. Haug Verlag.

Speroni, E. and A. Minghetti. 1988. Neuropharmacological activity of extracts from *Passiflora incarnata. Planta Medica.* 54: 488-91.

Steidle, H. 1931. Naunyn-schmiedeb. *Archive.* 161: 154.

Steinberg, R. and M. Soyka. 1989. Problems in long-term benzodiazepine treatment. *Scheizerische Rundschaufur Medizin Praxis.* 78: 784-7.

Stone, R. 1994. Study implicates second-hand smoke. *Science.* April 1, 264(5155):30.

Suzuki, O. et al. 1984. Inhibition of monoamine oxidase by hypericin. *Planta Medica.* 50: 272-4.

Terr, L. C. 1979. Children of Chowchilla: A study of psychic trauma. *Psychoanalytic Study of the Child.* 34: 547-623.

Theodoracopulos, T. 1995. The secret of success (afternoon napping). *National Review.* 47: 13. July 10. 68-70.

Thies, P.W. 1970. Therapeutic isovaleric acid esters. U.S. 3,485,857 (II260,345, CO7C) (CA 72: 114873).

Tierney, L. et al. 1996. *Current medical diagnosis and treatment.* Stamford, CT: Appleton and Lange.

Titcomb, M. 1948. Kava in Hawaii. *Journal of the Polynesian Society.* Sept. 8. 105-171.

Trousseau, A. and H. Pidoux. 1880. *Treatise on therapeutics.* New York: William Wood and Co.

Tschesche, R. et al. 1969. *Avena sativa. Chemische Berischte.* 102: 2072-82. In Spaich, W. 1978. *Moderne phytotherapie.* Heidelberg: Karl F. Haug Verlag.

Tutin et al. 1964. *Flora Europa.* Cambridge: Cambridge University Press.

United States Department of Justice. 1989-1992. *Cocaine: An overview.* Washington, D.C.: Federal Government Publications.

Ursin, H. et al. (Eds.). 1978. *Psychology of stress.* New York: Academic Press.

Van Voris, B. 1997. AG's claims mere smoke? Tobacco suits rest on less-than-certain legal theory. *National Law Journal.* April 28, 19(35):A1.

Vickery, D. 1990. *Lifeplan.* Evergreen, CO: Health Decisions, Inc.

von Anrep, B. 1879. Ueber die pshysiologische Wirkung des Cocain. *Pflueger's archiv fur die gesamte Physiologie.* 21:38-77, (29 Dec.).

Von Eickstedt, K.-W. 1969. Influence on the effects of alcohol by the valepotriates. *Arzneim.-Forsch.* 19: 995-7.

Von Hartungen, D. 1952. *Avena sativa. Hippokrates. 23: 154. In Spaich, W. 1978. Moderne phytotherapie.* Heidelberg: Karl F. Haug Verlag.

Wagner, H. and L. Sprinkmeyer. 1973. On the pharmacological action of lemon balm *(Melissa)* spirits. *Deutsche Apotehker Zeitung.* 113: 1159.

Weil, A. and W. Rosen. 1983. *From chocolate to morphine.* Boston: Houghton Mifflin.

Weiss, R. F. 1988. *Herbal medicine.* Beaconsfield, England: Beaconsfield Publishers, Ltd.

Weissbuch, B. 1996. Personal communication.

Whitcomb, B. et al. 1995. Failure of the community-based Vita State automated blood-pressure devide to accurately measure blood pressure. *Archives of Family Medicine.* May, 4(5):419-24.

Wichtl, M. 1986. *Hypericum perforatum L.—*

Das johanniskraut. *Zeitschrift für Phytotherapie.* 3: 87-90.

Windholz, M. (Ed.). 1976. *The Merck index* (9th ed.). Rahway, NJ: Merck Inc.

Wohlfart, R. et al. 1982. Nachweis sedativhypnotischer wirkstoffe im hopfen. *Planta Medica.* 48: 120-3.

Wood, H. C. et al. 1926. *The dispensatory of the United States of America (21st ed.).* Philadelphia: J.B. Lippincott.

Wren, R.C. 1988. *Potter's new cyclopaedia of botanical drugs and preparations.* Saffron Walden: C. W. Daniel.

www.alternatives.com/cfs-news/faq.htm

www.angelfire.com/pages0/ias/tr.html

www.nmia.com re cfs

www.ussc.gov/crack. Cocaine: an overview. U.S. Department of Justice, Drug Enforcement Administration.

Yamaji, K. et al. 1986. Chewing gums for anxiety inhibition. *Jpn. Kokai Tokkyo Koho JP.* 61: 47, 417.

Yudkin, J. 1967. Evolutionary and historical changes in dietary carbohydrates. *Amer. J. Clin. Nutr.* 20: 108-15.

Yudkin, J. 1969. Dietary sugar and coronary heart disease. *Nutrition News.* 32: 9-12.

Yudkin, J. 1971. Sugar consumption and myocardial infarction. *Lancet.* 1:292-97.

Zapatero, M. D. et al. 1995. Serum aluminum levels in Alzheimer's disease and other senile dementias. *Biological Trace Element Research.* 47: 235-40.

Zhukov, D. and K. Vinogradova. 1994. Inescapable shock induces the opposite changes of the plus-maze test behavior in rats with divergent coping strategy. *Physiology and Behavior.* November, 56(5), 1075-79.

RESOURCE DIRECTORY

Mail Order Sources for Herbs and Natural Products

Avena Botanicals
219 Mill St.
Rockport, ME 04856
207 594-0694
Teas, tinctures

Herb Pharm
20260 Williams Hwy.
Williams, OR 97544
800 348-4372
Herbal tinctures

Herbs, Etc.
1345 Cerrillos Rd.
Santa Fe, NM 87505
800 634-3727
Herbal tinctures

Living Arts
PO Box 2939
Venice, CA 90291-2939
800 254-8464
Audio and video meditation tapes; aromatherapy products

Mayway U.S.A.
1338 Cyperus St.
Oakland, CA 94607
510 208-3113
Chinese patent remedies and bulk herbs

Moonrise Herbs
826 G St.
Arcata, CA 95521
800 603-8364
Sleep pillows, herbs, essential oils

Oak Valley Herb Farm
PO Box 2482
Nevada City, CA 95959
Essential oils, massage oils

Rainbow Light
207 Macpherson
Santa Cruz, CA 95060
800 635-1233; (CA) 800 227-0555
Herbal tinctures and tablets

McZand Herbals
4063 Redwood Ave.
Los Angeles, CA 90066

800 800-0405
Herbal tinctures

Organizations

Academy for Guided Imagery
Box 2060
Mill Valley, CA 94942
415 389-9324

Alcoholics Anonymous General Service Office
Box 459
Grand Central Station
New York, NY 10163
Check local phone directory for listings.

American Association of Professional Hypnotherapists
Box 29
Boones Mill, VA 24065
703 334-3035

American Herb Products Association
4733 Bethesda Avenue
Suite 345
Bethesda, MD 20814
301 951-3204

American Herbalist Guild
PO Box 746555
Arvada, CO 80006
303 423-8800

Anxiety Disorders Association of America
6000 Executive Blvd., Ste. 513
Rockville, MD 20852
For list of self-help groups, call 900 737-3400

Association for Applied Psychophysiology and Biofeedback
10200 W. 44th Ave., Ste. 304
Wheat Ridge, CO 80033
303 422-8436

American Society of Clinical Hypnosis
2200 E. Devon Ave., Ste. 291
Des Plaines, IL 60018
708 297-3317

National Sleep Foundation
1367 Connecticut Ave., NW
Ste. 200
Washington, DC 20036

Narcolepsy Network
PO Box 42460
Cincinnati, OH 45242
513 891-3522

Recommended Reading

Aromatherapy
Keville, K. & M. Green. 1995. *Aromatherapy, a complete guide to the healing art.* Freedom, CA: The Crossing Press.

Breathing
Hendricks, Gay. 1995. *Conscious breathing.* New York: Bantam.

Chronic Fatigue Syndrome
Berne, K. 1995. *Running on empty.* Alameda, CA: Hunter House.

William, Collin. 1993. *Recovering from chronic fatigue syndrome: A guide to self-empowerment.* New York: The Body Press/Perigee.

World Wide Web Pages
www.alternatives.com/cfs-news

www.nmia.com

www.community-care.org.uk/ME/faq.html

www.angelfire.com/pages0/ias/tr.html

Use Altavista search engine to find CFS Internet Group sponspored by Roger Burns

Constitutional Types

Beinfeld, H. and E. Korngold. 1991. *Between heaven and earth: A guide to Chinese medicine.* New York: Ballantine Books.

Ladd, Vasant. 1984. *Ayurveda, the science of self-healing.* Santa Fe, NM: Lotus Press.

Sheldon, W.H. 1940. *The varieties of human physique.* New York, NY: Harper & Brothers.

Herbs

Hobbs, C. 1993. *Valerian, the relaxing and sleep herb.* Santa Cruz: Botanica Press.

Hoffmann, D. 1983. *The holistic herbal.* Findhorn, Scotland: The Findhorn Press.

Keville, K. 1994. *Herbs. An illustrated encyclopedia.* New York, NY: Friedman/Fairfax.

Keville, K. 1996. *Herbs for health and healing.* Emmaus, PA: Rodale Press.

Ody, P. 1993. *The complete medicinal herbal.* New York, NY: Dorling Kindersley.

Tierra, M. 1989. *Planetary herbology.* Santa Fe, NM: Lotus Press.

Weiss, R.F. 1988. *Herbal medicine.* Beaconsfield, England: Beaconsfield Publishers,Ltd.

Meditation

Chinmoy, Sri. 1978. *Meditation.* Jamaica, NY: Aum Publications.

Kornfield, J. *The inner art of meditation.* (audiotape)

Satchidananda, Sri Swami. *Guided relaxation and affirmations for inner peace.* (audiotape)

Melatonin

Reiter, R. J. & J. Robinson. 1995. *Your body's natural wonder drug, melatonin.* New York: Bantam Publishing.

Sahelian, R. 1996. *Melatonin, nature's sleeping pill.* Marina del Rey, CA: Be Happier Press.

Nutrition and Energetics of Food

Hobbs, C. 1992. *Foundations of health.* Santa Cruz: Botanica Press.

Pitchford, Paul. 1993. *Healing with whole foods.* Berkeley, CA: North Atlantic Books.

Santillo, H. 1993. *Intuitive eating.* Prescott, AZ: Hohm Press.

Tierra, L. 1992. *The herbs of life.* Freedom, CA: The Crossing Press.

Turner, K. 1987. *The self-healing cookbook.* Grass Valley, CA: Earthtones Press.

Inspirational Books

Chopra, Deepak. 1994. *The seven spiritual laws of success.* San Rafael, CA: New World Library.

Visualization

Gawain, S. 1978. *Creative visualization.* Berkeley, CA: Whatever Publications.

Miscellaneous

Criqui, M.H., et al. 1994. Does diet or alcohol explain the French paradox? *Lancet.* 344:1719-23.

Jacobs, M. R., & K. Fehr. 1987. *Drugs and drug abuse: A reference text* (2nd ed.). Toronto: Addiction Research Foundation.

Kahn, J. 1995. Red wine may be the healthiest alcoholic drink of all. *Medical Tribune.* February 2:10.

Keller, M. 1979. A historical overview

of alcohol and alcoholism. *Cancer Research*. 39. 2822-9.

Longnecker, Matthew P., et al. 1995. Alcohol consumption and the risk of cancer in humans: An overview. *Alcohol.* 12:87-96.

Maisto, S. A. et al. 1991. *Drug use and misuse.* Fort Worth, TX: Holt, Rinehart and Winston, Inc.

Mello, N. K. 1987. Alcohol abuse and alcoholism: 1978-1987. In H.Y. Meltzer (Ed.), *Psychopharmacology: The third generation of progress.* Pp. 1515-1520. New York: Raven Press.

U. S. Department of Health and Human Services (USDHHS). 1987. *Alcohol and health.* Rockville, MD: USDHHS.

Simeons, A. T. W. 1960. *Man's presumptuous brain: An evolutionary interpretation of psychosomatic disease.* New York: Dutton.

Journals

AHA Newsletter
PO Box 1673
Nevada City, CA 95959
916 265-9552

Herbalgram
PO Box 201660
Austin, TX 78270-1660
800 373-7105

Medical Herbalism
PO Box 20512
Boulder, CO 80308
303 541-9552

Protocol Journal of Botanical Medicine
PO Box 108
Harvard, MA 01451
800 466-5422

Audio Tapes, Inspirational

Chopra, D. *Seven Spiritual Laws of Success.*

Nhat-Hanh, Thich. 1996. *The long road turns to joy: A guide to walking meditation.* Berkeley: Parallax Press.

Nhat-Hanh, Thich. 1996. *Cultivating the mind of love: the practice of looking deeply in the Mahayana Buddhist tradition.* Foreword by Natalie Goldberg. Berkeley: Parallax Press.

Nhat-Hanh, Thich. 1993. *The blooming of a lotus: Guided meditation exercises for healing and transformation.* Translated by Annabel Laity. Boston: Beacon Press.

Nhat-Hanh, Thich. 1991. *Peace is every step: The path of mindfulness in everyday life. Edited by Arnold Kotler.* New York: Bantam.

Audio Tapes, Musical (for relaxation)

Eno, Brian. *Ambient #1.*
Davidoff, P.C. & Friends. *Bamboo.*
Thompson, Dr. Jeffrey. *Brainwave suite.*

Video

Yoga Journal's Yoga for relaxation.
Chopra, D. *Seven spiritual laws of success.*

INDEX